CREATIVE NEEDLEWORK

Jo Springer, Author

Solweig Hedin, Designer

Edith Noonberg, Editor

Publishers . WESTPORT CORP . New York

Contents

Acknowledgments

We wish to express our appreciation to Coats & Clark and Spinnerin Yarn Co., Inc. for supplying us with needlework designs and patterns; illustrations, diagrams and directions. The sources of these materials and the pages on which they can be found are listed below.

Let's Get Started

From the beginning of time, men have sought to beautify their environments. Prehistoric men embellished the skins they wore, decorated the walls of their dwelling-places and even put their talent to work in crafting their tools and weapons. This need to ornament our possessions has remained one of the most basic human characteristics. But the once highly personalized job has been taken over by experts—the fashion designers, the interior decorators—even the automobile manufacturers!

And what of the urge to add one's personal stamp to the elements of our physical world? It remains within us, but we have fewer and fewer outlets for expressing this basic need. We no longer build our own homes, make all our own clothing, develop all our tools. We are getting more and more leisure (or so we are told) which we fill with a variety of spectator activities—yet all the while, the urge to participate, to create, gnaws away at our peace of mind. Those lucky enough to have natural creative ability can pursue the fine arts—either as amateurs or as professionals. But for the great majority of us, there is the world of hand crafts to be explored, developed and enjoyed.

Needlework is an ideal outlet for one's creative spirit. A six-year old finds it fascinating—and so have some of the greatest modern artists, such as Pablo Picasso and Joan Miro.

Needlework is one of the least expensive of leisure time activities. Although a room-sized hooked rug may be quite costly, a charming piece of cross stitch can cost as little as 25¢. An additional bonus is the pleasure to be had from producing pieces of possible heirloom quality. In this computerized and "instant" world of ours, an hour with a needle and thread can be as valuable and therapeutic as an hour on the psychiatrist's couch. Few activities are as tranquilizing as knitting to music or the repetitive motions of hooking a rug.

Some people mistakenly object to needlework as a hobby since it seems to be a solitary one. On the contrary, the exact opposite is true—as it is for all dedicated enthusiasts. When one needleworker meets a fellow devotee at a yarn store, a county fair or in a museum, they soon begin comparing notes, swapping patterns and sharing techniques. Needleworkers frequently hold classes for friends and neighbors, and become ardent collectors of antique samples of their hobby.

No longer is needlework relegated to Victorian ladies who swoon at the drop of a crochet hook. Many men are beginning to discover that half an hour spent working needlepoint is as great a way to unwind after a hard day's work as two martinis on the rocks!

Suddenly in this, the last half of the 20th century, we have rediscovered the joys of producing fine handwork. This book is dedicated to introducing you, the reader, to the pleasures and rewards of needlework. Let's get started!

DESIGNER

AUTHOR

EDITOR

The good things of childhood are captured in the cross-stitch sampler design, page 5. (Directions, pages 18, 19.)

Let's Get Started

There really is no reason in the world why you can't start with any form of needlework that is the most appealing to you. You may well be a proficient knitter and now want to learn how to hook a rug, for example. We will assume, however, that you are a novice in every phase of needlework and want to start with the simplest techniques.

One of the easiest ways—and one that is often frowned upon by needlework purists—is to begin with a kit. Of course, we hope that every reader of this book will soon be designing her own projects, but the timid tyro may find it reassuring to begin with a stamped cross-stitch potholder or to fill in the background of a ready-made piece of needlepoint. Kits vary in the degree of skill required—from very simple to very intricate designs. The beginner should keep this in mind when making that first purchase.

There are a number of basic rules for needleworkers but there is one we cannot emphasize enough: Do not begin by reading lengthy pamphlets or directions! Nothing is more confusing than the mumbo jumbo of knitting directions, for instance. Directions have meaning only if you have the actual work in your hand. Follow them step by step without reading too far ahead. This may sound arbitrary but it will carry you over some rough spots painlessly.

A PLACE TO WORK

It is the recurrent dream of all needleworkers to have the perfect place in which to carry on the craft—a room dedicated to that activity alone. The room would always be bright and sunny, would have ideal worktables, comfortable chairs, infinite storage space and—as long as we're dreaming—would never need cleaning. Actually, most needlework can be done anywhere—on a commuters' train, at the beach, even in bed when you're getting over the flu! That's one of the joys of the craft.

There is one cardinal rule in this area, however. Always have excellent light. Make sure that it comes over your left shoulder (if you are right-handed). Also make sure that there is no glare.

EQUIPMENT AND ITS STORAGE

Since needlework requires only a few simple tools, it is only good sense to use the very best and to take excellent care of them.

Scissors

Specific equipment for each type of needlework will be discussed in later chapters, but **all** needle crafts require a good basic scissors. Keep yours for your work alone and don't let the kids use it to cut paper dolls or pry open paint cans. For all types of embroidery an embroidery scissors is also useful (but optional) equipment. These have short narrow blades which are sharply pointed. The points must close perfectly to snip threads properly, therefore they should be protected with a little sheath which you can make from a scrap of felt or leather.

Thimbles

For all types of needlework in which a true needle is used—embroidery, needlepoint and appliqué, for example—a thimble is useful. A metal one is less bulky than a plastic one. It should fit your middle finger perfectly, so try on several before buying one. You wouldn't hesitate trying on a great many shoes before buying a pair—and you'll have your thimble a lot longer. In fact, there is great ego satisfaction in owning a really elegant thimble. A gold or silver one is not too easy to find today but it is the needleworker's status symbol.

Needles

In earlier times the homemaker cherished her needles and kept them throughout her lifetime. Today fine steel needles are available in great variety. However, only two main categories of needles are used in most embroidery. Crewel (also known as embroidery) needles are used for stitching on most fabric backgrounds. These are rather short needles with a sharp point and a long eye. For work on canvas, burlap, and other open-weave fabrics where you must not split the threads of the background fabric, use a tapestry needle. This has a blunt point and a large eye. When using either type of needle, select the proper size for the work in hand. The eye should be large enough to accommodate the embroidery thread that you are using but the point should not be so big that it permanently separates the weave of the background fabric. The proper needle for each form of needlework will be listed in later chapters.

Strangely enough, we often become devoted to a particular needle. Keep yours in a needle case, a pincushion or a square of flannel. Even though your needlework may be kept in a large bag, a box or a drawer, it is a good idea to have a small soft drawstring bag in which to store your basic tools. In it they will be safe from scratches and nicks and won't be mislaid.

Knitting Needles and Crochet Hooks

Knitting needles and crochet hooks have a way of disappearing, too. Handsome ready-made cases are available for storing them neatly, but the new

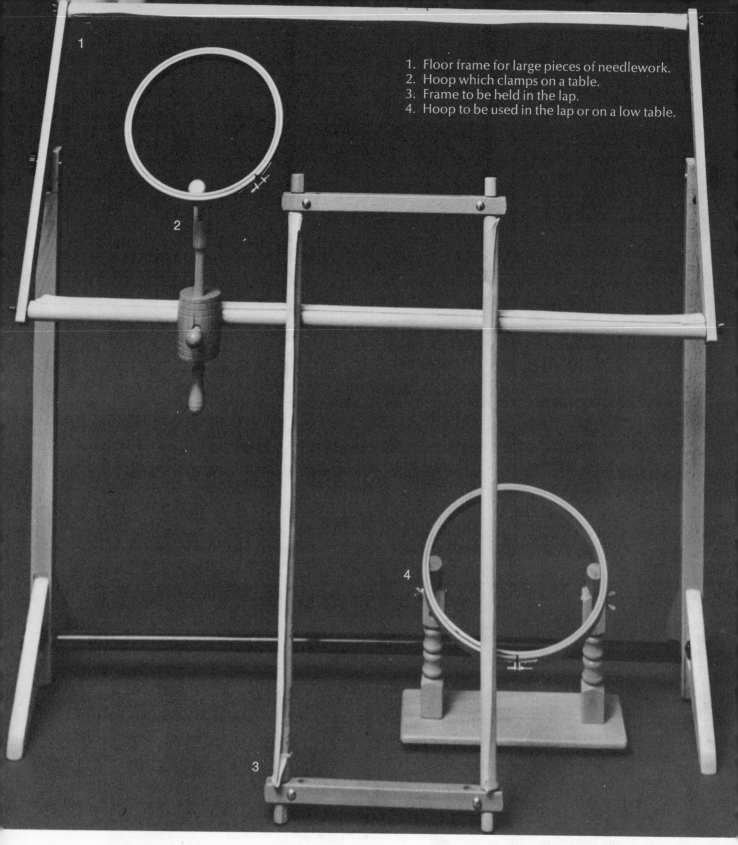

1. Floor frame for large pieces of needlework.
2. Hoop which clamps on a table.
3. Frame to be held in the lap.
4. Hoop to be used in the lap or on a low table.

jumbo-size needles and hooks never seem to fit in them—besides what do you do with that **extra** pair of No. 6 needles? Artists' wood or plastic brush cases make handy containers. Probably the cheapest storage method is one we devised years ago. Just slip your needles in a cardboard tube (an old paper towel roll, for instance) and close the ends with large corks. Do label the tubes—crochet hooks, double-pointed needles, etc.

Frames and Hoops

Most forms of needlework (even some hooked rugs) can be worked in the hand, but your work will be more accurate, even, and unpuckered if worked on a frame. No doubt you have seen or worked with embroidery hoops. These consist of two rings or ovals of wood or metal, one fitting inside the other. The best ones have a thumb screw on the outer ring to adjust the fit to the thickness of the fabric being held. Hoops are recommended only for small pieces of needlework. When used on larger designs, the hoops have to be moved as areas are completed, and the finished embroidery may be flattened. If this is unavoidable, it is wise to slip some tissue paper between the hoop and the embroidery.

To use a hoop lay the work on the smaller ring; place larger ring over it and tighten screw. **Note:** If fabric needs adjusting, be sure to pull only on the straight grain. Pulling on the bias will distort your embroidery. **Helpful Hint:** Always loosen the screw on your hoop before putting your work away. This will prevent permanent hoop marks on your fabric.

Rectangular frames can be purchased from well-stocked art needlework stores. The largest frames can hold work up to 36″ wide. Frames usually have rollers at the top and bottom or have adjustable sides so that they can be used for projects of various sizes. To use a frame, whip the top of your work to the tape at the top of the frame; roll up this end (or adjust side pieces if you have that type of frame) until lower end of your work is in position. Whip lower end to lower tape. **Note:** If your fabric frays easily, always overcast edges first, then fold back edges an inch or more so that you go through a double thickness when you whip fabric to tapes. Finish by lashing the sides of your work to the sides of the frame.

If a rectangular frame is not available, an old picture frame of the appropriate size can be used. Or artists' stretcher strips (from an art supply store) make a good substitute. Hammer the strips together, making sure that the corners are square. With either of these frames face down, center your work on the back, pull taut, and thumbtack or staple work to frame at the center of each side, then at the center of the top and bottom. Be sure the tacks are outside the area to be embroidered. Working from the center of sides out toward corners, continue to fasten work, alternating from side to side. Finally fasten at the top and bottom in the same manner as for the sides. If the frame is very large, work can be lashed in place with heavy thread.

To use these frames you will need to prop them up. Hold one edge in your lap and prop the opposite edge against a table or chair back.

Some hoops and frames come on stands which leave both hands free. If you are using a frame with a stand to be placed on a table, make sure that your table is low enough so that your work is at a comfortable working height. Floor hoops (such as a quilt hoop) and floor frames are particularly convenient to use. They can be adjusted to the proper working height and angle.

Materials and Their Storage

In the following chapters the appropriate materials for the various kinds of needlework will be discussed. But let's talk about storing materials — all kinds of materials — here.

Fabrics can be folded in large suit boxes or other types of packing boxes. If fabrics are kept for long periods of time, it is wise to refold them in another way occasionally so that the creases do not become permanent. However, it is strongly recommended that you roll fabrics whenever possible. This is particularly important with linen. Fabric such as burlap for rugs can be rolled on an old broom handle, linens on a cardboard tube. To keep the fabric roll clean, slip a paper bag over each end and fasten with rubber bands. If you have many rolls of fabric, they can be stored neatly in a closet by standing them in a carton or old waste basket.

Yarns and threads present the most difficult storage problem and there are almost as many storage methods as there are needleworkers. Shoe boxes are fine for strand cottons and small skeins of yarn. Although many wool yarns are mothproofed today, you will want to keep the wools separate from the cottons and synthetics so that you can add some moth preventive crystals or compounds — just in case. Bulky yarns, of course, require larger boxes.

There are quaint cloth embroidery thread organizers available but most needleworkers soon overflow such neat little packages. One way to cope with dozens of small quantities of yarns or threads is to wind them on cardboard tubes (from paper towels, for instance). Keep the ends from tangling by taping them in place. Shades of one color can go on one roll.

Note: Do label all storage boxes. It will save you endless searching later.

DESIGNS AND HOW TO TRANSFER THEM

Once you have become interested in needlework, you will be seeing designs in almost everything you encounter. A postcard in the morning mail might make a great design for a crewel picture. The back of your canasta deck suddenly looks like a handsome hooked rug. Handling the problems of converting an elaborate design from one medium to another is beyond the scope of this book. However, if you work out the various simple methods of developing the designs and patterns in the following chapters, you will soon have the skill to handle more complicated ones.

Often designs are not transferred directly to your working material. Needlepoint, for example, may be worked directly from charts. In most forms of needlework the design is applied to the fabric, however.

To apply a pattern to fabric you must first make

a clear tracing of the design. If the design comes from a book or a fine print, protect it by slipping a sheet of stiff clear plastic over the picture before tracing it on thin paper. Now transfer by the most applicable of the following methods:

Carbon Paper Method

Tape your fabric, right side up, to a smooth surface. Place carbon paper face down on it; tape in place. Position your tracing face up on the carbon paper; tape. With a sharp hard pencil go over all lines of the design. Check to see if you are using sufficient pressure to transfer the lines properly. **Note:** Although typewriter carbon paper may be used, it will be smudgy. Dressmakers' carbon paper is preferable. It comes in light colors for dark fabrics and dark colors for light fabrics.

Reverse Tracing Method

Working on the back of your tracing, go over all lines with a soft pencil. Tape the tracing, right side up, to your fabric and retrace all the lines, this time with a hard pencil. This is a somewhat smudgy method, but useful if carbon paper is not available.

Transfer Pattern Method

Many embroiderers prefer to use commercial transfers rather than develop their own designs. Transfers work very well on smooth fabrics like cotton or linen. Do not attempt to use a transfer pattern on textured weaves, coarse wools, velvets or other fabrics with a nap. First cut out just those parts of the transfer pattern that you plan to use. Make sure there are no loose flakes of transfer ink. Pin or tape your fabric to an ironing board. Place transfer, face down, on fabric and tape in place.

Make a test sample of a scrap of the transfer pattern on a scrap of your fabric, checking for the proper heat of your iron. "Low" or "rayon" is usually the correct setting. Use a firm stamping motion of the iron, not the usual gliding motion. When your test sample makes a clear transfer, repeat the process on the prepared fabric. Raise a corner to see if the transfer is complete. If not, repeat the process. Then run the warm iron over the surface of the pattern and lift it away from the fabric quickly. **Note:** Some transfer patterns have sufficient ink on the designs that they can be reused.

Hot Iron Pencil Method

Few needleworkers know that they can make their own hot iron transfers quite simply. All you need is a copying pencil, also called a hot iron pencil. First draw the design on tracing or tissue paper. Then, on other side of the paper, carefully go over all lines with the special pencil. Be sure the pencil point is sharp so that your lines will be fine. Since the dye in the pencil is difficult to remove once it is transferred to fabric, carefully erase any mistakes with an ink eraser before transferring.

Now apply the design to your fabric just as you would for any hot iron transfer (see preceding method). **Note:** Depending on the fabric, it is usually possible to reuse a transfer pattern made with a hot iron pencil.

DESIGNS AND HOW TO ENLARGE THEM

Even as a beginner, the needleworker must confront the problem of enlarging a design from a graph. You'll find such graphs under the sections on crewel, appliqué and hooking. The method seems quite formidable but is actually quite easy when worked out one step at a time.

1. Lay out a large sheet of wrapping paper or newsprint, a ruler and a sharp pencil.

2. Check the scale given on the diagram and draw the number of squares indicated, making sure that they are in the proper scale. For example, for the diagram shown, the scale is "each small square = 1" square." This means that you draw a grid 5 squares wide by 5 squares long and each square is 1" x 1". (Only part of enlarged design is shown, however.)

3. Now copy whatever is in any given square on the small diagram to its corresponding square on the grid which you have drawn.

4. When the design is complete, check the overall design, make any necessary corrections, and you are ready to transfer the design to your fabric.

ACTUAL SIZE

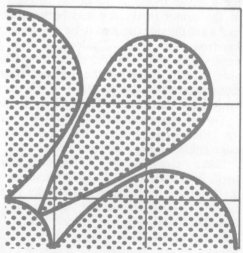

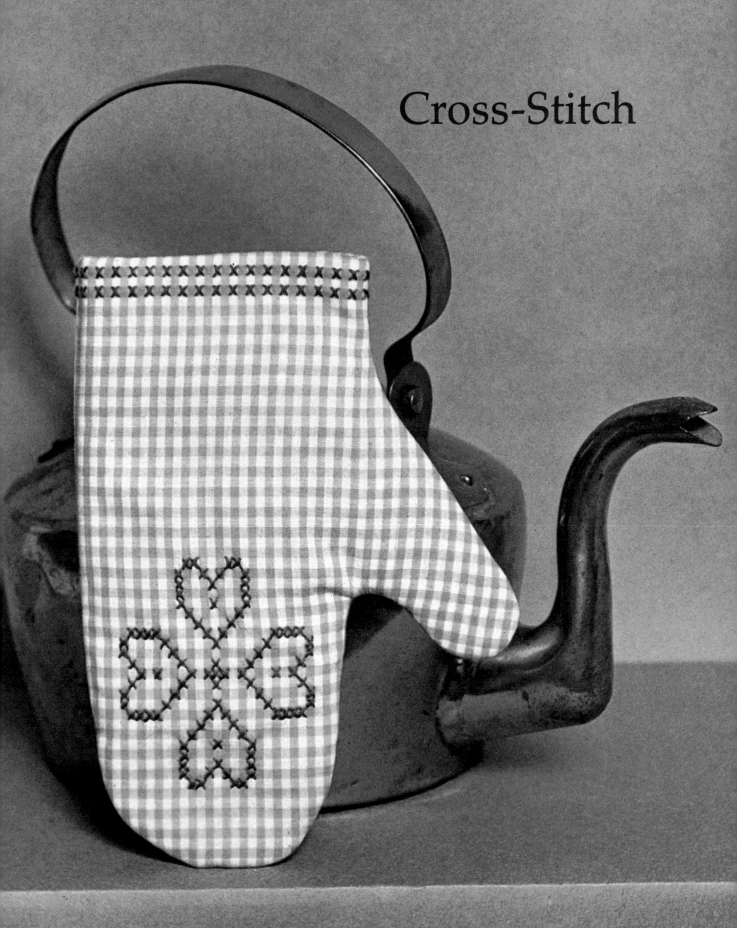

Cross-Stitch

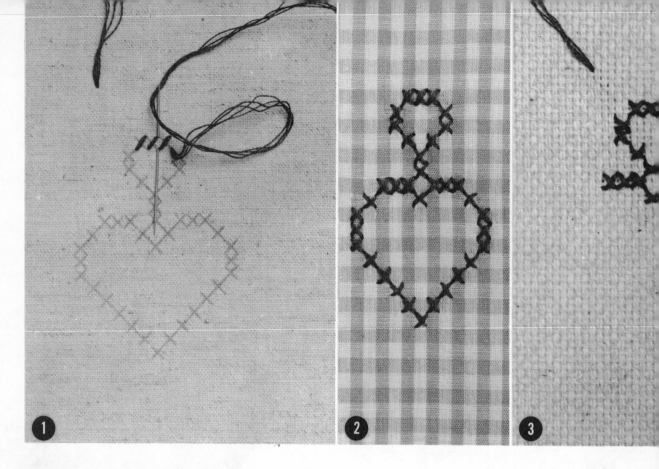

1

2

3

Cross-Stitch

Cross-stitch, simple or elaborate, seems to go on forever. When we come across a delightfully naive sampler in the clutter of an antique shop, we realize once again that cross-stitch is truly part of our American heritage. We must not forget, however, that our cross-stitch flourishes from roots that range the breadth of the European continent. When we start our adventures in needlework with even the simplest cross-stitch potholder we are joining a long line of needleworkers who have made the world a little bit more beautiful by stitching small crosses on fabric.

MATERIALS

Almost any fabric from voile to velvet can be used as the background. If you are using the thread-count method of working cross-stitch, even-weave fabric is by far the best background material. This means that the fabric (usually linen) has the same number of threads per inch lengthwise and cross-wise. Other linens may be used but your stitches may vary in size and you will find it more difficult to count the threads of the fabric.

The embroidery thread will depend on the background fabric used and the effect desired. Use a smooth hard-twist wool yarn on wools, possibly a silk or lightweight wool yarn on velvet and 6-strand embroidery floss or pearl cotton on cotton and linen.

CROSS-STITCH METHODS

Transfer Pattern Method

Bring needle up at the lower left corner of a cross. Insert needle into upper right corner. Draw thread tight but not so tight that work is puckered. You have completed a half cross-stitch. Make another half cross-stitch in the next cross to the right and in every cross across that section of work. On last cross bring needle up at lower right corner and insert into upper left corner. You have completed one whole cross-stitch. Continue working to the left until every stitch has been crossed.

You will notice that every stitch is crossed in the **same direction.** For really handsome cross-stitch, it is essential that all stitches cross in the same direction. Some workers prefer to complete each cross-stitch as they go. This is an acceptable method, but we feel that working one half a stitch across a row then completing the stitches on the return trip makes for more rhythmic strokes and evener stitches.

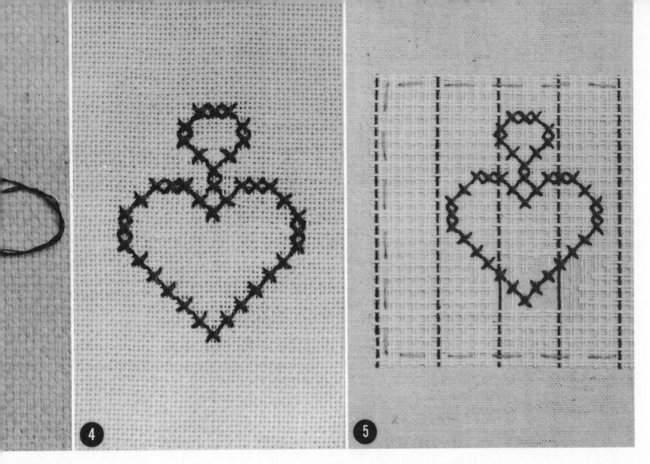

Five ways of working cross-stitch: (1) Transfer Pattern Method on stamped fabric; (2) Checked Fabric Method on checks of gingham; (3) Mesh Fabric Method on blocks of monk's cloth; (4) Thread Count Method on counted threads of fabric; (5) Canvas Method over a temporary canvas to aid in counting

Checked Fabric Method

This is a simple way of working cross-stitch that is highly recommended for the beginner. Choose fabric such as gingham, which has an even-weave check. This method is worked from a chart and no pattern is transferred to the fabric. The checked fabric acts as a guide for the stitches. Lay out the area to be worked by marking with a basting thread. For each symbol on the chart work a cross-stitch in the corresponding check of the fabric. **Note:** Designs limited to a very few colors are more effective than more elaborate ones when worked on checked fabric.

Mesh Fabric Method

Similar to the checked fabric technique, this method takes advantage of the weave of the fabric as the guidelines for the stitches. Some fabrics, such as monk's cloth, are woven so that the threads fall in blocks of equal size. These blocks can be used as a guide for stitches worked directly from a chart.

Thread Count Method

This method will produce the most perfect work and is generally used on samplers, fine table linens and pictures. No pattern is transferred to the fabric. The actual threads are counted, both horizontally and vertically. Each cross-stitch is worked over a square of 2, 3, or more threads.

Canvas Method

When you are using fabric whose threads cannot be counted and one on which transfer or pencil lines will not show (velvet or felt, for instance), this is the only possible method. Baste cross-stitch canvas (also known as Penelope canvas) to your working area. This canvas comes with from 7 to 15 meshes to the inch, so plan your piece accordingly. Work cross-stitches right over the canvas into your background fabric, using the canvas for counting stitches. Work stitches rather tightly. When the embroidery is complete, remove the bastings, then carefully snip the canvas in open spaces between the areas of cross-stitch. Draw out the threads of canvas one by one, using a tweezers if necessary. Wherever possible, snip canvas so that you do not have to pull a long thread through your cross-stitches. **Note:** Even-weave linen of the proper number of threads per inch can be used instead of the canvas.

CROSS-STITCH SQUARES

These two delightful little squares were specially designed to help you practice the thread count method of working cross-stitch. Neatly framed, they might add a bright note to your kitchen or breakfast room. Or just the border on Design A would be charming edging a table mat and the center motif could be worked on the napkin. If you are really ambitious, you might cross-stitch the motif on Design B all around a table cloth.

SIZE: 6″ finished squares.

MATERIALS: 36″ wide natural color even-weave linen, 22 threads to the inch (¼ yard will make 5 squares). **Note:** If you cannot find linen of the proper thread count, substitute one that is close. Just remember that fewer threads per inch will make a larger design, more threads per inch will make a smaller one. Plan your piece accordingly. 6-strand embroidery floss, 1 skein each medium blue and gray green for Design A, 1 skein medium blue for Design B; sewing thread.

EQUIPMENT: Embroidery hoop; fine tapestry needle.

PATTERN AND DESIGN: Cut linen 7½″ square. Be sure you cut straight along a thread of the fabric. If you are using an embroidery hoop, cut fabric large enough to fit your hoop. Overcast edges with sewing thread to prevent fraying. With a basting thread of a bright color mark the center lines of square both horizontally and vertically.

EMBROIDERY: Place square in hoop. Each square on the charts indicates a cross-stitch worked over 2 threads of the fabric. Work entire piece with 4 strands of embroidery floss. Begin by working all stitches on center line right over the basting threads. Complete one half of design by working from line A down to line B. For upper half of design turn chart upside down. Omit center horizontal line of stitches and complete rest of chart working from line A up to line B.

FINISHING: Block and frame or make ⅜″ finished hems (see Index).

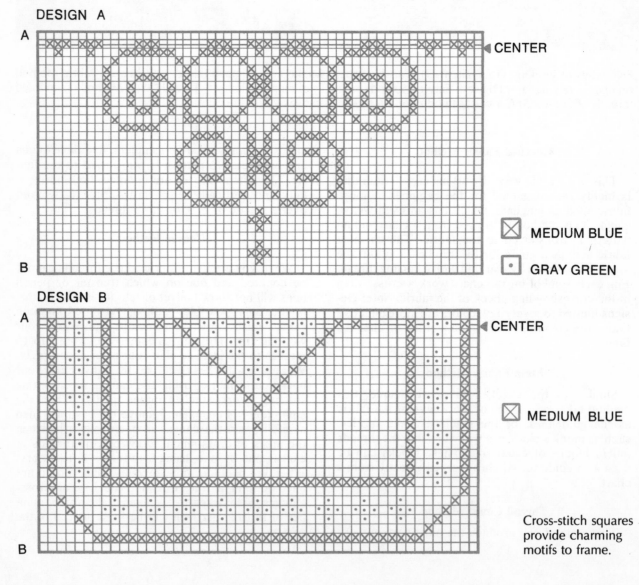

DESIGN A

A ◀ CENTER

B

⊠ MEDIUM BLUE

▣ GRAY GREEN

DESIGN B

A ◀ CENTER

B

⊠ MEDIUM BLUE

Cross-stitch squares provide charming motifs to frame.

CROSS-STITCH PLACE MATS

Now that you have some experience with cross-stitch you may want to try your hand at a design that requires just a little more concentration. We think the results more than justify your time. These place mats would enhance even the most elaborate luncheon table. If you prefer a luncheon cloth, these same designs can be translated easily into a continuous border.

SIZE: 14″ x 18″ finished mats.

MATERIALS: 36″-wide natural-color even-weave linen, 22 threads to the inch (1⅛ yards will make 4 mats. See note under materials for cross-stitch squares.) 6-strand embroidery floss, 1 skein each medium brown, dusty rose and hot pink for Mat A, 1 skein each warm brown, taupe and dusty rose for Mat B; sewing thread.

EQUIPMENT: Embroidery frame; fine tapestry needle.

PATTERN AND DESIGN: Cut linen 18″ x 20¼″, making sure that you cut straight along a thread of the fabric. This large size will give you enough material to attach to your embroidery frame. Overcast edges with sewing thread to prevent fraying. With bright colored thread baste outline of finished mat on fabric, centering it carefully. Make sure that your basting follows a thread of the fabric. Baste horizontal center line of mat.

EMBROIDERY: Mount mat in frame. Each square on the chart indicates a cross-stitch worked over 2 threads of the fabric. Work mats with 4 strands of embroidery floss throughout. Symbols on chart indicate the color placement. Start at the center basting line and work center row of stitches right over basting thread; the left edge of the design should be 1″ from left edge of mat. Work chart from A to B down side of mat. For other half of design turn chart upside down. Omit center horizontal line of stitches and complete rest of chart working from line A up to line B.

FINISHING: Block and make ⅜″ finished hems (see Index).

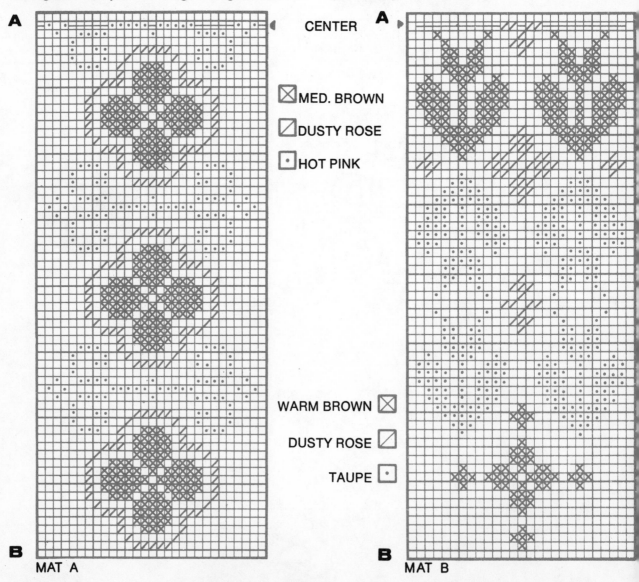

MED. BROWN

DUSTY ROSE

HOT PINK

WARM BROWN

DUSTY ROSE

TAUPE

MAT A   MAT B

Color photo right: Classic place mats to cross-stitch. (Mat A design is shown below, Mat B is above.)

CROSS-STITCH SAMPLER

Although traditionally samplers were made by very young girls, the charm of a cross-stitch sampler makes us all want to embroider one—even if we are just a bit over ten years old. The design of this particular sampler serves a dual purpose. In itself it makes a most appealing wall hanging, with its quaint motifs translated into a fresh modern idiom. These same motifs can be used in a dozen ways. Work just the center flower basket and you will have a picture to treasure. The country ladies or the birds would be delightful on a child's dress. The borders and other little motifs would brighten almost any household linens. Just give your imagination free rein.

SIZE: Embroidered area, about 14½″ x 19½″; hanging, about 18″ x 24″.

MATERIALS: 36″-wide natural-color even-weave linen, 22 threads to the inch, ¾ yard. (See note under Materials for Cross-Stitch Squares.) Pearl cotton, size 5, 1 ball each red, medium, blue, pink; sewing thread; picture frame or 2 thin dowels or brass rods 19″ long.

EQUIPMENT: Embroidery frame; fine tapestry needle.

PATTERN AND DESIGN: Overcast edges of fabric to prevent fraying. With sewing thread of a bright color baste center vertical line on fabric. Be sure that your basting line follows a thread of the fabric.

EMBROIDERY: Mount fabric in frame. Follow chart for design. Each square on the chart indicates a cross-stitch worked over 2 threads of the fabric. Symbols on chart show color placement. Start at vertical center line and work center row of stitches right over basting thread. Although entire chart is given for lower section of sampler, it shows just half of the upper design motifs. Work upper part of sampler following chart from A to B. When left half of sampler is completed work right half from center out, again following chart from A to B and omitting center vertical line of stitches.

FINISHING: Block and frame or make into a wall hanging (see Index).

B

A

CENTER

18

Because chart is so large, it had to be split. When you have completed the top row on page 18, continue up from bottom row of upper chart on this page.

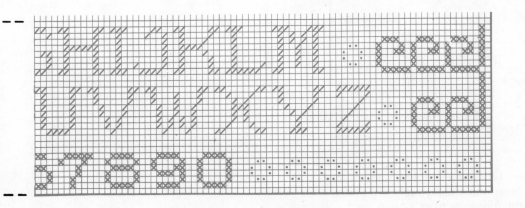

⊠ BLUE

⊡ RED

⊡ PINK

GINGHAM HOT MITT

Many of the projects in this book have been planned to give the beginner valuable experience in learning a particular technique. If you have never done any cross-stitch before, why not start with the practical and appealing little hot mitt — shown on page 11.

SIZE: Woman's medium size.

MATERIALS: $\frac{3}{8}$ yard blue and white checked gingham with $\frac{1}{8}''$ checks; pieces of old terry towel or other thick fabric for padding; 6-strand embroidery floss, 1 skein dark blue; sewing thread.

EQUIPMENT: Small embroidery hoop; crewel needle.

PATTERN AND DESIGN: Enlarge diagram for mitt (each small square = 1" square). Trace pattern once on gingham, placing wrist edge evenly on a row of checks. Cut out piece in the form of a rectangle, large enough to fit into your embroidery hoop. Place this piece in your hoop. With bright colored sewing thread baste a vertical line up center of mitt. Baste a horizontal line $2\frac{3}{4}''$ from finger-tip edge of mitt. Be sure that these lines run right along the center of a row of checks.

EMBROIDERY: Every cross on the chart for the design indicates 1 cross-stitch worked over 1 check of the gingham. Work entire design with 4 strands of embroidery floss. Begin by working all stitches on center lines right over basting threads. Then complete design following chart. Now work a border of cross-stitches near the wrist edge as follows: Skip one row of checks at wrist edge. Working on second row of checks from wrist edge, make a cross-stitch in every other check. Skip next row of checks. On following row work a cross-stitch in every other check as before so that stitches line up with those worked before.

FINISHING: Cut out mitt, adding $\frac{1}{2}''$ seam allowances on all edges. Cut out 3 more gingham and 4 padding pieces following mitt pattern, adding $\frac{1}{2}''$ seam allowances.

Right sides together, place a plain gingham piece on the embroidered piece. Place 2 padding pieces on each of these gingham pieces. Stitch together on all but wrist edges. Trim seam allowances, cutting away padding very close to seams. Also cut away seam allowances of padding at wrist edges. Clip seam allowances on curved edges. Turn to right side; press.

For lining, stitch together remaining 2 gingham pieces on all but wrist edges. Trim seam allowances. Do not turn. Slip lining into embroidered mitt. Turn in wrist edges and slip stitch together.

CHART FOR DESIGN

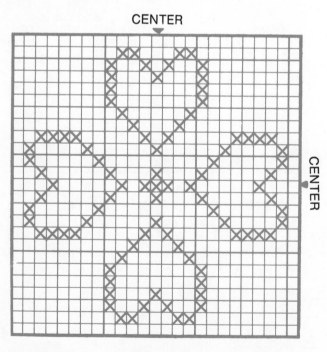

Making this quaint little gingham hot mitt is an excellent way to learn the checked fabric method of working cross-stitch designs from a chart.

DIAGRAM FOR MITT

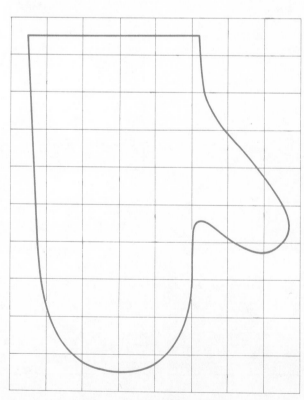

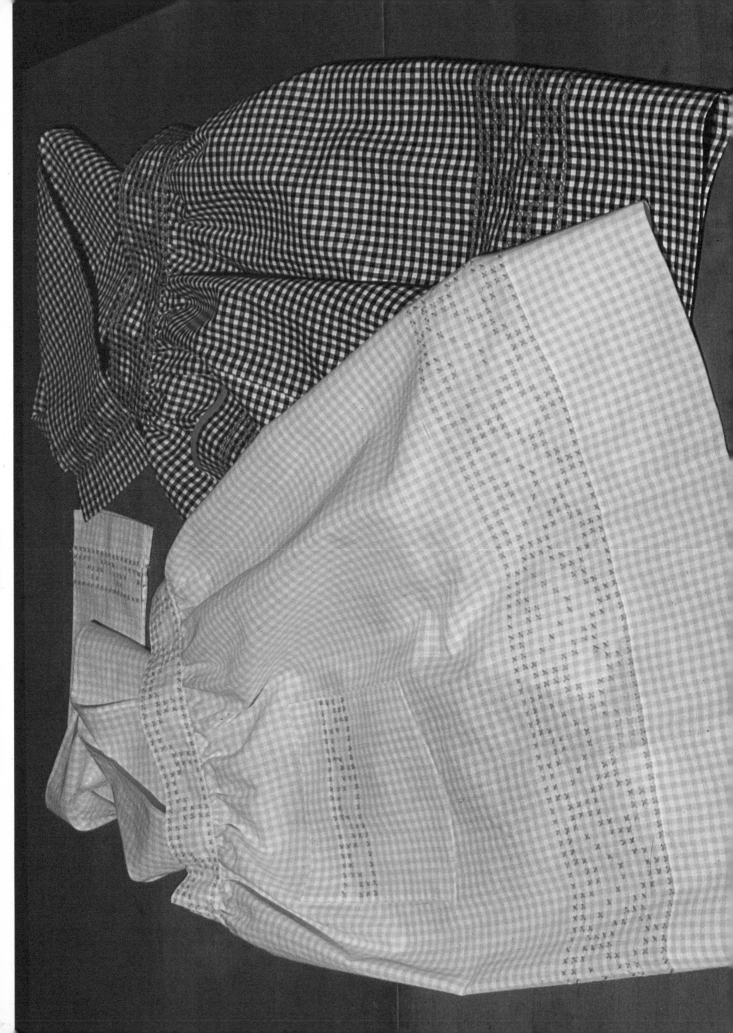

GINGHAM PARTY APRONS

Cross stitching on gingham can provide a decorative note as well as a practical one. You can be a well-dressed hostess at your next party while camouflaging your practicality with one of these pretty little aprons color-coordinated to the theme of the evening.

MATERIALS: 1 yard checked gingham with $\frac{1}{8}$-inch checks; 1 skein 6-strand embroidery floss in contrasting color; sewing thread.

EQUIPMENT: Medium size embroidery hoop; crewel needle.

PATTERN FOR APRON: Cut a rectangle of gingham 36″ x 24″ for apron; one strip for waistband, $3\frac{1}{2}$″ x 20″; two strips for ties, 4″ x 36″; one square for pocket, 6″ x 7″.

Ties: Turn under a narrow hem along each long edge and stitch. Turn under a 1-inch hem on one short edge and stitch. Pleat the raw edge to 1″ and baste. This edge is to be sewn to waistband.

Waistband: With a pin, mark the center of each short end for fold line. Turn $\frac{5}{8}$″ along one long edge to wrong side and press. At short ends, on right side of waistband, pin pleated edges of tie, matching raw edges and placing tie between fold line and $\frac{5}{8}$″ from raw edge. Fold waistband in half along fold line, right sides together. Note that $\frac{5}{8}$″ seam allowance will extend beyond pressed edge. Stitch $\frac{5}{8}$″

seam across short ends thus securing ties. Turn to right side and press.

Apron: Turn under 1″ along each 24-inch length for side hems and stitch. Turn under $3\frac{1}{2}$″ along 36-inch length for hem at lower edge and stitch. Baste a row of small running stitches $\frac{5}{8}$″ below raw edge at top and gather evenly to fit waistband.

Attach waistband: With right sides together pin gathered edge of apron to waistband, raw edges together, and stitch a $\frac{5}{8}$-inch seam. Turn waistband up, bringing pressed edge of waistband over stitching line and slip stitch in place. Press.

Pocket: Turn under and stitch a 1-inch hem at top. Pocket must be embroidered before attaching to apron. After embroidery is completed, press under $\frac{1}{2}$″ on three remaining sides of pocket. Top stitch in place on apron.

EMBROIDERY: The deceptively simple geometric design below provides an opportunity for you to test your creativity. It will be very effective in a monotone embroidery, or it can be striking through the use of gradations of color. Follow the same embroidery and transfer method as for the hot mitt on page 20. Use the complete pattern repeated across the lower edge of the apron placing the bottom row of embroidery on the row of checks above the stitched hem line. The top border of the pattern is embroidered along the waistband, ends of tie and just below pocket hem. Be sure to embroider pocket before stitching it to the apron.

The cross stitch designs on previous pages may also be adapted for embroidery on aprons.

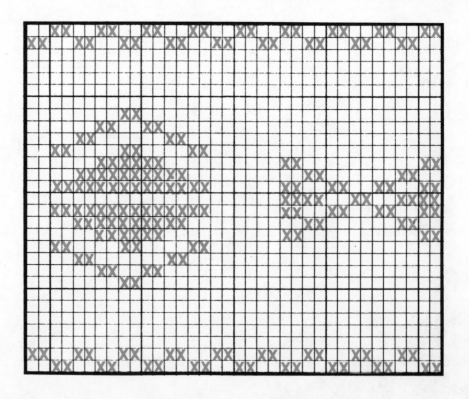

A Sampler of Embroidery Stitches

A Sampler of Embroidery Stitches

Having a wide variety of embroidery stitches at your fingertips is a little like having a large vocabulary. Although we can manage to communicate with a limited vocabulary, we become twice as interesting—maybe twice as smart—when we broaden our choice of words. You can do lovely embroidery even if you know only three or four stitches, but think of the excitement you can add to your needlework when you know the perfect stitch for a particular effect that you want.

In the Crewel section it is suggested that you familiarize yourself with running, Holbein, outline, chain and satin stitches as well as French knots.

Of course, cross-stitch is basic, too. Your repertoire of stitches can now be broadened to include many other fascinating stitches. Don't try to learn them all at once. It would be both boring and confusing. Practice one or two at a time until you become expert.

You may enjoy making a sampler of stitches. Mark 4″ squares on a long strip of fabric. When you have filled each square with a different stitch you will really know your stitches. And the sampler will be a charming memento of the days before you became an expert.

Arrowhead Stitch: This stitch is used for medium-width lines and for light filling. Bring needle up at top left corner, insert it below and to the right, then bring it out to the right on top line. For the second part of stitch insert needle back close to center of stitch and bring it out close to where thread emerges.

Backstitch: This stitch is a basic one used for lines, outlines and as a foundation for other stitches. Work from right to left. Bring needle up a short distance from beginning of the line to be covered; insert it at beginning of line. Bring needle out an equal distance ahead along line; draw it through. stitches should be very evenly spaced. **Note:** Backstitch can be threaded for a more decorative effect (see Holbein Stitch, Single-Threaded and Holbein Stitch, Double-Threaded).

Basket Filling Stitch: This stitch is used to fill the centers of large flowers or other areas. Alternate blocks of vertical satin stitches with blocks of horizontal satin stitches. Blocks can be made up of 3, 4 or more threads but all blocks must have the same number. Stitches may be touching or just slightly apart.

Basket Stitch: This stitch is used for solid lines and borders. Work from the top down. Bring needle up on left line; insert it lower down on right line and bring it out directly opposite on left line. Then insert needle on right line above stitch just made; bring out on left just below where thread just emerged. Insert needle on right line below lowest stitch and bring out exactly opposite. Take a stitch as shown, working in same holes that other stitches were worked into. Repeat these last 2 steps. The needle takes a step forward and backward alternately.

Blanket Stitch: This stitch is used for covering a turned-over edge (or a raw edge that will not fray). It is also used for outline or, when worked in a circle, to form flowers. Work from left to right. Bring needle up on lower line. Hold thread down with left thumb. Insert needle a little to the right of starting point but on upper line; bring out directly below on lower line; draw needle through over loop of thread.

Braid Stitch: This stitch is used for borders. Work from right to left. Bring needle up on lower line. Make a loop of thread as shown; hold down with left thumb, insert needle through loop and in fabric on top line; bring out on lower line. Pull loop on needle tight but not so tight that you lose the braid effect.

Braid Stitch, Edging: This stitch is worked along a hem or turned-over edge. Work from right to left. Bring needle to right side just below edge. Loop thread as shown, insert needle through loop, then behind fabric. Bring out a short distance below edge and over working thread. Pull thread through and away from you.

Brick Stitch: This stitch is used to fill in an entire area. Work straight stitches in a row, leaving the width of a stitch between each 2 stitches. Work a second row of the same size stitches but place them so that they interlock with the stitches of the previous row as shown. Completed stitches look like a section of brick wall.

Bullion Stitch: This stitch is used for a heavy encrusted effect especially when worked in gold or silver threads. The stitches are also often overlapped in a circle to form a rosebud. Bring thread up to right side of fabric; insert needle back the distance of the stitch desired, bring up in same spot thread first emerged. Do not draw needle through. Wind thread around point of needle (6 or 7 times or according to length of stitch required). Place left thumb on twists; draw needle and thread through the fabric and the twists. Pull needle and thread to the right and tighten by pulling working thread. Then insert needle through to the back as shown.

Buttonhole Stitch: This stitch is used to cover turned-over or raw edges or to outline. Examples are buttonholes, scallops, cutwork, lines and borders. Work the same as Blanket Stitch but work the stitches closer together.

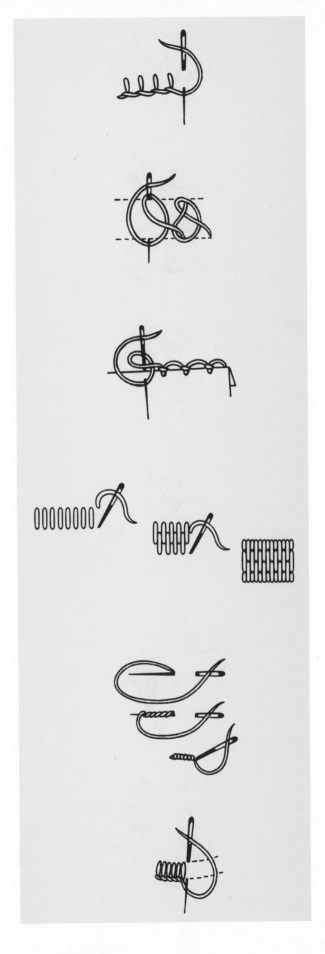

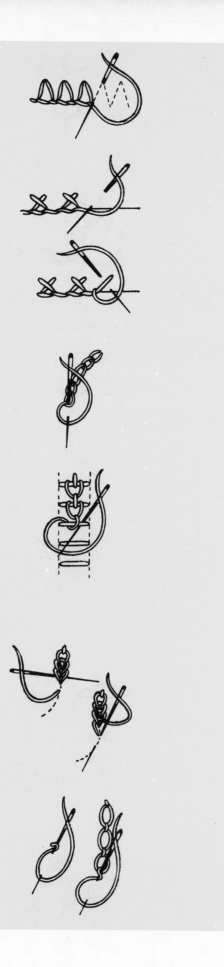

Buttonhole Stitch, Closed: This stitch is used for decorative borders and hems. Work the stitch the same as for blanket stitch but have the needle enter the fabric at the same spot for each pair of stitches.

Buttonhole Stitch, Crossed: This stitch is used for still more decorative borders and hems than the previous stitch. Work the stitch the same as for blanket stitch but cross each pair of stitches.

Chain Stitch: This stitch is used for lines and for outlines. Worked in close rows it is also used for a filling stitch. The stitches are worked from the top down. Bring needle to right side of fabric. Hold thread down with left thumb. Insert needle back where thread emerges. Bring out a short distance away. Draw out needle over loop.

Chain Stitch Band, Raised: This stitch is used for borders. First work a foundation of straight stitches spaced evenly apart. Work from the top down over the foundation stitches and do not pick up fabric. Bring needle up just above first foundation stitch; pass needle over and under this stitch, bring out toward left; then make a stitch as shown in diagram. Pass needle over and under next foundation stitch and repeat.

Chain Stitch, Broad: This stitch is used for lines, borders and stems. Work from top down. Bring needle up at top of line. Make a small straight stitch and bring needle out below. Pass needle back under straight stitch without picking up fabric; insert in same place it last emerged; bring out below. Make stitches in same manner, passing needle back under last chain stitch made.

Chain Stitch, Cable: This is just an interesting variation of the Chain Stitch and serves the same purposes. Bring needle up at top of line to be covered. Holding thread down with left thumb, pass needle from right to left under thread held down; twist needle into vertical position, thread twisted around it. Insert in fabric the desired length and draw it through over working thread.

Chain Stitch, Zigzag Cable: This is a simple variation of the preceding stitch. Work the same as Chain Stitch, Cable but make each stitch at right angles to the last stitch.

Chain Stitch, Checkered: This stitch is sometimes called a Magic Chain since one of the colors disappears each time a stitch is taken. Use it as you would any chain stitch but for especially decorative effects. Thread a needle with 2 colors of thread. Work as a regular chain stitch but when you are ready to pull the needle through, place dark thread over the needle and draw needle through over the light thread. Reverse for next stitch.

Chain Stitch, Double: This stitch is used for wide borders. Work from the top down. Bring needle up at A; insert at B and bring out at C. Place the thread over to the left and insert needle at A; bring out at D and work a similar stitch. Then insert needle at C and work a similar stitch. For fourth stitch, insert needle in second stitch. Alternate stitches in this manner.

Chain Stitch, Heavy: This stitch is used for wide lines, borders and broad stems. Work from top down. Make a small running stitch at top of line to be covered. Bring needle out a little below this stitch; thread under running stitch; insert needle in fabric where it last emerged. Bring out below this point and thread it again under running stitch; take it back into fabric where it last emerged. Each chain is made by working back under the 2 previous loops.

Chain Stitch, Knotted: This stitch is used for lines. Work from right to left. Bring needle up at end of line. Make a small vertical stitch on the line toward the left (a slightly slanted stitch is formed). Hold working thread down with left thumb; slip needle under slanted stitch from top to bottom (do not pick up fabric); pull thread through until a loop is formed; pass needle through this loop; pull thread away and toward the left.

Chain Stitch, Open: This stitch has many names— Roman Chain, Ladder Stitch, Broad Chain. Whatever you call it, it is used for borders, wide lines and even for casings through which a ribbon may be run. Work from the top down. Bring needle out at A. Hold thread down with left thumb; insert needle at B, bring out a little below A, draw thread through over working thread. Leave loop just formed a little loose as next stitch is inserted in it. Work next stitch as shown in diagram.

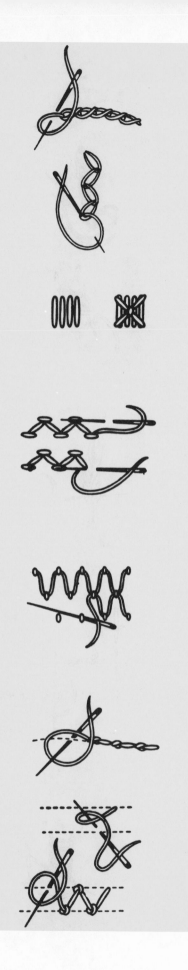

Chain Stitch, Twisted: Use this stitch for lines and borders. Work from right to left. Work as chain stitch but take a slanting stitch as shown and do not work back in previous stitch.

Chain Stitch, Zigzag: This is still another decorative variation of Chain Stitch. Work from top down. Work as for chain stitch but make each loop at an angle to the preceding loop. Run the needle through the thread of the preceding loop each time so that the stitch will lie flat.

Chessboard Filling: This stitch is used for light filling in fairly large areas. Make groups of 4 satin stitches (slightly spaced or close together). Make a cross-stitch over each group, then make a small stitch in the center where stitches cross.

Chevron Stitch: This stitch is used for lines, borders and, when rows are combined, for filling. Work from left to right. Bring needle up on lower line, insert needle to the right and bring out in the center of the stitch being formed. Make a stitch to the right on top line (first step in diagram). Then still on the top line, insert needle to the right and bring out in the center of the stitch now being formed. This step is similar to that shown in the lower half of the diagram. Continue in this manner on lower line then on top line.

Cloud Filling Stitch: This stitch is used for filling large areas. Make a foundation of rows of very tiny stitches as shown. Lace through these stitches (in another color if desired) first on the top row, then the row just below, alternating to the end of the row. On the next row lace stitches so loops meet under the same stitch as shown.

Coral Stitch: This stitch is used for lines, for outlines and sometimes as filling. Work from right to left. Bring needle up at end of line to be embroidered. Hold down thread with left thumb, then make a tiny slanting stitch across line. Draw needle under and over thread as shown.

Coral Stitch, Zigzag: This stitch is used for borders. Work the same as coral stitch but alternate stitches on an upper and lower line. Work over loops of thread as shown.

Couching Stitch: This stitch is used for outlines and lines. Place one or more threads along line to be covered, fastening them on the back at the right end of line and holding them with the left thumb as you work. With another thread, work small evenly-spaced stitches over these threads to hold them in place. At end of row draw all threads to back of work and fasten off.

Couching Stitch, Bokhara: This stitch is used for a solid filling. It is worked the same as couching but the same thread is used for the ground and the tying-down stitches. Carry thread from left to right across space to be filled; then work back as shown, making small slanting stitches at even intervals over this thread. The tying-down stitches should be rather close together and pulled tight.

Couching Stitch, Rumanian: This stitch is worked the same as Bokhara Couching but when you are working back over the thread, make the stitches longer and more slanted.

Cretan Stitch, Open: This stitch is used for lines, borders or filling. Work from left to right. Bring needle up on lower line. Make a small vertical stitch on top line as shown. Then with needle pointing up, make a similar stitch on lower line.

Cretan Stitch Leaf: This stitch is worked from the top down. Bring thread out at A. Make a small stitch B-C, drawing needle out over the loop of thread. Now make stitch D-E, again drawing needle out over the loop. Continue making stitches first one side then the other, adjusting the length of stitch to the outline. Note how decoratively the stitches interlock in the center.

Cross-stitch: This stitch is usually worked on crosses already transferred to fabric or on fabric which has threads that can be counted easily. Starting at lower left corner of a stitch and working from left to right, make a diagonal stitch (half cross-stitch) to upper right corner. Continue across, making a row of slanting stitches each going over an equal number of threads or over transferred pattern. Work back over these stitches as shown. You can work each cross-stitch individually and in any direction but they must all cross in the same direction.

Diamond Stitch: This stitch is used for borders. Work from the top down. Bring needle up on left line. Insert on right line and bring up directly below. Hold thread toward left; pass needle under the 2 threads as shown; draw needle through over working thread (knot made on right side of first stitch). Make a similar knot on left side of same stitch. Insert the needle in the left line right next to the knot just made; bring out below. Make a knot in the center on the lower of the 2 horizontal stitches. Make a stitch on the right line; make a knot, then make a knot on the left. Insert needle next to knot just made, bring out below. Then make a knot in the center.

Ermine Filling Stitch: This stitch is used for a spaced filling or for a border when worked in a row. Make a long straight stitch for center, then work an elongated cross-stitch over center stitch.

Eyelet Hole: This stitch is used in cutwork and eyelet embroidery. Draw circle of desired size on fabric. Work running stitches around it. Cut out center. Overcast all around circle, working over the running stitches.

Feather Stitch: This stitch is used for lines, borders, outlines, fern-like leaves and light filling. Work from top to bottom. Bring needle up a little to left of line to be covered. Hold thread down with left thumb; make a slanting stitch to the right and a little below this spot with needle pointing to the left; draw needle through over working thread. Carry thread to left side of line to be covered and make a similar stitch a little below this spot with needle pointing to the right; draw needle through over working thread.

Feather Stitch, Closed: This stitch is used for borders and wide lines. Work from the top down. Bring needle up at A; insert at B and bring out a little below. Note that needle is held perpendicularly on this and all subsequent stitches. Draw through over working thread. Insert needle just below starting point and make a similar stitch on left side (just like stitch being worked on diagram). Repeat, making stitches on right side then on left. Make stitches close together so that an almost unbroken line is formed at outer edges.

Feather Stitch, Long-Armed: This stitch is used for borders and filling. Work from the top down. Bring needle up at top of line to be covered. Insert to left and a little lower down; bring out at center; draw needle through over working thread. Make a similar stitch to right. Continue, alternating stitches.

Feather Stitch, Single: This stitch is used for lines, irregular outlines and smocking. Work from the top down. Bring needle up at top of line to be covered. Hold thread down with left thumb. Make a slanting stitch as shown and draw needle through over working thread. Repeat stitch on same side throughout.

Fern Stitch: This stitch is used for leaf veins or fern-like leaves. Work 3 straight stitches all radiating from the same center hole. Continue on so that the center stitches of each group form a continuous line.

Fishbone Stitch: This stitch is used to cover an entire area. Make a short stitch at top of area to be filled. Bring needle up on left edge; insert it a little below first stitch and just across center line; bring out on right edge. Make a similar stitch inserting needle to left of center line and bringing it out at left edge. Each succeeding stitch should slant and cross at the center.

Fishbone Stitch, Raised: This stitch, when finished, looks just like the preceding one but looks thicker and more cushiony. Make 3 stitches at top of area to be filled, ending with thread coming from left edge as shown in upper diagram. Insert needle on right edge, bring out on left edge directly opposite. Insert needle on right edge just below lowest stitch as shown in lower diagram; bring out needle on left edge directly opposite. Repeat these 2 steps shown in upper and lower diagrams.

Fly Stitch: This stitch is used for a light filling or, when worked in a row, for borders. Bring thread up at upper left corner of stitch; insert needle directly opposite (upper right corner of stitch) and bring out in center below; draw through over working thread. Make a small stitch to tie down loop. This tying-down stitch can be made various lengths for different effects.

French Knot: This stitch is used in groups for flower centers, for light filling and where the effect of a single dot is required. The thread is often used double or triple for a bigger dot. Bring needle up where dot is to be made. Wind thread 2 or 3 times around point of needle, insert in fabric as close as possible to spot where thread emerged (but not in exact spot) and pull to wrong side, holding twists of stitch in place.

Herringbone Stitch: This stitch is used for borders, wide lines and as a foundation for other stitches. Work from left to right. Bring needle up at A; insert at B, bring out at C; then insert at D, bring out at E. Continue in this manner.

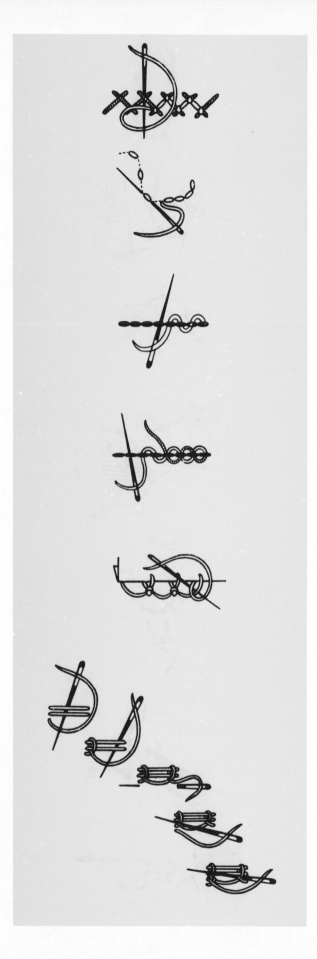

Herringbone Stitch, Tied: This is a more decorative version of herringbone and is used for borders. Make a foundation of herringbone stitches. Then work coral stitch over them, making a knot over intersections without picking up fabric.

Holbein Stitch: This stitch is used for lines and outlines. It is often used to outline solid areas of cross-stitch. Work running stitch along line to be covered, making sure that each stitch and space between stitches are all of equal size. Then work running stitch back over this line, filling in the empty spaces.

Holbein Stitch, Single-Threaded: This stitch is used for special emphasis on lines and borders. Work a foundation of Holbein Stitch. Then thread another color or weight of yarn through these stitches, not carrying it to back of fabric at all. Sometimes it is easier to insert the *eye* of the needle under the stitch rather than the point. Threading can be tight or loose depending on the effect you want.

Holbein Stitch, Double-Threaded: Complete the first 2 steps of Holbein Stitch, Single-Threaded. Then with thread of the same color as the first threading, (or a contrasting color), work back over the line of stitches to make loops on the opposite side of stitches.

Knot Stitch: This stitch is used to trim a hem or a turned-over edge. Work from left to right. Bring needle to right side at fold. With needle in vertical position, insert needle to right through hem and bring out below hem over working thread (do not pull tightly). Take another stitch over this loop as shown and pull into a knot.

Ladder Stitch: This stitch is used for wide borders and for filling. The sides are usually straight but an interesting effect can be achieved by expanding the width of the ladder as you work. Work from the top down. Make 2 horizontal stitches the desired width. Then pass needle under these horizontal stitches as shown. Do not pick up fabric. Make a similar loop stitch on right side (2nd step in diagram). Then insert needle in right edge; bring out on left edge (3rd step). Insert needle between 2nd and 3rd rungs of ladder, pass it under both threads of left-hand loop, draw through without picking up fabric (4th step). Work under right-hand loop in same manner (5th step). Repeat steps 3, 4 and 5. Pull thread slightly to the left after making left-hand loops but leave it a little loose when making right-hand loops. This will keep stitches even.

Laid Stitch: This stitch looks just like satin stitch but requires less thread and is somewhat flatter. Make a stitch like a satin stitch across area to be filled. Do not return to starting edge but make next stitch as shown, leaving size of a stitch between the two. Work all across the area then fill open spaces with another series of stitches.

Laid Work, Tied: This stitch is used for solid and very decorative filling. First fill in entire area to be worked in laid stitch. Then make a series of diagonal stitches over the laid stitch. Make another series of diagonal stitches crossing the first diagonal stitches at right angles. Tie down the diagonal stitches at intersections with a series of little stitches, as lower diagram. The laid stitches, the diagonal stitches and the tying down stitches may all be worked in different colors.

Lazy-daisy Stitch: This stitch is used for flowers and light filling. Bring thread up in center of "flower." Hold thread down with left thumb; insert needle close to or in exact spot where thread emerged and bring out desired distance (the length of the petal— see upper figure in diagram). Draw through over working thread. Then tie down with a tiny stitch made over loop as shown. Make similar stitches to form a circle around same center point. Diagram shows them slightly separated for clarity, but they can be made in same center hole.

Lazy-daisy Stitch, Long-tailed: This stitch is a simple variation of Lazy-daisy Stitch. It is worked in the same manner as the Lazy-daisy but the loop is smaller and the tying-down stitch is longer and is made toward the center.

Long and Short Stitch: This stitch is used for filling and for shading. Work the same as Satin Stitch, except that you stagger long and short stitches over the area to be covered. The irregular line makes a very softly shaded effect when closely related colors are used.

Long and Short Stitch, Surface: This stitch is used to save thread. It is worked the same as Long and Short Stitch but the Satin Stitches are worked on the surface (see Satin Stitch, Surface). The needle does not travel so far underneath the fabric.

Outline Stitch: This stitch is used for outlines, stems and any fine lines. Bring needle up at left end of line. Working from left to right, insert needle a short distance to the right and bring out a little way to the left at a very slight angle. Keep thread above the needle. **Note:** If thread is held below the needle, the stitch is known as Stem, or Crewel Stitch.

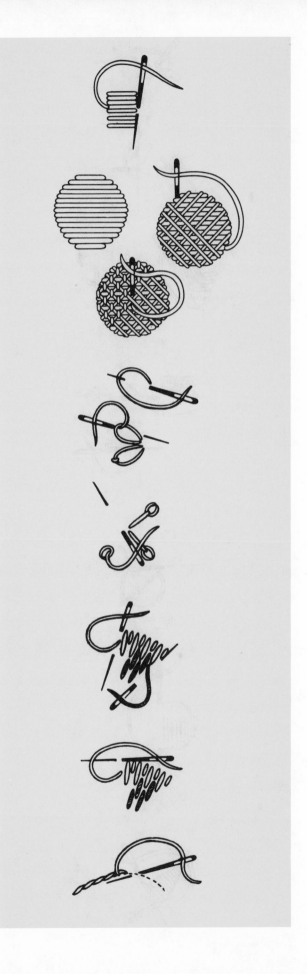

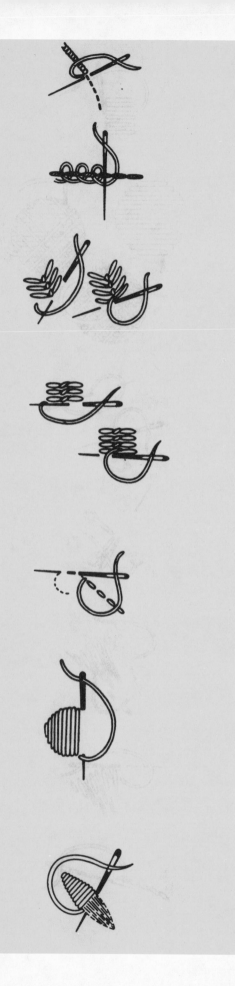

Overcast Stitch: This stitch is used for stems, outlines and monogramming. Work a row of running stitches along line to be covered. Then work small close stitches across these stitches. Pick up the smallest amount of fabric possible.

Pekingese Stitch: This stitch is used for borders. First make a row of back stitches. Without picking up fabric, lace second thread (in another color, if desired) through these stitches.

Roman Stitch: This stitch is used for borders or filling. Work from the top down. Bring needle up on left line; insert exactly opposite on right line; bring out in center. Then make a tiny stitch over this loop and bring needle out on left line (second step in diagram). Stitches can be made slightly curved as shown or perfectly straight.

Rumanian Stitch: This stitch is used for borders or filling. Work from the top down. Bring needle up on left line; insert exactly opposite on right line; bring it out about halfway back toward left line, draw through over working thread. Then tie this stitch down with a slanting stitch as shown.

Running Stitch: This stitch may be worked on a straight or curved line. It is used for outlines, a foundation for other stitches and for filling when worked in close rows. Work from right to left and make stitches even in size and evenly spaced. If work is in a hoop, only one stitch can be made at a time. If work is in the hand, 2 or 3 stitches can be made at a time. Running stitch may be threaded with another color (see Holbein Stitch, Single-Threaded or Holbein Stitch, Double-Threaded).

Satin Stitch: This stitch is used where background fabric is to be covered completely but over an area that is not too large. Bring needle up at one edge of area to be covered, insert at opposite edge and return to starting edge by carrying it underneath fabric. Stitches may be vertical, horizontal or diagonal but should always be parallel and close together.

Satin Stitch, Padded: For a slightly raised effect pad the area with stitches before working satin stitch. Straight stitches are used here. Padding may also be chain stitch or satin stitch. In any case, the padding is usually worked in the opposite direction to the final satin stitch.

Satin Stitch, Surface: This stitch is used to save thread. It is worked the same as Satin Stitch but the needle does not go all the way underneath area to be covered. Take a tiny stitch at the edge, then take a tiny stitch at opposite edge. For a closer alignment of stitches, however, use Laid Stitch.

Scroll Stitch: This stitch is used for borders. Work from left to right. Bring needle up at end of line to be covered. Make a loop of thread as shown. Insert needle in center of loop across line to be covered and pick up a small amount of fabric; pull loop tightly under point of needle, then draw needle through.

Seed Stitch: This stitch (sometimes called Seeding Stitch) is used for light filling and may be as dense as shown or more widely scattered. Make tiny straight stitches in any direction. The stitches are not worked in a regular pattern but should be of equal length. They can be made single or double as shown.

Shadow Stitch: This stitch is worked on sheer fabric so that the under part of the stitch shows through in a shadow effect. Work from right to left. Make a small backstitch on one side of area to be filled, slant needle to other side of space, make another backstitch. Shadow Stitch is worked on right side of fabric but main part of stitch appears on wrong side so that X's show through fabric while rows of continuous backstitches are on right side. This stitch may be worked across a variety of shapes — a leaf, a flower or a circle, for instance. The X's will vary in size but the backstitches will always be of equal size.

Sheaf Filling Stitch: This stitch is used for filling. Make 3 vertical satin stitches. Then bring needle out at center of left side; wrap thread around center twice without picking up fabric and insert where thread emerged.

Split Stitch: This stitch is used for outlines, stems and fine lines. When worked in close rows, it is used for filling. Close rows worked in closely related colors produce shading for leaves and flowers. Work split stitch like stem stitch (see Outline Stitch), then split working thread close to its base when you bring needle out.

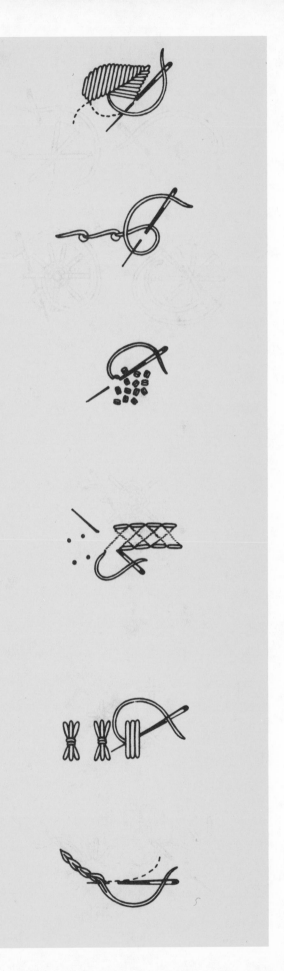

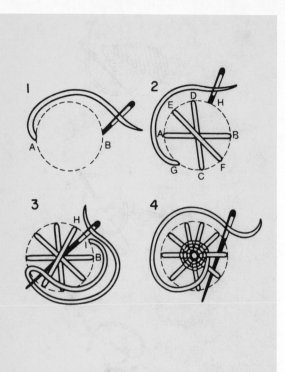

Spider Web, Whipped: This stitch is used as a highly decorative spot such as the center of a large flower. If your fabric is not too tightly woven, use a tapestry needle. Bring thread out at A; insert needle at B (diagram 1). Then bring needle out at C; insert at D (note that C-D is slightly off the true vertical). Bring needle out at E; insert at F; bring out at G; insert at H (note in diagram 2 that H is closer to D than to B). Bring needle out at I (halfway between H and B). Without inserting needle in fabric, run it under all the threads at the center; loop thread over needle as shown (diagram 3); pull needle through and pull upwards, knotting threads together in center. Continuing with the same working thread, run needle under 2 threads at the center; then run needle under the last thread used and 1 new thread (diagram 4). Repeat this process, going back over 1 thread and running needle under 2 threads, until the spokes are all covered. If desired, edge of Spider Web can be outlined with any basic stitch suggested for outlines.

Spider Web, Woven: This stitch is a slightly different version of Spider Web. Follow diagrams 1, 2 and 3 in preceding directions. When the spokes have been knotted together at center, continue on with same working thread. Weave under 1 spoke, over 1 spoke until entire web is filled. If desired, edge of Spider Web can be outlined with any basic stitch suggested for outlines.

Star Filling Stitch: This stitch is used for rather open filling of an area or combined with other stitches. Work a cross-stitch on the straight rather than the diagonal. Then work another cross-stitch of equal size right over the first one, this time placing it on the diagonal. Finally, work a tiny cross-stitch in the center over the intersection of the first two.

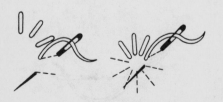

Straight Stitch: This stitch is used as an occasional single stitch scattered in a design or grouped in a ring to form a flower. Each stitch is always separated from the next one.

Thorn Stitch: This stitch is used for stems and leaves. First make a long center stitch from bottom of line to the top. Then work diagonal stitches over the center stitch from the top down.

Trellis Stitch: This stitch is used for filling especially where a lattice effect is desired. It is often used on flower centers. Work long horizontal stitches evenly spaced across area to be filled. Then work long vertical stitches across these. Work a cross-stitch, (sometimes only a half cross-stitch) at each intersection. A different weight or color of thread may be used to work cross-stitches.

Vandyke Stitch: This stitch is used for borders. Bring needle up at 1. Insert at 2 and bring out at 3. Then insert at 4 and bring out at 5. For next stitch insert needle under center crossed stitches and without picking up fabric draw needle through. Insert needle in right edge below last stitch, bring out directly below last stitch on left edge.

Wave Stitch, Open: This stitch is used for filling. Work a row of small straight vertical stitches from left to right across top of area to be filled (shaded stitches on diagram). Bring needle up on right edge below these stitches. Slip needle under first straight stitch and without picking up fabric, draw needle through. Make a tiny horizontal stitch below and on line with point where thread last emerged; then work under next straight stitch. The third and all following rows are slipped under the bases of two stitches of the previous row as shown.

Wheat-ear Stitch: This stitch is used for stems, borders and wheatlike stalks. Work from top down. Bring needle up on line to be covered (1); insert at 2; bring out at 3. Insert close to spot where thread first emerged and bring out a distance below. Then without picking up fabric, slip needle from right to left underneath the first 2 stitches (upper diagram). Insert needle in spot where thread last emerged and bring out to left as shown in lower diagram. Insert needle in bottom of loop and bring out above and to the right; insert again at bottom of loop and bring out a distance below.

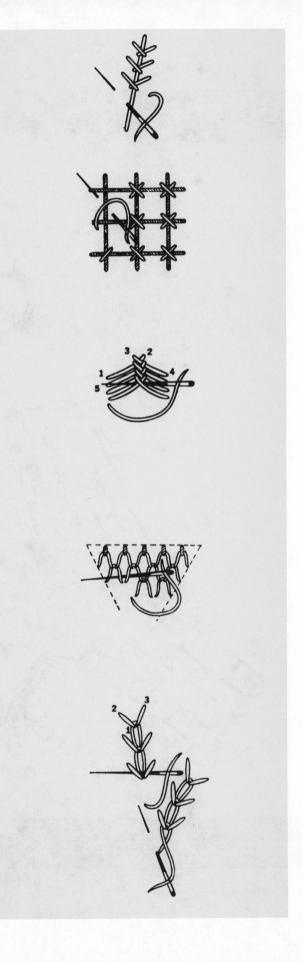

Crewel

Crewel

Crewel is a very old form of needlework combining European and Oriental elements with a modern American approach—and can be more fun to do than almost any other kind of needlework. Perhaps a warning is in order here. Crewel can be addictive! Don't start a piece unless you are willing to suffer the pangs of a guilty conscience for neglected chores and unfulfilled responsibilities. You will want to spend just five more minutes completing a new part of the design to see how your couching stitch works out. Another few minutes should finish that leaf. And that's the way the crewel—and the time—goes. As the word is used today, crewel is almost any type of embroidery done in a free manner with a variety of stitches and colored yarn or thread.

MATERIALS

Traditionally a twill linen in natural, cream or white was used as background fabric. But there were as many exceptions to the rule then as there are today. Cotton twill, firmly-woven wool, even silk were used. Although natural-color linen is still used most frequently, we no longer limit ourselves to neutral backgrounds.

When we study examples of antique crewel work, we find that the embroidery was worked most often with worsted yarns, frequently with linen yarns and even with silk threads on fine silk backgrounds.

Crewel wool, a fine two-ply yarn with a "crinkle," is available today in most yarn departments and needlework supply stores. Until recently, it was necessary to buy large quantities of each color. Now it is possible to buy crewel wool wound on cards containing only 30 yards. The two plies of some yarns can be split to give you a fine yarn for delicate effects. It may also be combined with a great variety of other yarns and cotton and linen threads for a wide range of effects.

Old crewel was often worked in shades of just one color such as green or blue. Now we work our crewel embroidery in a veritable rainbow of colors.

CREWEL STITCHES

A beautiful piece of crewel work may be embroidered in one basic stitch or in dozens of different stitches. It is suggested that you practice a few simple stitches to get the feeling of the work. Later on you can enlarge your repertoire. First draw some straight lines (using your thimble as a guide) some curved lines, some dots, and a few circles on scrap fabric of an appropriate weight. Put the fabric in a hoop and with whatever fine yarn or embroidery thread you have handy, practice stitches (see Index). Try a running stitch, Holbein stitch, outline stitch and chain stitch on the straight and curved lines. For really professional looking embroidery it is important to keep the stitches all the same length when working any given stitch. Work French knots on the dots, satin stitch in the circles. Now that you have practiced these stitches you are ready to tackle any of these four simple projects.

SIX BASIC CREWEL STITCHES

From left to right: Running Stitch, Holbein Stitch, Outline Stitch, Chain Stitch, French Knot, Satin Stitch. For detailed directions see Index.

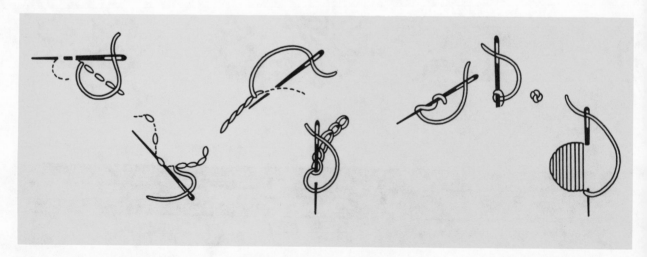

Right: Crewel napkins and napkin rings, eyeglasses case, pincushion, trayholder. See pages 42, 43, 44.

40

NAPKINS AND NAPKIN RINGS

Bright colored inexpensive napkins become conversation pieces with the addition of just a few embroidery stitches and their own matching napkin rings. In fact, when you become proficient at making these, you may want to use them as your contribution to the next bazaar.

SIZE: Napkin ring is 1½″ wide, 5¼″ around.
MATERIALS: Ready-made linen napkins (1 extra napkin will make about 10 napkin rings); pearl cotton, size 5, in 2 colors; dressmakers' iron-on interfacing, 1½″ x 5¼″ for each napkin ring; sewing thread to match napkins. **Color Note:** Napkins shown were worked in brown and white on turquoise, and pink and red on bright yellow-green. Choose your color combination to harmonize with your china, your dining room decor or a favorite tablecloth.

EQUIPMENT: Embroidery hoop; crewel needle.

Napkins

DESIGN: Transfer design (shown full size) to corner of your napkin, placing it 1″ from edges.
EMBROIDERY: Place napkin in embroidery hoop. Work lines in Holbein stitch in light shade, dots in French knots in dark color.

Napkin Rings

PATTERN AND DESIGN: On extra napkin mark areas 3¾″ x 6¼″ for number of napkin rings desired. In center of each marked area transfer design (shown full size).
EMBROIDERY: Do not cut out napkin rings. Place entire napkin in hoop and embroider all your rings before cutting out any of them. Work straight lines in Holbein stitch in light shade, dots in French knots in dark color. Complete by threading center line of stitches with dark color (see Index for double-threaded Holbein stitch).

FINISHING: Block piece. Cut out napkin rings. Cut interfacing 1½″ x 5¼″. Centering an interfacing piece on back of each embroidered piece, iron in place. Fold long edges of fabric to back; turn under one long raw edge, overlapping other raw edge and blindstitch in place. Turn in raw ends of fabric. Whip the two ends of napkin ring together.

PINCUSHION

There is something delightfully Victorian about a pincushion. No doubt we use pins as often as our ancestors—and therefore need a pincushion just as much—but they never seem quite twentieth century. Perhaps you'll sit a bit more primly with your feet neatly propped on a footstool when you embroider this plump little barrel pincushion.

SIZE: 2½″ in diameter, 2½″ high.
MATERIALS: Small piece (about 10″ square) unbleached linen or natural-color firmly-woven cotton; crewel wool, 1 card each bright green, forest green, chartreuse; small piece of stiff buckram; scrap cardboard; white glue; sawdust, cut-up nylon stockings or cotton batting for stuffing; sewing thread.

EQUIPMENT: Embroidery hoop; crewel needle.
PATTERN AND DESIGN: On fabric draw an area 2½″ x 8″, marking it on the straight of the goods. Do not cut out. Following diagram, work out design repeating from A to B four times. Design on diagram is shown full scale. Transfer design to marked area on fabric.

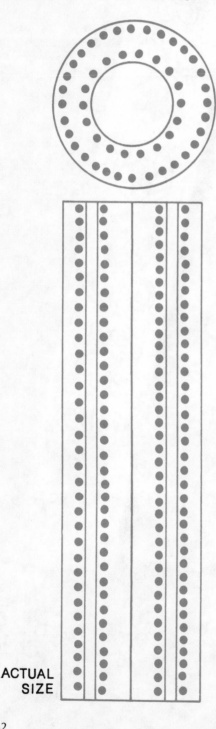

ACTUAL
SIZE

EMBROIDERY: Place piece in hoop. The only new stitches you will encounter are the single-threaded Holbein stitch and straight stitch (see Index). Embroider as follows: work spoke design in 1 strand, all others in 2. Work spoke design in about 16 straight stitches in bright green. Work all broken lines in Holbein stitch. Border lines are forest green; vertical lines, bright green. Thread all the vertical Holbein stitches (not the border) with forest green. On double straight lines use chartreuse and work chain stitch. Work all dots in French knots; join them with forest green running stitch.

FINISHING: When complete, block then cut out strip, adding ½" seam allowances on all edges. Also cut out 2 fabric circles each 3½" in diameter. Cut buckram 2½" x 8". Center it on back of embroidered piece. Fold seam allowances over buckram and fasten with a few spots of glue. Join narrow ends of embroidered piece, right side out, and whip together. Cut 2 cardboard circles 2½" in diameter. From center of one circle cut out a 1¾" circle and discard it, leaving only a narrow ring.

Run a double shirred thread near edge of each fabric circle. Place cardboard circle in center of wrong side of a fabric circle. Draw seam allowance over cardboard and pull up shirring thread. Repeat with cardboard ring and other fabric circle.

Whip covered circle to lower edge of embroidered piece. Stuff pincushion firmly. Whip covered ring to top edge of pincushion.

EYEGLASSES CASE

A handsome case for eyeglasses is always a welcome gift. This one uses modern colors in a particularly interesting mosaic pattern. Note how placing the stitches vertically and then horizontally makes the design seem to be in a dozen colors, when actually only four are used.

SIZE: 3" x 6".

MATERIALS: Small amount unbleached linen or firmly-woven natural-color cotton; crewel wool, 1 card each of light aqua, dark aqua, blue and bronze; small amount stiff buckram; white glue; sewing thread.

EQUIPMENT: Embroidery hoop; crewel needle.

PATTERN AND DESIGN: On fabric draw an area 3" x 6", marking it on the straight of goods. Do not cut out. Trace design as on diagram. (Diagram shows one half of design full scale.) Repeat from A to B once again for other half of design. Transfer design to marked area on fabric.

EMBROIDERY: Place work in hoop. Following the key accompanying diagram for colors, using 1 strand of wool, work squares in satin stitch throughout. The direction of the double lines in each square on diagram indicates the direction your satin stitches should take. Work dots in 2 strands of blue in French knots. With 1 strand of dark aqua work a row of Holbein stitch on each side of French knots.

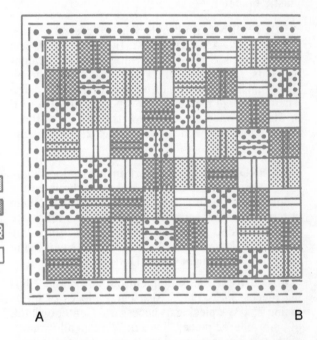

BLUE
DARK AQUA
BRONZE
LIGHT AQUA

FINISHING: Block then cut out embroidered piece, adding ½" seam allowance on all edges. Cut 3 more pieces of fabric the same size as the embroidered piece, including seam allowances. Cut out 2 pieces of buckram 3" x 6".

Center a buckram piece on the back of the embroidered piece. Fold seam allowances over buckram and fasten with a few spots of glue. Turn in seam allowances of a fabric piece and press. Whip this piece to the back of embroidered piece with wrong sides together.

Center a buckram piece on a plain piece and glue seam allowances as before. Join remaining plain piece to it as you did for the embroidered piece. Now right sides out, pin together carefully the front and the back of the eyeglasses case at the 4 corners. Whip together along one side, across the lower edge and up the other side.

TRAY HOLDER

Here's a project that will not only help you develop your crewel techniques but will also mystify your friends! We'll bet ten skeins of wool that they will never guess what you are making unless you enlighten them. Isn't this a wonderful way to turn a good looking serving tray into a handsome wall decoration? At the same time it is always ready for use. If you prefer, this same design may be adapted to a belt or bands for a luggage rack.

SIZE: To hold a tray up to 15″ wide.
MATERIALS: ⅜ yard 54″ unbleached linen or natural-color firmly-woven cotton; crewel wool, 1 card each olive, light olive, orange, scarlet, magenta, dark blue, blue and turquoise; ¼ yard dressmaker's non-woven interfacing; sewing thread; plastic bracelet.

EQUIPMENT: Embroidery hoop; crewel needle.
PATTERN AND DESIGN: In center of fabric draw 2 strips 3½″ x 40″, marking them on straight of goods. Do not cut out. Trace design on diagram. (Diagram shows one half of the design full scale.) Then complete the design by repeating from A to B in diagram once again. Down the center of the 2 strips transfer the design, starting 2¼″ from one end.

EMBROIDERY: Place work in embroidery hoop. Use 1 strand of the crewel wool throughout. In the colors shown on diagram work all lines in Holbein stitch. Stems and scroll-like leaves on the tulips are single-threaded Holbein stitch, the threading worked in light olive. All spiky elements worked in turquoise are straight stitch. Dots are French knots.

FINISHING: Block then cut out strips and 2 lining pieces 3¼″ x 39¾″. Also cut 2 pieces of interfacing 2″ x 39″, piecing as necessary. Center on back of embroidered pieces. Turn in ½″ seam allowances on both pieces; baste. Also turn in ½″ seam allowances all around both lining pieces. Slip stitch a plain lining to each embroidered piece. Lining is slightly smaller all around, therefore the embroidered pieces must be eased to the lining pieces. This will cause the finished strips to fold without wrinkles.

Wind dark blue yarn around bracelet so that it is completely covered. Tie ends or fasten with white glue or masking tape. Run an embroidered band through bracelet and whip ends together, working on wrong side, to form ring. Repeat with other band.

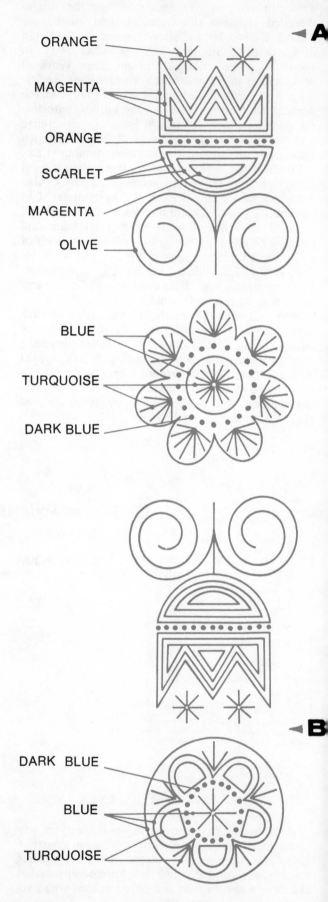

44

FISH PICTURE

This crewel fish is a show-off in its own golden sea. The simplicity of the stitches and interesting use of color combine to create an unusual effect. No poor fish, this!

SIZE: 16½″ x 18″.

MATERIALS: Coats & Clark's "Red Heart" 4 ply knitting worsted; ⅓ oz. each, mid-orange, canary yellow, tangerine, wood brown; a few yards each, Nile green, emerald, paddy green, black and white; a piece of gold burlap 16½″ x 18″.

EQUIPMENT: Embroidery hoop; tapestry needle; colored pencil; purple crayon; tracing paper, 12½″ x 14″.

ENLARGING THE DESIGN: Using a colored pencil, draw lines on the diagram from dots on one side to corresponding dots on opposite side, forming squares. On tracing paper make the same number of squares, each square measuring ½ inch. Within each square on the paper, draw the portion of the design shown in the corresponding square of the diagram.

TRANSFERRING DESIGN TO FABRIC: The simplest method is to have the wrong side of the tracing paper sketch toward you, and with a sharpened crayon go over the lines of the drawing which show through the paper. Leaving a 2-inch margin on all sides of fabric, place the tracing paper over the fabric, crayon side down. Press with a warm iron. It is wise to test with scraps of fabric before transferring the design to large piece of fabric.

EMBROIDERY: Follow diagram and key for stitches and colors for all parts indicated on diagram. All parts similar to numbered parts on diagram are worked in the same stitch and color.

Chevron Filling: This is borrowed from the Florentine stitch of needlepoint, but it makes an effective filling and may be carried out in as many colors as desired. It looks best if it is not outlined, so make sure that edges are kept neat. Start across the widest space to be filled, since the first row acts as a guide for all shorter rows. With canary yellow lay 5 parallel line across width of fish in area to be worked. Lines are to be made approximately ½″ apart. Bring thread up underneath line 1, pass over line 2 and down closely below line 3. Make four stitches this way, close together. Bring needle up underneath line 2, pass over line 3 and down closely below line 4. Make four stitches close together. Bring needle up under line 3, over line 4 and down under line 5. Continue these blocks of four stitches, going down three lines and up three lines until row has been completed. With mid-orange work next row as before, bringing needle through same hole made by previous thread. Work third row with tangerine and fourth row with wood brown. Alternate colors as shown on stitch detail. Always complete one row before starting the next.

KEY FOR STITCHES AND COLORS

1. Chevron filling — Canary yellow, mid-orange, tangerine, wood brown. (Alternate these colors.)

2. Feather stitch — Canary yellow

3. Feather stitch — Paddy green

4. Feather stitch — Emerald

5. French knots — Wood brown (fill area)

6. French knots — White

7. Van Dyke stitch — Mid-orange

8. Stem stitch — Wood brown

9. Couching — Emerald

10. Couching — Paddy green

11. Couching — Nile green

12. Couching — Tangerine

13. Couching — Yellow

14. Couching — Black

BIRD PICTURE

What a beautiful way to express affection and friendship! A gift of needlework lovingly embroidered by you would be cherished by anyone lucky enough to receive it. This happy portrait of two doves is symbolic of Peace. The flowers represent Beauty, the bright colors Joy. And your contribution is that of Love. (See pages 38 and 39.)

SIZE: 8½″ x 17½″.

MATERIALS: ½ yard unbleached linen or natural-color firmly-woven cotton; crewel wool, 1 card each light pink, medium rose, dark rose, dark turquoise, medium turquoise, medium aqua, medium French blue, dark French blue, medium olive green, dark olive green, medium rust, dark orange, dark yellow, brown; materials for framing.

EQUIPMENT: Embroidery frame; crewel needle.

48

DESIGN: Trace design directly from the color photograph or enlarge diagram (each small square = ½″ square) so that your pattern is the size the piece was actually worked. Transfer design to center of fabric cut 12½″ x 21½″.

EMBROIDERY: Place work in frame. Use 1 strand of wool throughout. Follow photograph for colors. Broken lines on diagram indicate coral stitch. Unbroken lines are worked in Holbein stitch.

The only exceptions are the birds' tails. The lines across each feather should be worked in a large straight stitch. All shaded areas are laid stitch.

The only new stitch on this piece is the star filling stitch (see Index). Only half of the final little cross-stitch used to hold the larger stitches together was worked on this piece, however. These are worked on all the little star-shaped motifs on the diagram.

FINISHING: Block and frame picture following directions (see Index).

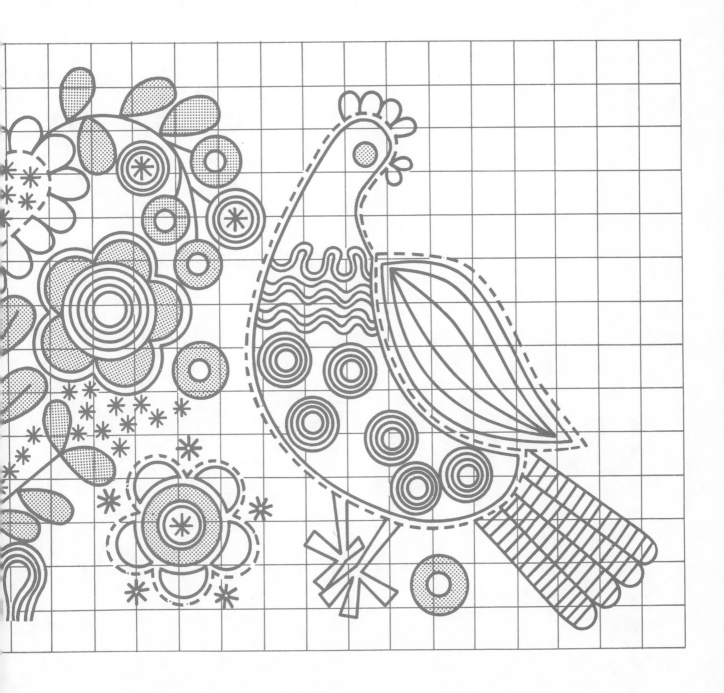

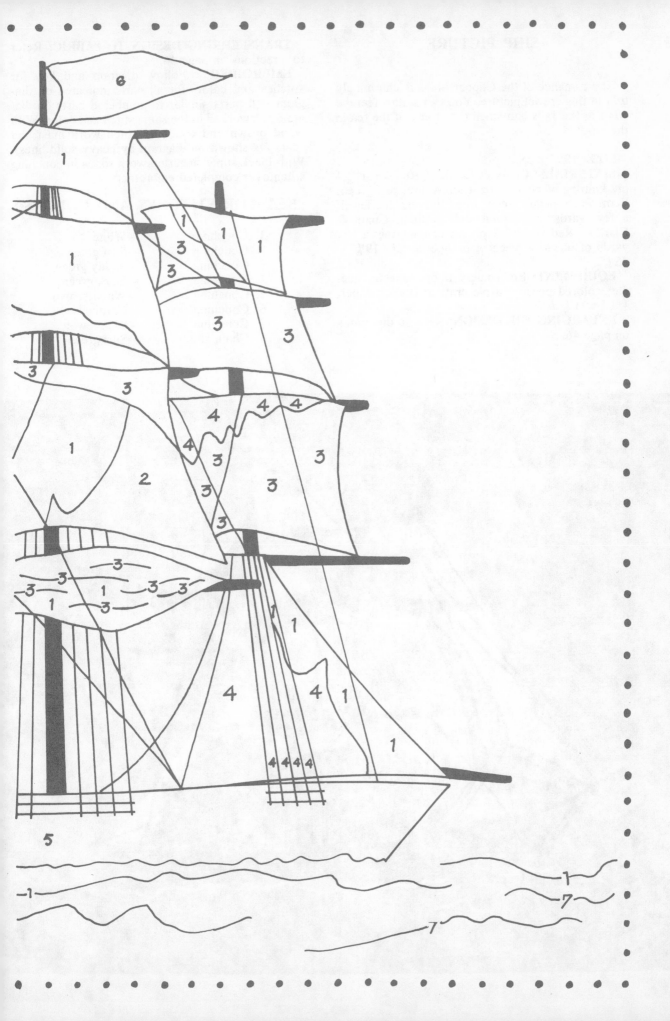

SHIP PICTURE

The romance of the Clipper Ships is charmingly told in this crewel picture. You can almost feel the wind in the sails and smell the aroma of the tea in the hold.

SIZE: 19½″ x 25½″.

MATERIALS: Coats & Clark's "Red Heart" 4 ply knitting worsted: 1 oz. each, white, surf green; ⅓ oz. each, paddy green, wood brown, blue jewel; a few yards dark green and cardinal. Coats & Clark's "Red Heart" 3 ply super fingering: a few yards of black; a piece of orange burlap, 19½″ x 25½″.

EQUIPMENT: Embroidery hoop; tapestry needle; colored pencil; purple crayon; tracing paper, 15½″ x 21½″.

ENLARGING THE DESIGN: Refer to directions on page 46.

TRANSFERRING DESIGN TO FABRIC: Refer to directions on page 46.

EMBROIDERY: Follow diagram and key for stitches and colors for all parts indicated on diagram. All parts similar to numbered parts on diagram are worked in the same stitch and color. With wood brown and couching stitch work mast and spars (as shown on diagram by heavy solid lines). With black super fingering work ropes in couching stitch over completed embroidery.

KEY FOR STITCHES AND COLORS:

1. Couching — White
2. Couching — Surf green
3. Couching — Paddy green
4. Couching — Dark green
5. Couching — Wood brown
6. Couching — Cardinal
7. Couching — Blue jewel
8. Chain stitch — Surf green

FLORAL PILLOW TOP

Doesn't this floral design remind you of an English country garden bright with asters and delphiniums? Even the straight lines of the background are reminiscent of a proper picket fence. Although the design was planned as a pillow top, framed it would make a charming picture. Or you might make two and convert them into a smashing tote bag.

SIZE: 10″ x 11¼″.

MATERIALS: ½ yard 36″ unbleached linen or natural-color firmly woven cotton; crewel wool, 1 card each light bronze, medium green, dark olive, pink, orange, dark rose, medium blue, French blue and turquoise; other materials depend upon how the embroidery is used.

EQUIPMENT: Embroidery frame; crewel needle.

DESIGN: Enlarge diagram for design (each small square = 1″ square). Transfer design to fabric.

EMBROIDERY: Place work in embroidery frame. The key accompanying the diagram indicates the stitches to be used. If you have not encountered the trellis stitch, the laid stitch and coral stitch before, practice them on scrap fabric (see Index).

Now start your embroidery using colors as follows: All vertical lines are light bronze. All leaves are medium green with a border of dark olive Holbein stitch. On Flower 1 **working from outer edge in,** use light rose, dark rose, pink, dark rose. On Flower 2 use dark rose, orange, pink, dark rose, pink. On Flower 3 use French blue, medium blue, turquoise, French blue, medium blue. Flower 4 colors are in the same order as Flower 3. Flower 5 is same as Flower 1. On Flower 6 use dark rose, orange, pink, orange, dark rose, pink. On Flower 7 use medium blue, turquoise, French blue, medium blue, turquoise. Flower 8 is same as Flower 6.

FINISHING: Block and make into a pillow or tote bag or frame following directions (see Index).

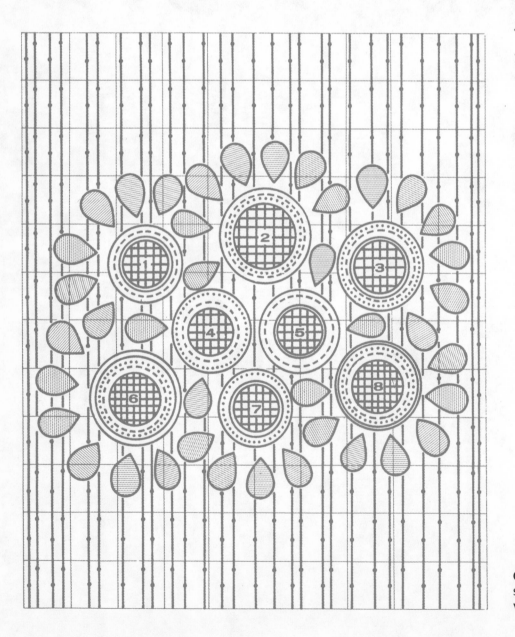

	OUTLINE STIT[CH]
	CHAIN STITCH
	FRENCH KNOT
	CORAL STITCH
	TRELLIS STITC[H]
	LAID STITCH

Garden flowers make b[o] spots of color on this versatile crewel design.

54

SEA FLOWER PICTURE

Sea flowers in deep cool tones are observed by a perky sea horse. A variety of interesting stitches are used so that doing the embroidery is as enjoyable as the end result.

SIZE: 14½" x 26½".

MATERIALS: Coats & Clark's "Red Heart" 4 ply knitting worsted: ⅓ oz. each, Nile green, dark turquoise, black; a few yards amethyst, light turquoise, lilac, olive green; a piece of light green burlap, 14½" x 26½".

EQUIPMENT: Embroidery hoop; tapestry needle; colored pencil; purple crayon; tracing paper, 10½" x 26½".

ENLARGING THE DESIGN: Refer to directions on page 46.

TRANSFERRING DESIGN TO FABRIC: Refer to directions on page 46.

EMBROIDERY: Follow diagram and key for stitches and colors for all parts indicated on diagram. All parts similar to numbered parts on diagram are worked in the same stitch and color.

Weaving Stitch: This stitch is made by laying down vertical satin stitches over the leaf shapes. Then weave in and out of these stitches with contrasting color as indicated on key for stitches and colors.

KEY FOR STITCHES AND COLORS:

1. Van Dyke stitch — Olive green
2. Stem stitch — Olive green
3. Weaving stitch — Amethyst and olive green
4. Weaving stitch — Lilac and Nile green
5. Weaving stitch — Olive green and Nile green
6. Weaving stitch — Lilac and dark turquoise
7. Weaving stitch — Lilac and olive green
8. Straight stitch — Nile green
9. Straight stitch — Lilac
10. Straight stitch — Olive green

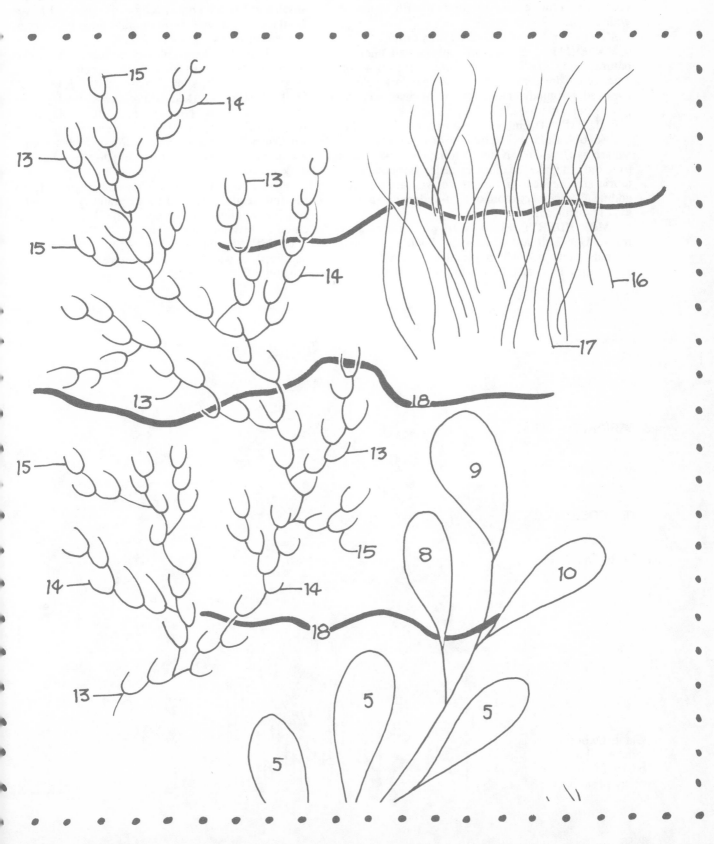

FLOWER BASKET

Baskets of flowers—fresh, artificial or crewel—enhance the decor of any room. Even the experienced needleworker will enjoy creating this basketful, although the stitches are easy enough for a beginner. The giant stitches work up in no time. Use your own color scheme to contrast with or match your decor.

SIZE: 15″ x 17″ (embroidered area only).

MATERIALS: ⅝ yard 36″ unbleached linen or natural-color firmly woven cotton; crewel wool, 1 card each dark orange, bright orange, dark yellow, dark red, burgundy, dark rose, bright rose, tea rose, pink, grape, marine blue.

EQUIPMENT: Embroidery frame; crewel needle.

DESIGN: Enlarge diagram for design (each small square = 1″ square). **Note:** Shading on flowers was used only to make the diagram easier to follow. Plan fabric size needed for the project you are making, adding all necessary seam or turn-under allowances, etc. Transfer design to fabric.

EMBROIDERY: Place work in embroidery frame. Use 2 strands of yarn for all stitches except French knots (for which you use 3 strands). See Index for all stitches. First work petals of all round flowers in straight stitch. To save yarn as well as make stitches neater, work these on the surface only, somewhat like the method used in working laid stitch. Use the color indicated by number in center of flower. Using same color as petals, work a circle of Holbein stitch around inner edge of petals. Now finish flower centers with circles of Holbein stitch and French knots in colors as follows: Flower 1—dark red; flower 2—burgundy; flower 3—bright orange; flower 4—grape.

Work the fan-shaped blossoms (in color indicated by number) in 8 to 10 straight stitches the full length of the blossom. Anchor these down with Holbein stitch worked where the curved line is shown on diagram. Now on outer half of each blossom work a straight stitch between each of those worked before in colors as follows: On blossom 4 use grape; on blossom 5 use pink; on blossom 6 use dark yellow.

Work basket in marine blue in straight stitches the full height indicated on diagram. Anchor with running stitches worked across the basket as indicated by broken lines.

FINISHING: Block piece. Remove from frame and finish as wall hanging or picture (for directions, see Index).

1 BRIGHT ROSE

2 DARK ROSE

3 DARK RED

4 BURGUNDY

5 TEA ROSE

6 DARK ORANGE

Giant stitches quickly fill a basket full of pretty posies.

WALL HANGING

Even the most modern room setting would be enhanced by this design of stylized tulips, daisies and asters. Just two basic stitches worked in only one color—rich warm brown—will produce a piece of needlework that is truly in the heirloom category.

SIZE: 19″ x 21″.

MATERIALS: ⅝ yard unbleached linen or natural-color firmly woven cotton; warm brown color linen or cotton-and-rayon thread or crewel wool or pearl cotton, size 5 (see below for amounts).

EQUIPMENT: Embroidery frame; crewel needle.

DESIGN: Enlarge diagram (each small square = ½″ square). Complete other half of design. Transfer to fabric.

EMBROIDERY: Place work in frame. Actual piece was worked with 1 strand of cotton-and-rayon thread. Since you may be using any of a variety of threads, try using 1, 2 and 3 strands. When you have found the effect you prefer, work with that number of strands throughout. **Note:** Since the amount of thread needed to complete the wall hanging depends on the number of strands you are using, be sure to start with a sufficient amount. Unused skeins or balls can often be returned to the store for refund.

Work all lines in stem stitch (see Index). All dots are in French knots.

FINISHING: Block and make into a wall hanging following directions (see Index).

Only one color and two simple embroidery stitches add up to a hanging worthy of a place of honor on any wall.

MALLARD DUCK PICTURE

This mallard duck is a perfect companion for the fish on page 45. Make them both and hang them side by side for a handsome effect.

SIZE: 15½" x 18".
MATERIALS: Coats & Clark's "Red Heart" 4 ply knitting worsted: 1 oz. skein paddy green; few yards white, beige, taupe, coffee, yellow, periwinkle, olive green and surf green; Coats & Clark's 3 ply super fingering: few yards black; a piece of yellow burlap, 15½" x 18".
EQUIPMENT: Embroidery hoop; tapestry needle; colored pencil; purple crayon; tracing paper, 11½" x 14".

ENLARGING THE DESIGN: Refer to directions on page 46.
TRANSFERRING DESIGN TO FABRIC: Refer to directions on page 46.
EMBROIDERY: Follow diagram and key for stitches and colors for all parts indicated on diagram. All parts similar to numbered parts on diagram are worked in same stitch and color.
Detached Buttonhole Stitch: The first row of this stitch is worked exactly as for the buttonhole stitch. The second row is worked into the first row but the needle enters the fabric only at the end of each row.

KEY FOR STITCHES AND COLORS:

1.	Long and short stitch	—Paddy green
1a.	Chain stitch	—Paddy green
2.	Couching	—Yellow
2a.	Stem stitch	—Black
3.	Satin stitch	—Taupe
4.	Satin stitch	—Black
5.	Couching	—White
6.	Buttonhole stitch	—Coffee
7.	Satin stitch	—Taupe
8.	Feather stitch	—Beige
8a.	Chain stitch	—Beige
9.	Detached buttonhole stitch	—Beige
10.	Feather stitch	—Taupe
11.	Buttonhole stitch	—Coffee
12.	Detached buttonhole stitch	—Double rows of coffee, taupe, beige
12a.	Stem Stitch	—Coffee
13.	Buttonhole stitch	—Periwinkle
14.	Buttonhole stitch	—White
15.	Fly stitch	—Beige
16.	Fly stitch	—Black
17.	Fly stitch	—Paddy green
18.	Fern stitch	—Surf green
19.	Couching	—Periwinkle
20.	Couching	—Olive green
21.	Couching	—Surf green
22.	Couching	—Coffee
23.	Couching	—Paddy green
24.	Stem stitch	—White

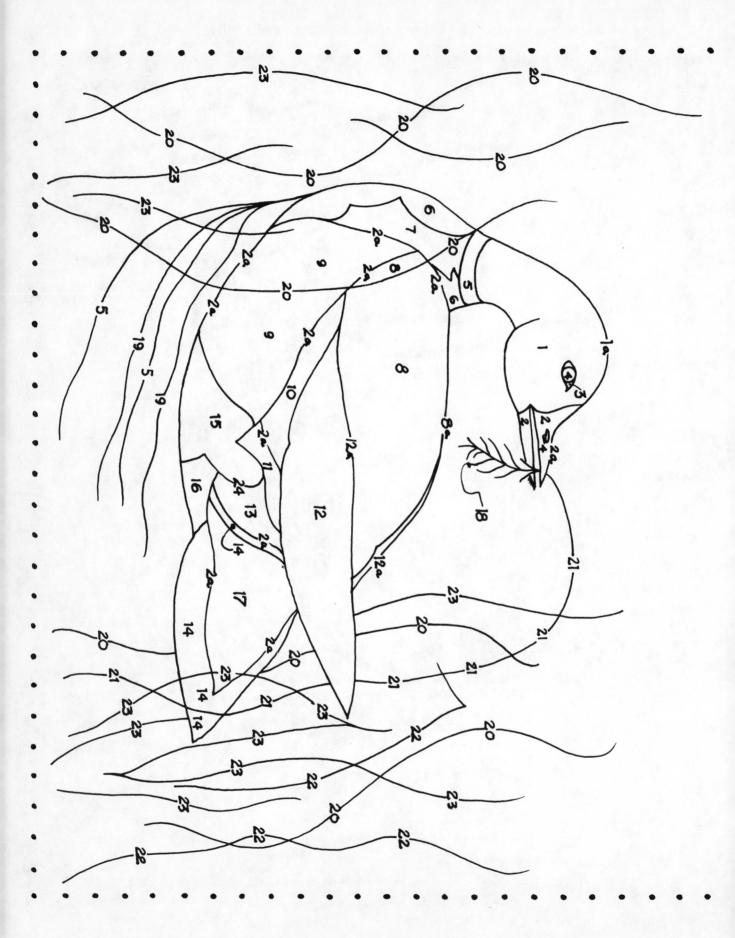

Monogramming

Monogramming

Perhaps the most personal gift imaginable is one bearing a monogram. It can never have been meant for anyone except the recipient. If it is a handmade gift, it indicates just that much more that it was lovingly worked for no one else in the world. If you want to make a gift demonstrating your sincere affection or true love, none will express it better than one with a monogram.

In a more leisurely era, a girl marked every item in her trousseau with an elaborate cipher of initials. A woman replaced every worn sheet, even kitchen towels, with one marked with a carefully worked monogram. She also marked her own lingerie, her husband's shirts, even her children's clothing with an appropriate monogram. Today laundry marks and camp labels take care of the identification. We enjoy our monograms purely as decoration.

There are commercial transfers available for many kinds of initials. Or you can easily find interesting letters in magazines and newspapers. To give you some useful background in working monograms, however, we shall present some basic information here and complete sets of initials for you to use as shown or to adapt to your needs.

THE ETIQUETTE OF MONOGRAMS

For men: If the letters are to be all the same size, use his first initial, middle initial, last initial—in that order. If you want a large center letter flanked by two smaller ones in your design, use his first initial, last initial, middle initial—in that order.

For women: The rules for men's monograms apply to unmarried women as well. The married woman replaces her middle initial with that of her maiden name. If she was Mary Jane Smith and married Mr. Brown, her new monogram is MSB if the letters are all one size. If there is to be a larger center letter, her monogram is MBs.

Placement of monograms is generally a matter of good common sense. Obviously you would not monogram a sheet on a corner which will be tucked under the mattress. Sheets are monogrammed in the center just above the top hem so that the monogram falls in the right position when the sheet is turned down over the blanket. Pillow cases are usually monogrammed in the center just above the hem.

Tablecloths may be marked at one end (or both ends if the cloth is large) in the right-hand corner. Or the monogram may be centered at each end just above the area of the place settings. Table mats are marked on the left side either vertically or horizontally (near the top). Napkins are usually monogrammed in one corner in a style similar to that used on the cloth or mat but on a smaller scale.

METHOD

Trace the initials desired from the alphabet shown. Letters are about 1″. If you want larger letters, enlarge them in the usual way. If more elaborate letters are desired, add the curlicues as on the S or the HJ in the photographs. Or you might frame the letters like the sample S or the towels marked

G and IU. Note how the addition of an embroidered dot enlivens the J and the design of LO.

When you have worked out your entire design on paper, transfer it to your project. Place work in an embroidery hoop. Monograms shown were all worked with 4 strands of 6-strand floss. Satin stitch is used most often for monogramming. For a luxurious quality to the letters the satin stitch is usually padded. (For all stitches see the Index). Split stitch or chain stitch can also be used for the padding. Work the padding with a slightly heavier thread than the satin stitch.

For informal monograms, many different stitches may be used. The sample letter S was worked in Holbein stitch with a scattering of French knots. The frame circling it consists of 2 lines of chain stitch separated by a line of Holbein. The sample letters HJ were worked in Holbein stitch with a trim of French knots.

The towel marked IU has satin stitch letters outlined with Holbein stitch. The interlocking circles are coral stitch. The letters LO are chain stitch with a trim of French knots. The letter G is all chain stitch. Its frame consists of a ring of chain edged with rings of Holbein. The scallops are Holbein.

Occasionally we'd like a monogram on a garment or a heavy bath towel that doesn't lend itself to embroidery. A sweater is a good example. To embroider on knit goods first apply monogram design to a firm lightweight fabric—organdy, muslin or the like—cut large enough to fit in your embroidery hoop. Baste this fabric to your sweater exactly where you want the decoration to be, making sure that you do not stretch the knitting. Place work in hoop. Embroider the monogram then carefully cut away the extra fabric so that only the monogram remains.

Just a reminder: Cross-stitch monograms can be handsome too. They are particularly appropriate on children's garments and informal household linens. Don't forget there is a complete alphabet on the sampler in the cross-stitch section.

Perhaps the precise nature of a monogram does not appeal to you. In that case, try a first name written out in your own handwriting. A child's name in his own wobbly script is delightful worked in chain stitch on a play outfit.

Helpful Hint: Very often a sheet or pillow case or tablecloth wears out long before the monogram which embellishes it. Just cut out the monogram leaving a narrow border around it. The monogram can then be applied (see section on appliqué) to a similar object.

Just for fun we put a simple embroidery motif on a towel in the grouping. You will notice how well it combines with the monogrammed towels. If you want to copy it, here is a full size design to transfer to your towel. Using 3 strands of 6-strand embroidery floss throughout, work as follows: In center alternate straight stitches of rose and blue. Work a ring of medium blue outline stitch, then dotted area in medium blue laid stitch. Work spiky units in straight stitch, the top 3 in medium blue, the lower 2 in dark blue. Work petal areas in Holbein stitch, the inner line in dark blue, the outer 2 in rose.

ACTUAL SIZE

67

Trace the initials desired from the alphabets shown. They can all be worked in the given size; however, you may want to enlarge yours. To do so, draw in a grid as in the first alphabet. Draw a similar grid to the size you want and copy the letters square for square.

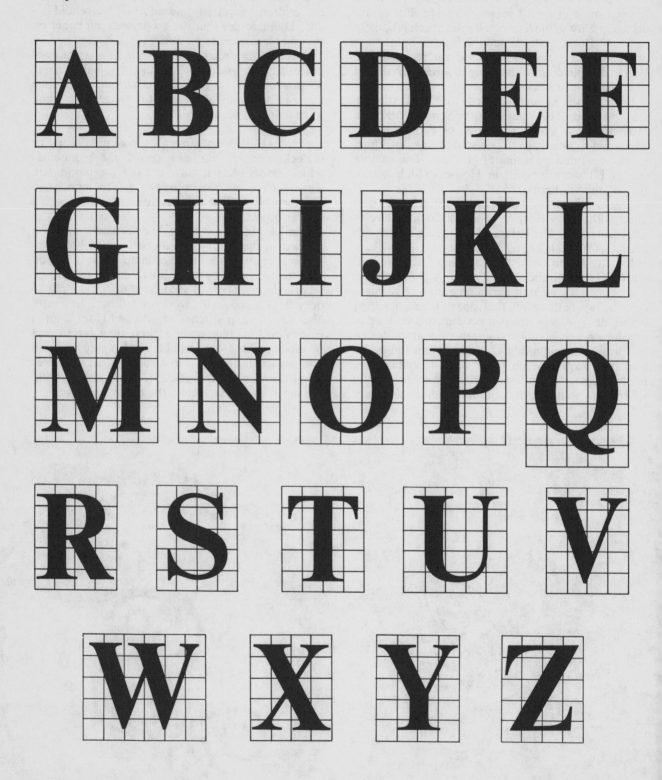

ABCDEF
GHIJKL
MNOPQ
RSTUV
WXYZ123
4567890

ABCDEFG

hijklmn

opqrstu

vwxyz12

34567890

ABCDEF
GHIJKLM
NOPQR
STUVW
XYZ1234
567890

A B C D E

F G H I J K

L M N O P

Q R S T U

V W X Y Z

1 2 3 4 5 6 7 8 9 0

Hemstitching

All pieces began with a ¼″ hem held in place with plain hemstitching.

1. 3 threads were drawn beyond the hem. Plain hemstitching was worked tightly on the bottom and top of the drawn thread section.

2. No threads were drawn. Two bands of Italian hemstitching were worked over 3 horizontal threads each. The stitches were pulled up rather tightly to produce the little openings.

3. 1 thread was drawn beyond hem, 3 threads were skipped, then 1 more thread was drawn. Italian hemstitching was worked over the 3-thread area.

4. Standard crossed cluster hemstitching worked over a 6-drawn thread section. The crossings seem to go in the opposite direction to those in the diagrams for this stitch. Actually, the sample was worked exactly as the stitch in the diagrams but the work happened to be held with the hem above the drawn threads rather than below.

Hemstitching

Hemstitching is a method by which a hem is sewn in place while working a decorative border. This border is usually made by drawing threads, then stitching remaining threads into neat little groups.

MATERIALS AND EQUIPMENT

Almost any fabric of plain weave can be hemstitched. It is advisable to work on cotton or linen in which threads are easy to see and count.

Hemstitching may be worked with the actual threads drawn, but you will find it more practical to use a good quality sewing thread, preferably linen. The working thread should be approximately the same weight as the fabric thread. Occasionally a slightly heavier thread is introduced in detailed stitches such as the crossed cluster. Hemstitching may be worked in a contrasting color, but it is usually done in the same color as the fabric, or a shade darker.

It is worked in the hand; you need only a fine tapestry needle to easily separate the background threads.

METHOD

First true up the piece of fabric by pulling a thread and cutting on that line. (To pull a thread: life one thread with the point of a pin so you have an end to hold, then carefully draw out the thread.) Turn hem of desired width to wrong side and baste. Miter corners of napkins and tablecloth. (See Index.)

Then draw threads for hemstitching. Generally, threads are not pulled across hems at sides of work. Our designer has adapted an ingenious method which eliminates the cut threads and possible fraying. Clip the thread to be drawn in the **center** of the row. With a pin draw out the thread as far as the side hem. Do not cut off. Repeat with the other half of thread. Insert a pin in each side hem and wrap drawn threads around pins. When hemstitching is complete, work the drawn threads into hem and clip excess.

Plain Hemstitching: Draw out 2, 3 or more threads just beyond hem. The diagram shows just one method of plain hemstitching. It is usually worked on the wrong side, from left to right. Hide end of working thread in the hem and fasten with a few little stitches. Bring a needle up a little below drawn thread section, catching about 2 threads of hem. (The hem does not show in diagram.) Put needle from right to left under desired number (2,3,4) vertical threads in the drawn thread section. Draw thread up tight. Then insert needle into hem section. Alternate these two steps across row. Other edge of drawn thread section may be worked in same manner.

Italian Hemstitching: Draw out 2 or 3 threads beyond basted hem. Skip 3 threads; draw out the same number of threads as before. To fasten hem, work plain hemstitching picking up groups of 3 threads.

Now fasten working thread at right side of drawn thread section (arrow in diagram). Working from right to left, bring needle up at 1 and insert back at arrow. Bring needle up at 2 and go around the same 3 threads in upper drawn thread section. Then continue stitch back to lower drawn thread section. Continue across row. Keep each group of threads in line with those on first row of hemstitching. Top edge of upper drawn thread section may also be hemstitched.

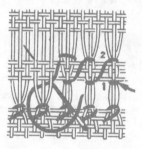

Crossed Cluster Hemstitching: Beyond basted hem draw out a wide area of threads (8,9,10 or more). Work plain hemstitching at each side of drawn thread section making groups of 4 threads. Be sure that these groups line up at top and bottom of drawn thread section. On right side of work fasten thread at right edge in middle of drawn thread section. Also fasten down 2 threads of first group in the same place. Pick up 2 threads of second group (see diagram A) with needle pointing from left to right. Pull this group of threads over and to the right of the remaining 2 threads of the first group and, with needle pointing from right to left, scoop up the remaining 2 threads of the first group (see diagram B). Continue across row.

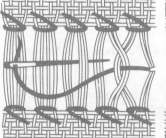 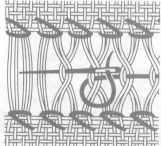

Faggoting

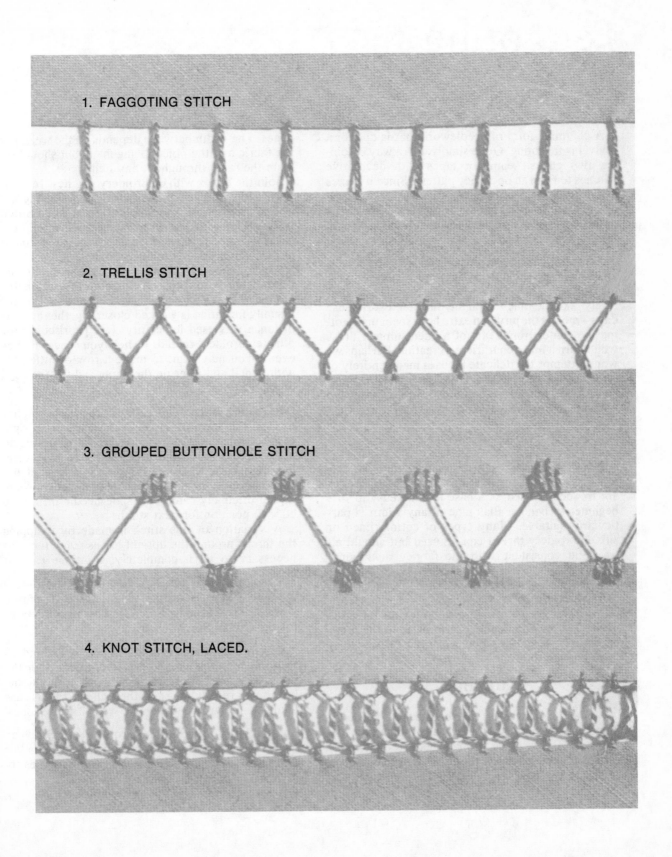

1. FAGGOTING STITCH

2. TRELLIS STITCH

3. GROUPED BUTTONHOLE STITCH

4. KNOT STITCH, LACED.

Faggoting

A charming form of needlework that is due for a revival is faggoting. Quite simply, it is a way of joining two edges, seams or tapes with decorative stitches to form an open lacy pattern. Since it makes use of traditional embroidery stitches, its history is a long and obscure one, but it was last fashionable in the early 1920's—a period which is having a high fashion revival today!

Faggoting can be used on table linens, guest towels and some household items but is even more suitable for clothing. Those of us who make our own clothes rarely take the time to add any fine handwork these days—more's the pity! An extra hour spent in faggoting the center front seam of a linen summer dress would turn it into a couturière's creation. Perhaps we won't attempt the delicate blouses made entirely of satin stripes faggoted together such as our great-aunts made, but we can certainly trim a baby sacque with a bit of lace neatly joined by a row of faggoting.

MATERIALS

Most fabrics can be used for faggoting, but cotton, linen or silk are the most appropriate. Tapes are frequently used as a base and are easy for the beginner to handle. Bias tape of any width is particularly suitable. Many types of cotton, linen or silk embroidery thread can be used but should always be consistent with the fabric background.

EQUIPMENT

A crewel needle of a size to hold your thread is needed. A sewing needle is also basic to the preparation for faggoting. You will need heavy paper large enough to fit the edges you are joining.

METHOD

Prepare the edges of your background fabric by hemming invisibly. If you are using bias tape (or strips of fabric), place wrong sides together, edges turned in, and slip-stitch the edges. Baste the pieces to the heavy paper, leaving $1/8''$ to $1/2''$ between the edges. The width between depends on the weight of the fabric and the object being made but should remain the same throughout any item.

Join the edges with embroidery stitches. In addition to the stitches shown here, the following are also appropriate: Coral Stitch, Zigzag; Braid Stitch on each edge joined with a lacing; Sheaf Stitch. **Note:** All stitches mentioned or shown can be found in the section on embroidery stitches.

To practice faggoting stitches slip-stitch the edges of single-fold bias tape together. Baste lengths of tape to heavy paper, placing them about $1/2''$ apart. Usually faggoting is worked closer together but this distance was used for clarity. Use pearl cotton or other embroidery thread. To help you space stitches evenly you may want to make a row of little dots with pencil and ruler on the paper right at the edge of each tape.

Faggoting Stitch: This is one of the basic stitches used in this form of needlework. Work from right to left. Bring thread out at top edge. Bring needle directly across space and insert in lower edge, coming from back to front. Wrap thread around upright bar once, then insert needle in top edge where thread originally came out; slide needle inside top edge to position for next stitch.

A variation of this stitch is made by wrapping the thread around the upright bar as many times as necessary to fill it completely. Continue to next position as before.

Trellis Stitch: This stitch should not be confused with the Trellis Filling Stitch. Follow the directions for the Cretan Stitch, Open.

Grouped Buttonhole Stitch: This is a standard Buttonhole Stitch worked first in one edge, then the other. The number of stitches in a group is optional but should remain the same throughout. In this case 2 longer stitches are worked between 2 shorter ones.

Knot Stitch, Laced: Make a row of Knot Stitch on each edge. With a thread of a heavier weight and/or a contrasting color, lace the 2 rows of stitches together.

Appliqué

Appliqué

If you have ever had a secret yearning to paint a great picture but are sure that you "can't even draw a straight line," appliqué is the needlecraft for you. By sewing bits of fabric to a fabric background—which is just what appliqué is—you will be able to indulge your desire to create objects of real charm that combine many of the elements of fine art. In galleries they call it "collage." We (with the modesty of all needleworkers) simply call it appliqué. Look at the wonderful way you can combine colors—even without the use of a palette. Composition and design? Just move your little snippets of cloth around until you achieve a thoroughly satisfying effect and you become a creator. Texture? Perhaps wool tweed will make that shape look even more like a tree. Suddenly the mere pieces of cloth in your hands become your own contribution to the hand arts.

Although fabric has been applied to a background fabric in a decorative manner wherever fine needlework has been done, appliqué became one of the basic forms of American needlework. When our great-grandmothers finally had the leisure to do something more than the necessary weaving and sewing to keep their families clothed, they looked around for ways to make their simple homes more beautiful. What better way than to embellish the bedcovers that warmed them during the long cold winters? The scraps of calico carefully hoarded from years of dressmaking were used to make gay patterns on their linen and cotton coverlets. Although we may not have the time to produce the dozens of quilts and bedcovers that our ancestors did, we can derive the same pleasure in appliquéing bright pieces of fabric to a cosy sofa cushion or a lovely wall hanging.

MATERIALS

Calico, percale, broadcloth, muslin are generally used for both the background and the appliqué pieces, but any closely-woven fabric that does not fray easily will do. Be sure that fabrics are preshrunk and colorfast. If washability is not a factor (as in a wall hanging), wools, velvets, and silks might be used. Fabrics of many textures will also add to the character of your work. Often a new sheet (plain white or in a color) is used as a background for a quilt.

For the stitchery, regular sewing thread in a color to match each individual appliqué piece is used. If the piece is being appliquéd with embroidery stitches, 6-strand floss or other embroidery threads are used.

EQUIPMENT

A regular sewing needle is used when the appliqué is blindstitched in place. A crewel needle is required if embroidery stitches are used. Appliqué is usually worked in the hand and a frame is not necessary.

METHOD

If your design (as for a quilt) requires many identical pieces, cut an actual-size pattern from cardboard for each element of the design. Place pattern on wrong side of fabric; pencil around. Repeat as many times as necessary, being sure to leave $\frac{1}{2}$" between pieces. If edges of pattern become worn with repeated use, replace with a new one. Repeat this process with each part of the design. Cut out pieces leaving $\frac{1}{4}$" seam allowance all around (see illustration-Step 1). Separate pieces and place similar shapes in small plastic bags. They will remain clean and are easily identified in the transparent bags. **Note:** If only one or two pieces of a particular shape are needed, the design can be transferred directly to the fabric (see Index) without the use of a cardboard pattern.

Setting Pieces: Transfer entire pattern to background fabric. Prepare each appliqué piece by placing the cardboard pattern on wrong side of fabric, then press seam allowances over pattern (see illustration-Step 2). Clip seam allowances on curves and slash at corners to make them lie flat. It is wise to baste the seam allowance flat around all pieces. Place each piece right side up in its appropriate place on the background fabric. Baste in place.

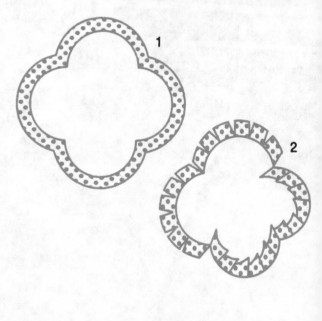

Page 77 shows two simple appliqué projects for beginners. Directions for the tote bag and pillow are on page 79.

78

Appliquéing: Blind Technique: With sewing thread and sewing needle blind hem pieces in place. Slip stitch and overcast stitch can also be used for this method. The choice of stitch is not so important as the neatness and even length of the stitches. The edges of the appliqué pieces may then be decorated with a variety of embroidery stitches such as couching, feather stitch or chain stitch, but they are usually left plain. **Embroidery Technique:** After the appliqué pieces are basted in place, attach them permanently to the background fabric with embroidery stitches only. No sewing stitches are used in this technique. Buttonhole stitch is most commonly used (see Index). Work the stitches as closely together as necessary to hold the pieces neatly in place. Often the stitches can be so widely spaced that you are actually working a blanket stitch. Other stitches, such as satin or feather are also used to appliqué pieces in place. **Note:** The experienced needleworker may not bother pressing the seam allowance to the wrong side of the appliqué pieces. She will just turn in the edge and baste it. In this case it is helpful to mark the outline of the piece on the right side of the fabric at the very beginning.

TOTE BAG

With all the things that a woman finds it necessary to carry these days, a tote bag is almost as vital to her well being as a lipstick. The tote, in a particularly convenient size, was designed to introduce you to the basic technique of appliqué in the easiest manner possible. There are no difficult curved seams to turn and sew, no odd shapes to handle. On the other hand, the strict design of squares and stripes will lend itself to any number of color combinations. By the way, to keep the project simple we appliquéd just the front of the bag. You may want to gain extra experience in appliqué by decorating both the front and the back, however.

SIZE: $8\frac{3}{4}'' \times 14'' \times 2\frac{1}{2}''$.

MATERIALS: 36''-wide firmly woven cotton, $\frac{1}{2}$ yard each aqua and bright blue, small pieces of navy, cream and chartreuse; 36''-wide white non-woven stiffening, $\frac{3}{8}$ yard; sewing thread in colors to match fabrics; $2\frac{1}{2}'' \times 8\frac{3}{4}''$ piece stiff cardboard (optional).

EQUIPMENT: Sewing needle.

CUTTING: Bag (aqua): For front and back cut 2 pieces $9\frac{3}{4}'' \times 15''$. For side gussets cut 2 pieces $3\frac{1}{2}'' \times 15''$. For bottom gusset cut 1 piece $3\frac{1}{2}'' \times 9\frac{3}{4}''$. For handles cut 2 pieces $2\frac{5}{8}'' \times 11''$. **Lining** (bright blue): Cut pieces as for bag, omitting the 2 handle pieces. **Stiffening:** Cut pieces as for bag. **Appliqué Pieces:** Cut $2\frac{1}{2}''$ squares as follows: 2 cream, 2 bright blue, 4 navy. Cut $1\frac{1}{4}'' \times 9\frac{3}{4}''$ strips as follows: 2 cream, 2 navy, 2 chartreuse, 1 bright blue.

APPLIQUÉ: Press $\frac{1}{4}''$ seam allowances to wrong side on each edge of squares. On strips, on long edges only, press $\frac{1}{4}''$ seam allowances to wrong side. Baste appliqué pieces to front of bag following photograph for color placement. Start with bottom strip $\frac{3}{4}''$ above lower edge. Strips are $\frac{1}{4}''$ apart. To position squares properly, work from center out to sides. Squares are $\frac{3}{16}''$ apart. When all pieces are basted, appliqué in place using the Blind Technique.

FINISHING: Baste stiffening to the wrong side of all bag pieces. Right sides together, pin and baste together all bag pieces (except handles) with $\frac{1}{2}''$ seams; stitch. Trim stiffening close to seams. Turn bag to right side. Assemble all lining pieces as for bag, making seams just a fraction wider than $\frac{1}{2}''$. Do not turn. On handles turn under $\frac{7}{8}''$ on each long edge. Turn under $\frac{1}{4}''$ on long raw edge; slip stitch in place. Pin handles inside lining, raw ends at top edges and $1\frac{1}{2}''$ from side seams. Stitch across handles $\frac{1}{2}''$ from raw ends. Repeat stitching for extra strength.

Turn $\frac{1}{2}''$ at top edges of bag and lining to wrong side. Place lining in bag. Slip stitch together at top edge. If desired, place piece of stiff cardboard in the bottom of bag so that bag will retain its shape. For a neater appearance cardboard may be covered with fabric.

PILLOW

This chubby pillow with its bold confetti dots would make a cosy addition to a teenager's room or look just right tossed on an old-fashioned porch chair. You might consider this pillow as Step 2 in learning the various techniques of appliqué. You will learn how to handle curved edges on your appliqué pieces as well as how to appliqué with embroidery stitches. Even after mastering these skills you will probably want to make a second pillow. They are so pleasant to make, why stop with just one?

SIZE: 13'' square.

MATERIALS: 36''-wide firmly-woven cotton, $\frac{3}{8}$ yard pink, $\frac{1}{2}$ yard red, small pieces of rose, orange and maroon; 6-strand embroidery floss in rose, orange and red; sewing thread in pink, red and white; $\frac{1}{2}$ yard 36''-wide muslin (or good parts of an old sheet); 1 bag shredded foam rubber.

EQUIPMENT: Sewing needle; crewel needle.

CUTTING: For pillow form cut 2 pieces of muslin 14'' square. For pillow cover cut 2 pieces of red cotton 14'' square. For background of appliqué cut pink cotton 13'' square. For appliqué pieces cut circles $4\frac{1}{2}''$ in diameter as follows: 1 red, 1 rose, 1 orange. Cut circles $3\frac{1}{4}''$ in diameter as follows: 2 red, 3 orange, 4 rose. Cut 12 maroon circles $2\frac{1}{4}''$ in diameter.

APPLIQUÉ: Enlarge diagram (each small square = 1'' square) for pattern. Transfer pattern centering it on cotton square. On all circles press ¼″ seam allowances to wrong side. Base appliqué pieces in place on background following photograph for color arrangement. Circles should overlap (see broken lines on diagram). Join circles to background fabric with blanket stitch worked with 3 strands of floss in the same color as the circle being appliquéd. The only exceptions are the small maroon circles. Work these in rose floss in blanket stitches that are quite close together. **Note:** Work only those edges of circles that are exposed—not where they are overlapped.

FINISHING: For pillow form stitch the 2 muslin pieces together around edges with ½″ seams, leaving 3″ opening. Turn. Fill with foam rubber. Sew opening closed.

On pink square that has been appliquéd, press ½″ seam allowances to wrong side. Center pink square on a red square; baste, then blind appliqué in place. **R**ight sides together, stitch the 2 red squares together with ½″ seams, leaving 10″ open on 1 side. Turn and press. Slip in the pillow form. Turn in seam allowances on raw edges; slip stitch closed.

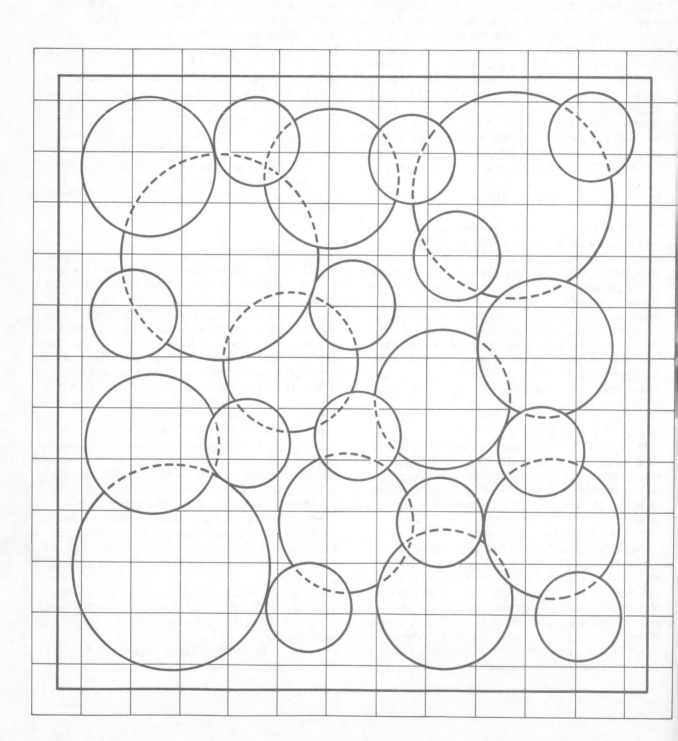

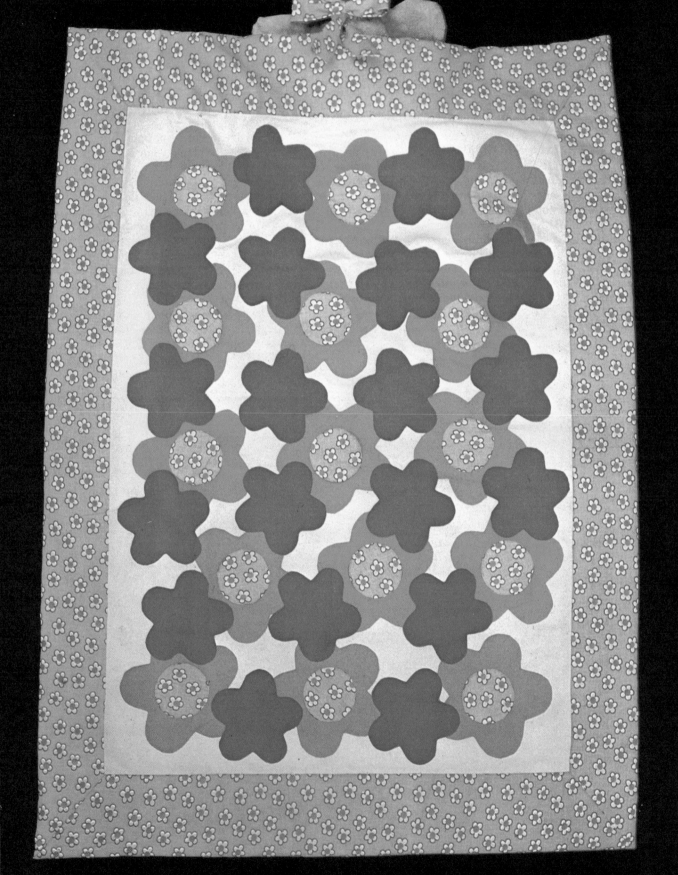

COVERLET

You don't have to be a grandmother to want to make a lavish layette for a new baby—but it helps. However, this gay young coverlet is so appealing that even a very young mother-to-be will want to try her hand at appliqué.

The design is similar to the little five-petal flowers of the print, although any pretty small-scale print is suitable. We feel that the bright colors are a new look for the very young, but you may prefer pastels for babies. In that case, choose the print first, then buy three suitable pastel cottons to combine with it.

SIZE: 25″ x 33″.

MATERIALS: 36″-wide cotton, 1¼ yards print, ¾ yard white, ⅜ yard each red, rose and orange; good section of an old blanket or ¾ yard blanketing or quilted fabric; sewing thread in red, rose, orange and background color of your print.

EQUIPMENT: Sewing needle.

CUTTING: Cut print backing 32″ x 40″. **Note:** The backing and print border for the front are in one piece. For background fabric for appliqué cut white cotton 25″ x 33″. For interlining cut blanket fabric 25″ x 33″. Trace the actual-size patterns below and make cardboard patterns for the flowers and flower center. Add ¼″ seam allowances on all the following pieces: Using large flower pattern cut 7

orange and 8 rose pieces. Cut 19 red pieces following small flower pattern. From print cut 15 centers.

APPLIQUÉ: Enlarge the diagram given on the "end papers" of this book (just inside the front or back cover), each small square = 1″ square. Transfer to white background fabric, centering design on fabric. On all appliqué pieces, press seam allowances to wrong side, clipping and slashing as necessary. Baste a center in place on each large flower. Appliqué by blind method. Baste large flowers in place on design following photograph for color arrangement. Blind appliqué to background. Blind appliqué all red flowers in place.

FINISHING: Put print backing face down on table. Center the blanket fabric on the backing. Pin and baste carefully from the center out. Stitch around edges of the interlining.

Place appliquéd section face up on interlining. Again working from center out, pin and baste carefully. Fold print edges to right side of carriage cover. Miter corners (for directions, see Index). Turn in ½″ on raw edges; blindstitch, taking care that your stitches do not go through to the back of the carriage cover. Also blindstitch down each miter at corners.

If desired, a few stitches can be worked right through the print centers of flowers to the back of cover to hold the interlining securely in place.

Large flower pattern (actual size) at left. Small flower pattern (one-half, actual size) above. Complete small flower pattern before cutting.

82

Pretend
Appliqué

Pretend Appliqué

In this hectic age of superhighways, intercontinental jets, and trips to the moon, there is something incongruous about a needleworker spending endless hours on a single project (unless it is of heirloom quality). Although most of the designs in this book are not too time-consuming, we were particularly anxious to provide you with some activities which produce a great big effect without requiring too many of your precious minutes. Since the stitchery used in appliqué is what takes time, we've just eliminated thread and substituted glue instead. And that's why we've invented the new name—pretend appliqué.

Obviously this technique is suitable only for those items which will not get hard usage. Even if you are dedicated to delicate stitchery, do try the wall hanging or the picture! We think that you will enjoy the process so much that you may want to work out a picture frame, even a cover for a special book—or think of a dozen other uses for pretend appliqué.

MATERIALS

Any textured fabric—cotton, linen or wool—will make a suitable background. For the appliqué pieces, felt is the ideal material. It does not fray and therefore needs no turning in of the edges. Felt come by the yard in 36″ or 72″ widths and is also available in 9″ x 12″ pieces, all in a wide range of colors. A number of glues are suitable. There is even a special fabric cement available. Ordinary liquid white glue (not paste) is recommended, however. A wonderful new iron-on bonding material also works well in this form of appliqué.

EQUIPMENT

A small brush is needed for use with glue; an iron and press cloth is needed to apply the bonding material. Use a soft pencil on felt.

METHOD

First transfer your prepared pattern to the background fabric. (Once you are experienced in this work it may be necessary to mark only a few key places on the background.) With a soft pencil, outline the appliqué pieces of felt; cut out. Working on one appliqué piece at a time, spread glue all over the back, making sure that you carry it right out to the edges. Place the piece in position on the background fabric and smooth it down, working from the center out. As each section of the design is completed, cover with a piece of paper, weight it down with a few books or magazines until the glue is dry.

Interesting new notions and needlework supplies are constantly being introduced. One that may be useful for your pretend appliqué is a bonding material which fuses fabric to fabric. It is available in sewing or notions departments. Cut out a piece large enough to fit your felt piece. With steam iron and press cloth fuse to the back of the felt, following directions that come with the bonding material. Remove backing. Your pattern pieces can be easily traced directly on this new material. Cut out pieces and fuse them to your background fabric, again following directions that come with the bonding material. **Note:** Touch up any loose felt pieces on overlaps, etc. with glue.

All outdoors is captured in the wall hanging on the preceding page. Composed of snippets of purple, orange and fuschia felt and joined to the background by the "pretend applique" technique, it is easy enough for a youngster to do.

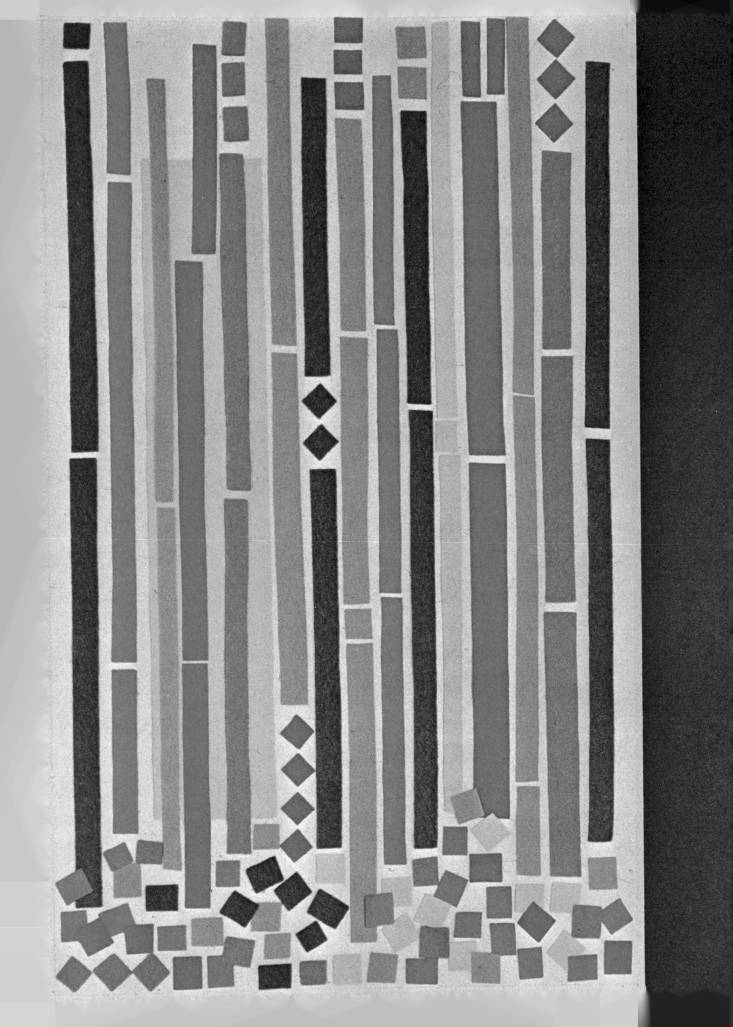

BUTTERFLY WALL HANGING

A warm afternoon sun, golden field flowers, any number of bright vacation-time memories might be evoked by this wall hanging. Any butterfly expert would be hard pressed to give this gaudy creature its scientific name but we call it Midsummer. Do revive your memories of summers past—or build dreams of summers to come—by making a pretend butterfly in pretend appliqué.

SIZE: About 19″ x 23″.

MATERIALS: $\frac{3}{4}$ yard 36″-wide unbleached linen or natural-color textured cotton; for lining $\frac{3}{4}$ yard 36″-wide orange cotton; 9″ x 12″ felt pieces, 1 each of purple and orange, 2 of fuschia; white glue or $\frac{5}{8}$ yard bonding material; sewing thread; 3 dressmaker's weights (optional).

EQUIPMENT: Soft pencil; glue brush; iron and press cloth.

CUTTING: Enlarge diagram for pattern, page 87 (each small square = 1″ square). Complete other half of pattern reversing design. Cut linen or cotton background fabric 20″ x 24″ and 1 long hanging strip 2½″ x 27″. Cut orange cotton lining 20″ x 24″. Baste vertical center line on the longer dimension of the background fabric, then transfer pattern to background fabric, centering it on center line and placing it so that lower point of butterfly comes 5″ above lower edge of fabric. Following pattern for flower marked X on diagram, transfer 9 flowers across background fabric 1¼″ above lower edge. Center first flower on center line and mark others ½″ apart.

If you are using bonding material, follow preceding directions under Method, as well as directions that come with the material. Following pattern, cut 2 fuschia felt wings. From purple felt cut pieces for all shaded areas on diagram. Cut all other shapes from orange felt. Also cut 9 orange flowers following flower X on diagram. Cut 9 purple circles ½″ in diameter.

APPLIQUÉ: Join felt wings to fabric background by gluing or bonding them in place, then join flowers and decorative trim to wings. Join little curved pieces around edges of wings. Adhere the flowers to lower edge of hanging, then add a purple circle to center of each.

FINISHING: Turn in ½″ seam allowances on all edges of hanging and lining. Wrong sides together, slip stitch lining to hanging on sides and lower edge. Press hanging, turning in ½″ seam allowances at top of hanging and lining. Fold hanging strip in half lengthwise. Stitch raw edges together with ¼″ seam. Turn; press. From this piece cut 9 hanging tabs 3″ long. Fold each in half crosswise. Insert ½″ of raw ends of each in top of wall hanging, spacing them evenly across. Slip stitch hanging closed across top edge, catching in hanging tabs as you sew. If desired, sew weights to lining at lower corners and center of lower edge. See Index for general directions for wall hangings.

PRETEND APPLIQUÉ PICTURE

This exciting contemporary picture is a particularly good example of the creative possibilities you will discover in pretend appliqué. Even if you develop it from the pattern given, you will find yourself shifting the pieces to satisfy your own esthetic sense.

SIZE: 12½″ x 20″.

MATERIALS: ½ yard 36″-wide unbleached linen or natural-color textured cotton; 9″ x 12″ felt pieces, 1 each of light olive, dark olive, grass green, emerald and jade; $\frac{1}{8}$ yard 36″-wide chartreuse felt; white glue or 1 yard bonding material; 12½″ x 20″ piece of firm but lightweight cardboard.

EQUIPMENT: Soft pencil; glue brush; iron and press cloth.

CUTTING: Enlarge diagram on page 88 (each small square = ½″ square). Transfer pattern, centering it on a 16½″ x 24″ piece of linen or cotton background fabric. This allows a 2″ turn back all around. Following pattern, cut felt appliqué pieces in colors indicated by various shadings on diagram. **Note:** Cut a 2½″ x 13½″ piece of chartreuse felt to go behind the 3rd, 4th and 5th main strips from the left on the diagram (see dotted lines). If you are using bonding material, follow preceding directions under Method, as well as directions that come with the material.

APPLIQUÉ: Join felt pieces to fabric background by gluing or bonding them in place. Overlap pieces where indicated by broken lines on diagram.

FINISHING: Press finished appliqué. Mount on cardboard (see Index for directions). Frame as desired.

Simple felt strips play one subtle shade against another to produce a handsome contemporary picture. Even the novice needleworker can achieve professional results with the "pretend applique" technique above.

Pretend Appliqué Chart:
Butterfly Wall Hanging.
Directions, page 86.

TOP

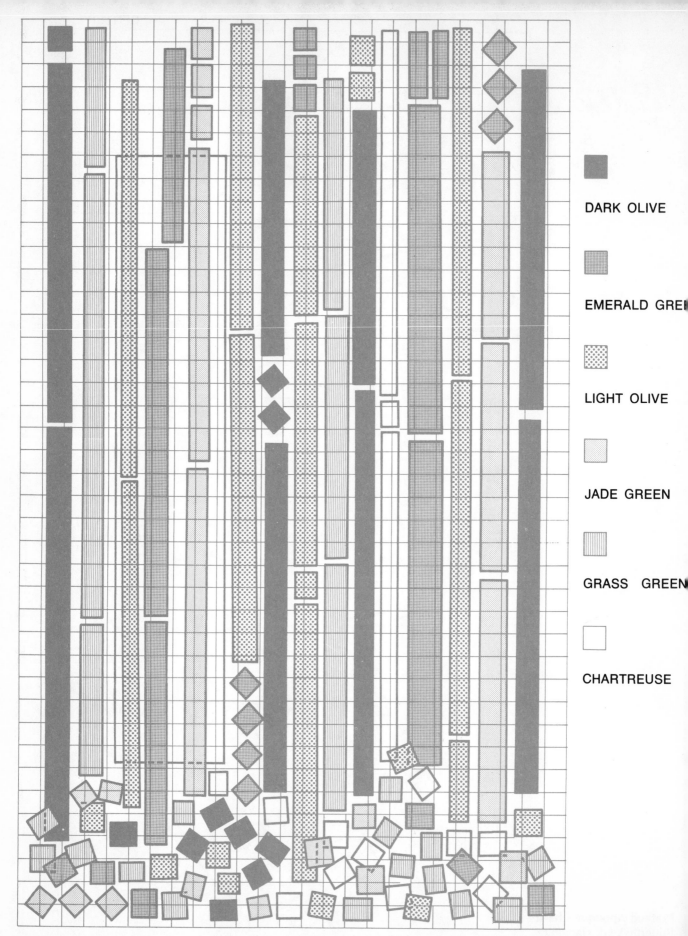

Pretend Appliqué Chart:
Contemporary Picture.
Directions, page 86.

DARK OLIVE

EMERALD GREEN

LIGHT OLIVE

JADE GREEN

GRASS GREEN

CHARTREUSE

Needlepoint

Needlepoint

Visit any proud showplace of the American past and you will come across handsome examples of exquisite needlepoint worked by the great ladies who dwelt there. Mount Vernon treasures ten elegant chair cushions made by Martha Washington. Williamsburg is the home of any number of pieces of fine furniture upholstered in needlepoint lovingly worked over two centuries ago. How exciting to think that your needlework may be beautiful enough—and durable enough—to live down through the ages.

What is this special form of needlecraft that is marked by such elegance that it is as much at home in a palace as in a studio apartment? Very simply it is a form of embroidery in which stitches (usually worked in wool) completely cover the square meshes of canvas especially woven for the purpose. Often called tapestry, it took its name—and often its designs—from the woven tapestries that graced the great baronial halls of Europe.

Traditionally, needlepoint was the handwork of ladies of wealth and leisure. The materials were expensive, the product unsuited to the rough log cabins of the American frontier. Fortunately that is no longer true. Excellent yarn and canvases are readily available. The designs and uses for needlepoint are as varied as the full range of contemporary taste. Since any department store carries needlepoint in traditional patterns, we have developed designs for you in a more modern idiom. They were also planned to give you experience in working different needlepoint stitches and, hopefully, to introduce you to a new leisure-time activity to be enjoyed for a lifetime.

TYPES OF NEEDLEPOINT

Since you are going to become an expert, it is wise to learn the proper terminology for the various forms of needlepoint. **Petit Point:** When the needlepoint is worked on canvas with 20 or more meshes to the inch, it is called petit point (little stitch). This delicate work is usually found on expensive imported evening bags or on the faces or other details of antique needlepoint pictures. **Needlepoint:** Beside being a general term, this word applies specifically to those pieces worked on canvas with 14

A rose is a rose . . . so much so that the vibrant needlepoint roses on this modern pillow top have even fooled the butterfly.

to 18 meshes to the inch. **Gros Point:** The average piece of needlepoint worked today is on canvas with 8 to 12 meshes per inch and is called gros point (big stitch). **Large Gros Point:** Handsome rugs— even wall hangings and cushions—can be worked on canvas with 3½ to 7 meshes per inch. For want of a better name it is called large gros point.

HOW TO BUY NEEDLEPOINT

Finished Design Details: Until recently most needlepoint pieces available in department stores had the design already worked. Only the background was left to be filled in. This may provide experience for the beginner but, hopefully, you will soon graduate to the more advanced—and more interesting— ways of working needlepoint. **Tramé Designs:** Sometimes you will find needlepoint pieces with the design indicated by long laid threads on the surface

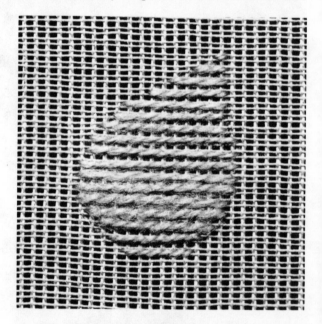

of the canvas (see photograph). These threads (called tramé threads) also indicate the color to be worked as well as the design. Half cross-stitch is always used on tramé pieces and is worked right over the tramé threads. This gives a slightly padded effect to the work. When the entire design is finished, the background is filled in in the usual manner. **Painted Designs:** It is now possible to find excellent needlepoint designs, both traditional and contemporary, painted directly on the canvas. These are easy to follow since your stitches are always worked in approximately the color indicated on the canvas. **Charted Designs:** Designs such as those on the following pages are worked out, stitch by stitch, on charts. The key accompanying each chart indicates the colors to be used. Each square on the chart indicates one stitch on the canvas.

MATERIALS

Canvas: Needlepoint is worked on canvas specially woven to produce evenly-spaced stitches of a given size. The size of the stitch depends on the number of meshes per inch of the canvas. Rug canvas may have as few as $3\frac{1}{2}$ meshes per inch; petit point canvas as many as 40 meshes per inch. If a design calls for a particular size canvas, you may switch to another size. Remember, however, that the size of your finished piece of needlepoint will change. For example, if the design calls for canvas with 10 meshes to the inch and you use canvas with 14 meshes to the inch, your object will be smaller. Conversely, if you changed to canvas with 8 meshes to the inch, your finished piece will be larger.

Canvas comes in various widths, the most common being 27″ and 36″. Purchase the width that is the most economical for the work being planned. Canvas is available in single-thread and double-thread weaves (see photographs). Most needlepoint worked today is on double-thread canvas but delicate work (petit point) is always done on single-thread. Double-thread is usually ecru in color; single-thread is usually white.

Yarns: Although many smooth yarns may be used for needlepoint, so-called tapestry yarn is generally used. It is a firmly twisted yarn that does not fray easily, comes in handsome color ranges and in about 10 and 40 yard skeins. One or more strands of crewel embroidery wool is also frequently used for needlepoint. Occasionally one wants to introduce a shiny look to small areas of a design and embroidery thread in cotton, silk or synthetics may be added. **Note:** Dark backgrounds are often found on antique pieces and they make a fine contrast for modern designs. It is often more subtle, however, to use a very dark gray, a greenish black or a very dark blue rather than a true black on designs such as the rose pillow which follows.

In any case, the yarn must be the proper thickness to cover the canvas completely and yet not be so thick that it separates the threads of the canvas or frays when being worked. It is not easy to estimate the amount of yarn needed for a particular design but you can judge fairly well by working one square inch on your canvas in the yarn and stitch desired. Keep track of the amount used and multiply by the number of square inches of any given color in your design. Add an extra skein for loss by clipping ends, ripping, etc. Buy all the yarn (particularly for the background) at one time since later dye lots may differ slightly.

EQUIPMENT

Although most Americans work needlepoint in the hand (since the work can then be carried anywhere), it is highly recommended that you use a frame. It makes for much evener work and the canvas will remain in better shape and require less blocking when the piece is finished. The only other equipment necessary is a thimble, a scissors (since the yarn should be cut—never broken off) and a tapestry needle. This is a blunt needle with a large eye. Needle sizes range from 18 to 22, the largest number being the finest needle. You may want to have a few needles since it is convenient to have one threaded with each color that is on your piece.

METHOD

Preparing Work: Always allow at least 2″ on all sides of the canvas beyond the area to be worked. To prevent fraying bind edges of canvas with masking tape or paint with white glue. If your canvas does not have the design already worked and you are not working from a chart, you may want to paint in the design. First trace the outline with waterproof ink on the canvas. Paint in each color area.

Although oil paints have always been used for this purpose, the new acrylic paints are particularly suitable. They are comparatively odor-free, dry rapidly and need only water for cleaning brushes.

If you are using a frame, turn back 1″ of canvas all around to form a double edge and lash to frame.

General Details: Use yarn cut not longer than 18″. Repeatedly pulling a longer length through the canvas will cause fraying and breaking. The design areas may be worked first and the background filled in later. If you are working from a chart, it will be easier to work the needlepoint row by row, however.

Begin a new yarn by making a knot. Leaving knot on right side, run yarn down through canvas about 1″ from where you want to begin. Bring needle up at starting point. After the stitches worked later cover the loose end of yarn, clip off the knot. When ending a length of yarn, run it back under a few stitches on wrong side of work.

BLOCKING

Frequently in doing needlepoint one pulls the canvas out of shape. Blocking will straighten out the work and will also make the stitches appear more even. If work is on a frame, it can be blocked right on the frame. If you have worked it in the hand, sponge **the wrong side** of the needlepoint until yarn and canvas are wet but not saturated. Stretch piece into proper shape and fasten to a board with rust-proof tacks placing them not more than 1″ apart. Let dry thoroughly. If work is still out of shape, repeat the process.

BASIC STITCHES

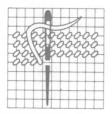

Half Cross-stitch: The simplest of all needlepoint stitches is the half cross-stitch (see diagram). Always work from left to right. Start at the bottom of a stitch. Cross over 1 mesh of the canvas (diagonally) and insert needle for next stitch. Notice that the needle is always inserted in the vertical position. When the row of stitches is completed, turn work upside down so that next row can be worked from left to right.

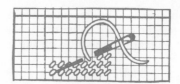

Tent Stitch: Petit point is always worked in this stitch. Since the work covers the back of the canvas as well as the front, it is also used for gros point when a particularly durable piece is required such as for chair seats, footstools or rugs. Remember that it requires more yarn than the half cross-stitch and is worked from right to left. Bring needle out at bottom left corner of a stitch. Cross over diagonally to upper right corner. Insert needle and cross behind stitch just completed to new stitch on left. When 1 row of stitches is completed, turn work upside down so that next row can also be worked from right to left. It is also called the Continental Stitch.

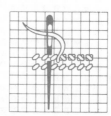

Diagonal Stitch: This stitch (also called Basket Weave) is similar to tent stitch but is worked diagonally across the canvas. Note on the diagram that the needle is inserted horizontally. On the following row it will be inserted vertically. This stitch is used on backgrounds when a particularly even appearance is desirable.

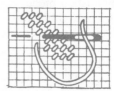

Cross-Stitch: When a slightly more textured effect is desired, cross-stitch is often used for needlepoint. It is also used frequently with crosses 3½, 5 or 7 to 1″ for rugs. In working designs each cross-stitch is completed individually. On backgrounds, however, a row of half cross-stitch is completed, then the second half of the stitch is completed on the return (see diagram). In either case the stitches must all cross in the same direction.

Other Stitches: There are literally dozens of handsome stitches used in embroidery on canvas. A few that you may enjoy experimenting with are shown on the following pages. Worked in rich colors, some are so decorative in themselves that they need no further pattern to produce a handsome effect.

ELABORATE NEEDLEPOINT STITCHES

This is just one for you to experiment with. It can be worked in 1 or 2 colors. Make a square of 16 small half cross-stitches as shown. Alternate with a square of 7 stitches graduated in size. Follow diagram for number of threads to work over.

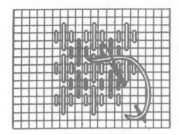

Hungarian Stitch: This is a variation of the Florentine Stitch, also called Bargello Work, also called Flame Stitch. The terms are used interchangeably. Make groups of 3 upright stitches, working over 2, 4 then 2 horizontal threads of canvas. Alternate rows so all spaces are filled. This stitch may be worked in 1 color or in 2 as shown.

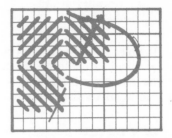

Checkerboard Shadow Stitch: This variation of the Checker Stitch was used on the beautiful belt shown on page 105. Start by forming a square of 7 diagonals as in the Checker Stitch. Using only these graduated squares, work each group of 7 diagonals at right angles to the adjacent group. This creates the shadow effect.

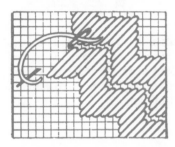

Byzantine Stitch: This stitch is used to cover large areas quickly. It gives the effect of a woven fabric. Work satin stitches diagonally over 4 vertical and 4 horizontal threads and form steps as shown.

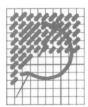

Scottish Stitch: Effectively worked in two colors, this stitch uses Tent Stitch to frame the graduated diagonals of the Checker Stitch. As you continue the pattern, work only one row of Tent Stitches between the diagonal squares. Use a contrasting color for the Tent Stitch.

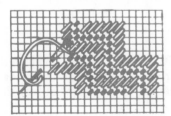

Jacquard Stitch: Make rows in steps, working 1 row over 2 vertical and 2 horizontal threads of canvas and the next row half cross-stitches over 1 intersection.

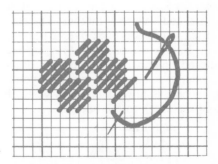

Tile Stitch: This is a diagonal stitch worked from the upper left hand corner of the canvas to the lower right hand corner. Stitches are worked crossing 2 vertical and 2 horizontal threads, then 3, 4, 3, 2, 3, 4, 3 vertical and horizontal threads; continuing in this sequence. The next row of diagonals is dovetailed into the first row so that the diagonal that crosses 2 verticals and 2 horizontals is aligned with the diagonal that crosses 4 verticals and 4 horizontals.

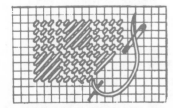

Checker Stitch: There are a number of variations of Checker (sometimes called Checkerboard) Stitch.

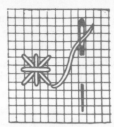

Cross-stitch, Double: This stitch works up faster than the usual small cross-stitch. Make a cross-stitch over the number of threads shown, then work another cross-stitch diagonally over it.

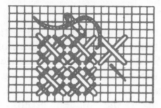

Rice Stitch: First cover background with large cross-stitches worked over 4 vertical and 4 horizontal threads of canvas. Over corners of each cross-stitch make small diagonal stitches at right angles to each other. Cross-stitches are often worked in a heavier weight yarn.

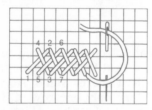

Plait Stitch: This variation of the Cross Stitch creates a textured effect. It is worked one cross stitch at a time. The first half of the stitch is over 2 horizontal and 2 vertical threads. The second half of the stitch is crossed back over 2 horizontal and 1 vertical. Follow the diagram, bringing the needle up in the odd numbered squares and down in the even numbered squares. As you work you will note that the needle is always inserted vertically from the top of the stitch to the bottom.

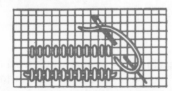

Gobelin Stitch, Upright: This stitch is usually worked on single-mesh canvas. Work stitches over 2 horizontal threads as shown at top of diagram. Sometimes a thread is laid across the canvas first and the stitches are worked over it as shown in lower part of diagram.

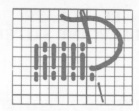

Parisian Stitch: A variation in the Gobelin Stitch is achieved by changing the size of the stitches. Using a single horizontal thread of the canvas as a base, work alternate Gobelin Stitches over 2 and 4 horizontals. In the second and succeeding rows, long and short stitches will be alternated vertically.

Gobelin Stitch, Encroaching: This stitch is often used for shading or to cover large areas quickly. Work stitches over 5 horizontal threads and slant diagonally over 1. The next row overlaps the last by 1 thread of canvas.

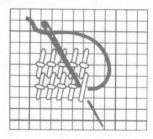

Knotted Stitch: This stitch is completed simply by working a row of tent stitches over the third horizontal thread of the Gobelin Stitch, Encroaching.

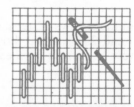

Florentine Stitch: This stitch forms zigzag patterns known as Florentine work. Work straight stitches over 4 threads of canvas, making each stitch 2 threads above (or below) the last one. This stitch is particularly attractive when worked in 3 or 4 shades of 1 color, each row across being worked in just 1 shade.

NEEDLEPOINT PILLOW

Roses and needlepoint are as closely related in our minds as hearts and Valentine's Day. On this lovely pillow, shown on page 89, an exotic new breed of roses unknown to any horticultural society makes its first appearance. Worked in vibrant shades of orange, magenta, scarlet and hot pink, these full-blown beauties are scattered on an inky black background to produce marvelous color impact.

The color areas were deliberately kept bold and sharp so that the chart can be followed easily by the beginner. A simple half cross-stitch is used throughout.

SIZE: About 11″ x 14″.

MATERIALS: ½ yard 27″ double-mesh needlepoint canvas, 10 meshes to 1″; 30-yard cards of crewel yarn, 1 orange, 1 magenta, 1 scarlet, 2 hot pink, 6 bright green and 7 black; masking tape; 12″ x 15″ piece of firm black cotton or wool for pillow back; 2 pieces of muslin 12″ x 15″ for inner pillow; sewing thread; 1 bag shredded foam rubber.

EQUIPMENT: Embroidery frame; tapestry needle.

PREPARING CANVAS: Cut canvas 15″ x 18″. Bind edges, turn them under and place piece in frame following general directions given at the beginning of this section.

NEEDLEPOINT: Use 3 strands of crewel wool throughout. Using half cross-stitch, work from chart, page 97. Each square on the chart indicates 1 stitch in the color specified by the key. Once you have the "feel" of working needlepoint, you may want to work an entire area of a single color (such as a leaf) rather than complete a row at a time.

FINISHING: Block piece. Cut off excess canvas, leaving ½″ all around. Turn this under and baste around edges. For inner pillow stitch the 2 muslin pieces together around edges with ½″ seam allowances, leaving a 3″ opening. Turn and stuff with shredded foam rubber. Sew opening closed. Turn under and press ½″ seam allowances all around piece of black cotton or wool. With wrong sides together whip (with small stitches) this piece to needlepoint piece, leaving an 8″ opening on 1 end. Slip in inner pillow and whip opening closed.

NEEDLEPOINT PICTURE

A make-believe ship sails a make-believe sea on this imaginative picture. Even a make-believe wind blows East and West at the same time! Or how could those little flags be carrying on the way they do?

The variety of rich colors and the amusing design make this picture a delight to work and a pleasure to own. The simple square shape can easily be converted to a pillow as well. Although the stitch used is the basic half cross-stitch, the frequent color changes will give the less-experienced needleworker valuable practice.

SIZE: About 12″ square.

MATERIALS: ½ yard single-mesh needlepoint canvas, 12 meshes to 1″; 30-yard cards crewel yarn, 5 blue gray, 5 medium aqua, 3 marine blue, 1 peacock blue, 1 bright orange, 1 burnt orange, 1 magenta, 1 gray violet; masking tape; piece of firm but lightweight cardboard.

EQUIPMENT: Embroidery frame; tapestry needle.

PREPARING CANVAS: Cut canvas 16″ square. Bind edges, turn under and place piece in frame following general directions given at the beginning of this section.

NEEDLEPOINT: Use 3 strands of crewel wool throughout. Using half cross-stitch and working a stitch in each mesh of canvas, work directly from chart. Each square on chart indicates 1 stitch in the color specified by the key. **Note:** To make the chart easier to follow we omitted the color changes on the background. The background alternates rows of blue gray and medium aqua. Work bottom row of picture in blue gray; work next row in medium aqua. Alternate these 2 rows all the way to the top row which is blue gray. The center 9 stitches of each flower are also blue gray.

FINISHING: Block piece. Cut cardboard the exact size of your needlepoint area. Attach needlepoint to cardboard (see Index for directions). Frame as desired.

Needlepoint designs don't have to be serious! The happy little ship sailing in a sea of flowers on page 95 is an example of the modern approach to needlework design. This picture would add a bright note to any room.

⊞	GREEN	⊠	MAGENTA
⊟	HOT PINK	⊡	SCARLET
⊡	ORANGE	⊞	BLACK

 MARINE BLUE

 PEACOCK BLUE

 BRIGHT ORANGE

BURNT ORANGE

 MAGENTA

GRAY-VIOLET

NEEDLEPOINT DESK SET

There are many times you will want to create a gift that is not too personal but that shows you cared enough to spend time and effort on it. Perhaps you are a patient who wants to express her gratitude to her doctor beyond the prompt payment of a bill. Or you may want to produce a gift that is just right to present to a husband or an employer, or as a house gift. For this reason we have come up with this design for a desk set that would look great on a teak desk in a modern family room yet is elegant enough for a traditional desk in a living room or in an office. The needlepoint pieces work up quickly and will also give you experience in working cross-stitch on canvas.

SIZE: Blotter strips, about $1\frac{7}{8}$" x $12\frac{1}{4}$"; pencil cup, about 4" high x $3\frac{1}{4}$" in diameter; telephone book, about $4\frac{3}{8}$ x $6\frac{3}{8}$".

MATERIALS: For a 3-piece desk set: $\frac{1}{2}$ yard 36" single-mesh needlepoint canvas, 14 meshes to 1"; 10-yard skeins tapestry yarn, 7 black, 5 camel, 3 off-white; masking tape; pencil cup 4" high x $3\frac{1}{4}$" in diameter; $\frac{1}{2}$ yard 36" firmly-woven black cotton; $12\frac{1}{4}$" x 19" piece of firm cardboard; desk blotter; looseleaf telephone book $4\frac{3}{8}$" x $6\frac{3}{8}$"; black sewing thread.

EQUIPMENT: Tapestry needle; sewing needle.

PREPARING CANVAS: Mark the 2 blotter strips $1\frac{1}{8}$" x $12\frac{1}{4}$" on canvas so that they are at least 2" apart and 2" from edges of canvas. Cut out this area. Mark area for pencil cup 4" x 10" and for telephone book $6\frac{3}{8}$" x 10" on remaining canvas, leaving 2" spaces as before. Bind edges of both pieces of canvas following general directions given at the beginning of this section. Since the needlepoint areas are small, it is not necessary to use a frame.

NEEDLEPOINT: Use cross-stitch throughout and work each stitch over **2** horizontal and **2** vertical threads of the canvas. Work directly from the charts. Each square on charts indicates 1 stitch in the color specified.

Blotter Strips: For each strip follow chart working from bottom row up to the top. Omitting the row marked Center, repeat chart from top down to bottom row.

Pencil Cup: Work entire chart. However, if your basic cup differs in size from the given measurements, adjust the design accordingly. If your cup is higher, add a black border to top and bottom edges; if cup is lower, omit a row or two on top and bottom edges. If diameter of cup is larger, add rows at sides of strip; if smaller, omit a row or two at sides.

Telephone Book: Follow chart from A to B then continue on for back cover of book by omitting center row of stitches and repeat chart back to A. If your book differs slightly in size, add (or subtract) a row or two of border stitches.

FINISHING: Block pieces.

Blotter: Cut out blotter strips leaving $\frac{1}{2}$" of canvas all around each. Fold allowances to wrong side and sew invisibly in place. Cut black cotton $13\frac{1}{4}$" x 20". Hem long edges so that width of piece is exact size of needlepoint strips. Turn in $\frac{1}{2}$" at 1 end of cotton piece. Lay needlepoint strip over end and whip in place around the 3 outer edges, leaving inner edge of strip free. Repeat at other end. Slip cardboard under blotter strips. A regular desk blotter may then be cut to fit the cardboard and slipped in place.

Pencil Cup: Cut out needlepoint piece leaving $\frac{1}{2}$" allowances all around. Fold allowances on each short end to wrong side and fasten down with masking tape. Bring the 2 short ends of piece together and join with whip stitch. Fold remaining 2 seam allowances to wrong side and fasten with masking tape. Slip needlepoint over pencil cup.

Telephone Book: Cut out needlepoint piece leaving $\frac{1}{2}$" allowances all around. Fold allowances to wrong side and sew invisibly in place. Cut 2 pieces black cotton $5\frac{1}{4}$" x $7\frac{1}{2}$" (or to fit 1 side of your needlepoint cover—not including the spine—and adding $\frac{1}{2}$" all around). Turn $\frac{1}{2}$" allowances to wrong side all around each piece. Wrong sides together, pin a cotton piece to 1 side of needlepoint cover, starting at side edge and reaching as far as spine. Whip cotton to needlepoint around outside edges. Hem black cotton along edge that meets spine but do not fasten down. Repeat with the cotton piece of other side of cover. Cut 2 black cotton pieces $1\frac{3}{4}$" square. Fold about $\frac{1}{4}$" to wrong side all around. Pieces should be exact width of spine. Sew a piece in place at top and bottom of inside of spine to cover bare canvas. Slip telephone book into needlepoint cover.

Any writing penned on this elegant desk blotter on page 99 is sure to have literary merit—even if it's only a grocery list. Directions are for blotter, pencil cup and telephone book. See opposite page for the charts.

CENTER OF SPINE

TELEPHONE BOOK

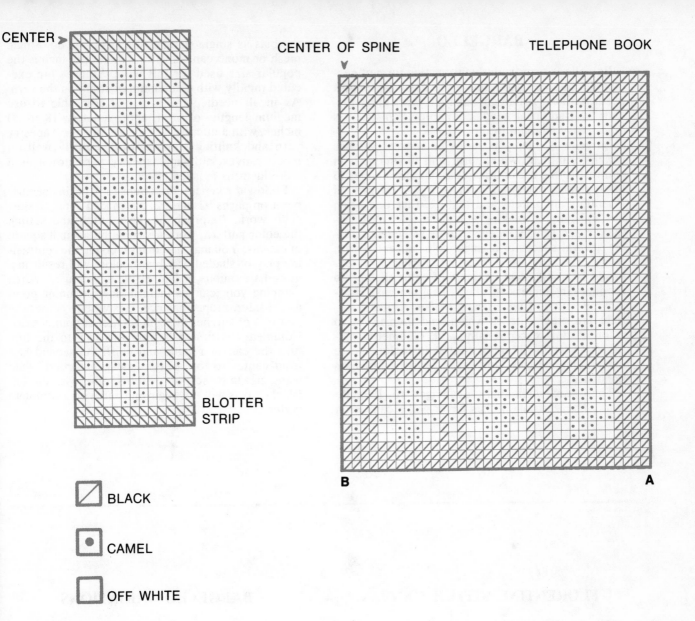

BLOTTER
STRIP

B

A

◻ BLACK

▣ CAMEL

☐ OFF WHITE

PENCIL CUP

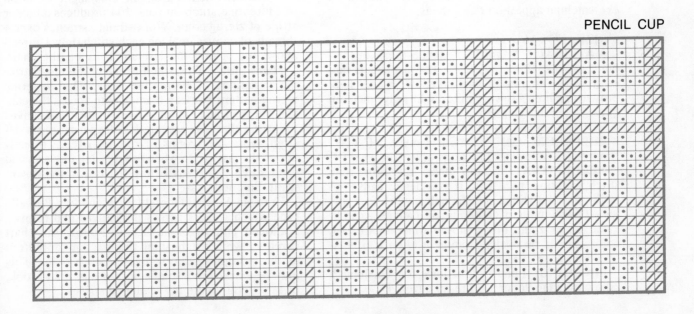

BARGELLO

Bargello is a particularly fascinating form of needlepoint adopted with great enthusiasm by today's needleworker. Although regarded with great disdain by traditional needlepoint precisianists, it is quick, easy, and fun to do.

Bargello is simply a series of vertical stitches which form their own pattern. This technique is in contrast to the use of individual slanting stitches to fill in painted or charted designs. It also offers such versatility of pattern and texture, that one often has difficulty in making a choice. The most authentic and striking effects can be achieved by using several shades of a single color accented with white or black. The Florentine stitch canvas opposite is an excellent example of color shading to produce an impressive effect using an easy, fast-moving stitch. Hungarian, Parisian, Gobelin upright are other stitches which lend themselves to color shading exceptionally well. Geometric patterns worked in vibrant or contrasting colors create outstanding designs, and are effectively used on upholstery.

There are additional advantages to Bargello work. The vertical stitches never pull a canvas on the bias as single slanting stitches often do. Single mesh or mono canvas with 14 holes per inch is the popular size used for this work. Stitches are executed rapidly with a minimum of strain on the yarn. As in all needlepoint, it is still advisable to use medium lengths of yarn, approximately 18 to 20 inches, with a number 20 tapestry needle. Tapestry yarn and knitting worsted work equally well on mono canvas, although tapestry yarn produces a more lustrous finished effect.

Follow the general directions for working needlepoint on pages 91 and 92, which also apply to Bargello work. Before choosing a stitch and setting the color pattern, work a sample on a small square of canvas. You may find that reversing the contrasting play of shaded or vibrant colors will result in a more harmonious or impressive appearance. When planning your canvas there is one remaining point to consider, proper balance. It is wise to center the first row of stitches along the center of your canvas. Complete the first half from this row to the top, turn the canvas around and finish the second half from center to top. This is most important when using zigzag or scallop patterns, otherwise the finished canvas will not begin and end with a complete pattern.

FLORENTINE STITCH CANVAS

Waves of dramatically shaded color present an eye-catching appeal on this canvas.

SIZE: 17″ x 16″.
MATERIALS: ⅝ yard 27″ single mesh needlepoint canvas, 12 meshes to 1″; 10-yard skeins tapestry yarn, approx. 2 each, yellow, beige, light brown, medium brown, white, light gray, medium gray, black; masking tape.
EQUIPMENT: Tapestry needle.
PREPARING CANVAS: Cut canvas 21″ x 20″. Bind edges following directions given on page 91.
NEEDLEPOINT: Follow chart for Florentine stitch variation, page 104. If you desire canvas to begin and end with a specific color, work first row to establish pattern centering on canvas as indicated on diagram. For a most harmonious blend, colors should be shaded from light to dark as illustrated on page 103.
FINISHING: Follow directions for finishing a pillow on page 96, or picture on page 247.

BARGELLO VARIATIONS

Florentine Stitch Variation: This slight variation of Florentine stitch on page 104 produces a bolder stripe of zigzag color. Work straight stitches over 4 threads of canvas, making each stitch only 1 thread above (or below) the last stitch as on the chart.

Flame Stitch: This stitch is one of the most striking variations of Florentine work. The wavering zigzag pattern marks a flaming path across the canvas. Work straight stitches over 4 threads of canvas following chart for pattern. If a deeper zigzag is desired, work the groups of stitches over 2 threads above the last group when progressing upward, and each stitch 2 threads below the last in the downward direction.

Hexagon Stitch: This stitch is another Bargello type which wavers across the canvas and forms a scalloped pattern of hexagons. Follow the chart carefully while establishing the first row of pattern as the hexagons seem to overlap each other. This may be worked in a solid color for a jacquard-look, or in several colors for scalloped stripes.

Florentine Stitch Variation

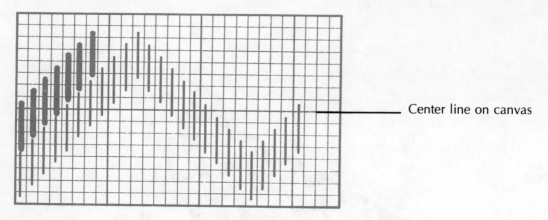

Center line on canvas

Flame Stitch

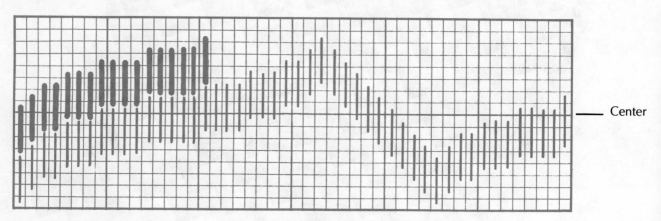

Center

Hexagon Stitch

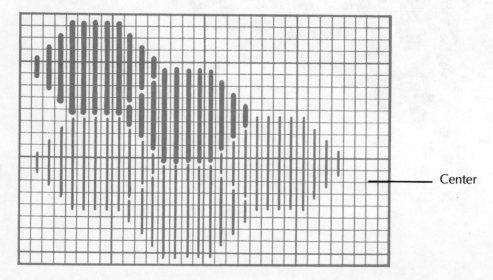

Center

104

PATRIOTIC HANDBAG

Makes you think of George M. Cohan, the Fourth of July and all those grand old things, doesn't it? It's amazing just what the colors red, white and blue can do to a design. This handbag is in the same basic pattern as the desk set yet in this combination of colors the design takes on an entirely new look.

Even though you may have made the desk set, don't hesitate working the design again. This time around you will learn a brand-new needlepoint stitch and will also learn how to combine two stitches in one design.

SIZE: About 8½″ x 10½″.
MATERIALS: ⅜ yard 27″ single-mesh needlepoint canvas, 12 meshes to 1″; 10-yard skeins tapestry yarn, 4 red, 2 white and 6 blue; masking tape; piece of blue textured wool or cotton for back of bag and handles; blue silk for lining; small amount dressmaker's non-woven interfacing; 9½″ zipper; blue sewing thread.
EQUIPMENT: Tapestry needle; sewing needle.
PREPARING CANVAS: Cut canvas 12½″ x 14½″. Bind edges following directions given at beginning of this section. It is not necessary to use a frame.
NEEDLEPOINT: Follow chart for color placement. Each square on the chart indicates 1 stitch in the color specified by the key. First work all the

blue, then all the red sections in twist stitch (see diagram). Lastly work all white areas in cross-stitch.
FINISHING: Block piece. Trim canvas so there are ½″ seam allowances all around. Cut interfacing 8½″ x 10½″; center on back of needlepoint and tack with a few stitches. Turn under seam allowances of canvas and baste.

Back of Bag: Cut 1 piece of wool or cotton 8″ x 11½″ and 1 piece 2½″ x 11½″. Cut interfacing 7″ x 10½″ and 1½″ x 10½″. Center interfacing pieces on similar wool or cotton pieces (interfacing pieces have no seam allowances); baste. Join long edges of the 2 pieces, stitching only at each end, leaving center 9½″ open for zipper. Insert zipper. (**Note:** Zipper is near top of bag.) Turn under seam allowances on all outer edges; baste.

Handles: Cut 1 piece of wool or cotton 1½″ x 11″. Fold in thirds lengthwise; turn in raw edge ¼″. Slip stitch closed. Tack ends of handle to wrong side of needlepoint piece 2½″ from each side edge. Make another handle and tack to back of bag in same manner.

Lining: Cut lining pieces 9½″ x 11½″, 8″ x 11½″ and 2½″ x 11½″. Turn in ½″ seam allowances on edges of all pieces. Slip stitch to back of corresponding parts of bag. **Note:** It may be necessary to turn in a fraction of an inch more along zipper edges.

Wrong sides together, pin back of bag to needlepoint piece carefully and whip together around all sides.

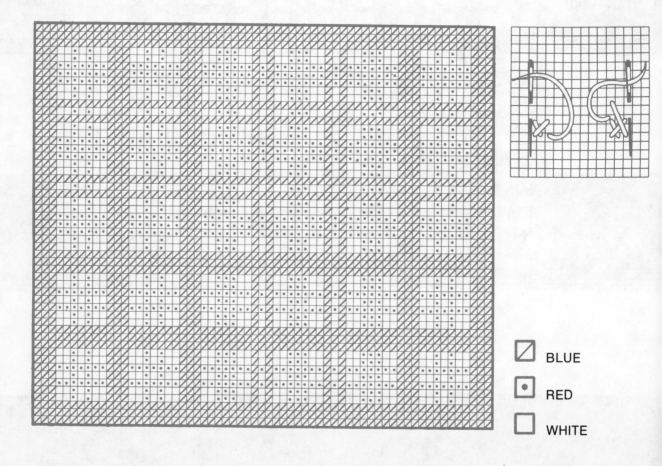

BLUE

RED

WHITE

CHAIR

Do you have an old needlepoint chair that is drab and dated and that you would like to freshen up? That is what was done with the chair pictured on page 107. Such a project is an exercise in creativity, patience and endurance. It takes a long time to do the needlework, but the results are well worth it.

SIZE: Depends on the size of the chair to be covered. See note on measuring, below.

MATERIALS: 3 pieces of single mesh canvas, 10 meshes to 1"; needlepoint yarn; masking tape. **Note:** Your needlework salesperson will advise you on the quantity of yarn to buy. It is a good idea, for such a big project, to purchase no-dye-lot yarn.

EQUIPMENT: Tapestry needle.

PREPARING CANVAS: Measure the seat, front and back of chair, add 1" to each side of each piece to tuck-in. Cut canvas with an additional 2" on each side of area to be worked. For example: If the chair seat measures 21" x 23", work over an area 23" x 25"; cut canvas 27" x 29". Bind edges with masking tape. **Note:** A very good idea is to take your chair to the upholsterer and ask him to measure it for you. Then you will be certain that your pieces are the correct size.

NEEDLEPOINT: This particular design cannot be transferred. Follow the chart or create your own pattern. Start each piece at the exact center with exactly the same point of the design (see below). This design is worked on the diagonal and one entire diagonal row of basket weave squares should be worked before starting the next row of stitches. Complete an entire diagonal row of diagonal stitches before starting a row of tent stitches, and so forth. The diagonal stitch is worked over 2 vertical and 2 horizontal threads of canvas in direction opposite to the basket weave. One row of tent stitches separates each row of diagonals.

FINISHING: Take chair and needlepoint pieces to the upholsterer for blocking and covering. If you have had experience in upholstering furniture, you may wish to do it yourself. Be sure to block your needlepoint before you proceed. (See Index.)

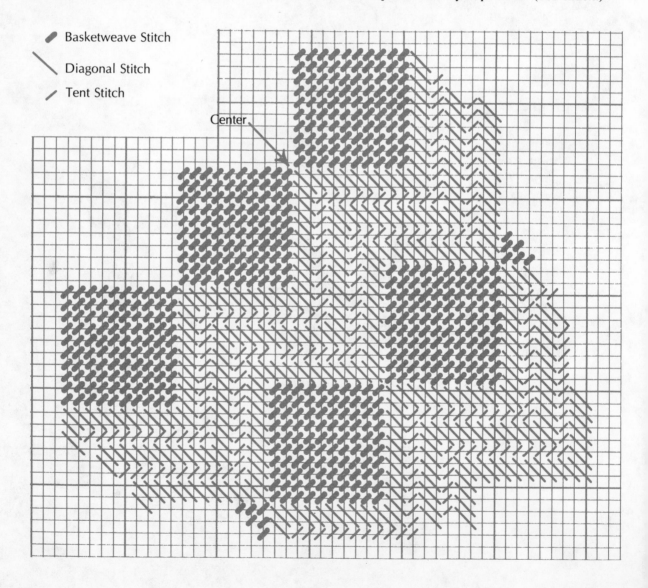

Basketweave Stitch

Diagonal Stitch

Tent Stitch

Center

ABSTRACT DESIGN IN LARGE GROS POINT

Now that you are an expert you may want to try your hand at needlepoint where you can exercise your creativity. Here's a bold design in large gros point for you to play with. Perhaps you would enjoy working it in other colors. The photograph shows a sketch of an alternate color concept.

You could make the piece just as it is for a pillow top. Or you could extend the design, work it on even larger mesh canvas and come up with a breathtaking hall runner. Worked on a finer mesh canvas, the design might make a smashing modern handbag. Give your imagination free rein!

SIZE: About 14″ square.

MATERIALS: ½ yard double-mesh needlepoint canvas, 5 meshes to 1″; 1-oz. skein wool rug yarn, 1 each brick red, purple, deep rose, pink; masking tape.

EQUIPMENT: Large tapestry or rug needle.

PREPARING CANVAS: Cut canvas 18″ square. Bind edges; turn them under and place piece in frame following general directions given at beginning of this section.

NEEDLEPOINT: Use 1 strand of rug yarn throughout. Using half cross-stitch, work directly from chart. Each square on the chart indicates 1 stitch in the color specified by the key.

FINISHING: Block piece. Finish as desired.

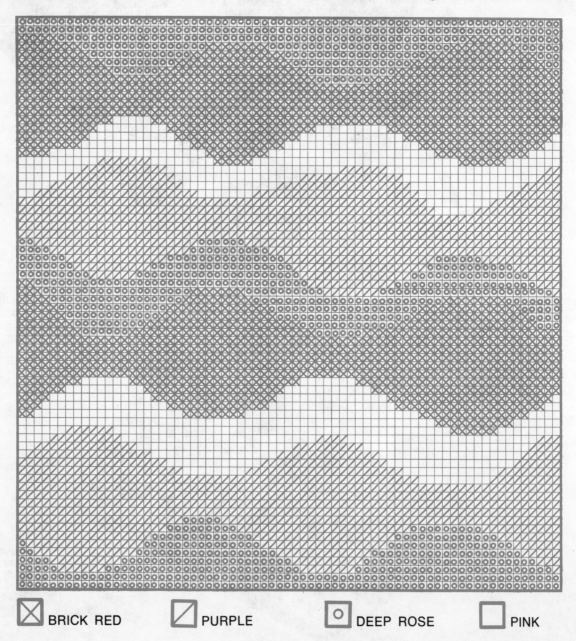

☒ BRICK RED   ▧ PURPLE   ⊡ DEEP ROSE   ☐ PINK

110

OWL PICTURE

Owls are usually described as wise, but whimsical is a better adjective for this bird. He's fun to make and will fit into today's modern decor. If the color is not suitable for your use, try another monochromatic scheme or experiment with contrasting colors.

SIZE: 10″ x 11″.

MATERIALS: ⅜ yard single mesh needlepoint canvas, 10 meshes to 1″; 10 yard skeins tapestry yarn, approximately 4 white, 3 baby blue, 2 light blue, 1 yellow and a few yards of black.

EQUIPMENT: Tapestry needle.

PREPARING CANVAS: Cut canvas 12″ x 13½″. Bind edges following directions given at the beginning of this section. Enlarge and transfer design to canvas following directions beginning on page 91. Each small square on diagram is equal to a square of 4 meshes on the canvas.

NEEDLEPOINT: Use tent or continental stitch throughout, taking care not to pull the yarn too tightly and cause the canvas to go on the bias. Follow the chart carefully using the color key. For the outlines not numbered, use medium blue for curved feather lines on the body and black for the eyelashes.

FINISHING: Block. Follow directions for finishing pillow or picture. (See Index.)

1 BABY BLUE   4 ROYAL BLUE   7 WHITE

2 LIGHT BLUE   5 YELLOW

3 MEDIUM BLUE   6 BLACK

Rug Making

Rug Making

When we talk of primitive peoples, we sometimes classify them by the kind of floor they had. We even speak of a certain historic figure of more recent times as having come from a "dirt-floored cabin." Actually the earliest furnishings were probably a pile of leaves or perhaps animal skins, which served as bed and sitting area. It's hard to imagine that these "rugs" were the forebears of our rugs today!

Perhaps it's human nature to want to protect ourselves from the cold and hardness of our floors, whether they are made of packed earth, parquet or marble. For many centuries, people used whatever large fur or textile items they had as floor coverings. Old tapestries came down from the walls to serve as rugs. In the cold north countries of Europe, the heavy bed covers moved down to the floors.

We have access to such handsome and practical floor coverings today that we had better have some pretty strong motivation to put our efforts into producing a rug. In case you need some reasons to bolster your resolve to make a rug, here are a few that we believe are valid.

1. A rug, if you plan it carefully, may cost almost nothing to make—and saving money is one of the best reasons for rug making that we can think of. Yarn raveled from old sweaters, woolen strips cut from garments gathered from friends, mill ends—all may be the basic material of an exquisite rug. The writer of this book worked in a large institution many years ago where the floors were covered with hundreds of beautiful Oriental-type rugs hooked and woven by the patients from the ravelings of old burlap potato sacks!

2. There are fashions in rugs as there are in everything else. When low pile rugs are in style, just try to find a high pile one! If almond green is the current color and you have your heart set on a rug with a gray background, you can cover every store in town and never find the one you really want. Make your own rug and you can have the exact color, size, type and design that you know is perfect for your home.

3. If the two preceding reasons for making a rug have not already put you to work, let's talk about satisfaction. Perhaps there is no more gratifying experience than surveying a job well done. Just think how great you would feel if the rug that greets your guests at the front door was a product of your own hands. Unlike many items of needlework, a rug is never put away. It is always there to attest to your skill, persistence and artistry! Need we say more?

TYPES OF RUGS

There are almost as many ways to make a rug as there are forms of needlework. Although giving directions for all of them is beyond the scope of this book, let us mention a few. Knitting and crocheting are excellent ways of producing rugs with a "country" look. They work up fast and are especially good in kitchens or family rooms where washability is a factor.

Braided rugs are known to all of us. Even if the colonial style of decorating (where they are used most often) is not yours, a braided rug can find a place in almost any home.

Woven rugs may be as simple as the old-time "rag rug" or as elaborate as the most exquisite tapestry. We sincerely hope that a few of our readers will "graduate" to this exciting craft.

Rugs can also be embroidered. Occasionally examples are found in which the entire rug consists of basic embroidery stitches worked in heavy wools on burlap. More often one sees lovely cross-stitch rugs worked in wool on burlap or on rug canvas. Rugs can be worked in many of the other needlepoint stitches. In fact, some designs in the needlepoint section (the pillow, the purse or the abstract designs, for example) would make handsome rugs worked on a large scale.

Although the preceding methods of making rugs (and many other methods) are fascinating, we shall concentrate on the rya rug and the latch hooked rug. General information about the techniques and directions for making a rug by each method follow.

RYA RUGS

In Scandinavia, the early peoples slept on and under animal skins to find a measure of warmth in the endless, bitterly cold winter nights. The skins were always used with the fur side in. It may not have been very sanitary but it must have been cozy. Generations later when skills had been developed and sheep had been domesticated, the people of these Northern lands began to make their bed covers—and quite naturally they made them as much like animal skins as possible. The smooth surface was used on top, the warm pile on the bottom of their rya. These primitive covers were woven on a loom.

Much later, as further skills developed, the Scandinavian bed began to be dressed with hand-woven linen sheets and hand-woven wool blankets. But the thrifty peasant was not about to discard his beloved rya. He just turned it over and, pile side up, began using it for a day-time coverlet. It was not too long before it occurred to some smart Scandinavian that a rya would be ideal to keep the cold winds from whistling up through the floor boards.

MATERIALS

To discuss materials for these rugs it is necessary to talk a little about techniques. The original rya was woven on a loom, the basic thread being wool or linen. The pile which was knotted in during the weaving was most often wool but could also be linen, cut-up rags or a combination of all three. Later a new technique (see Method) was developed in which the pile was sewn to a fabric background. This fabric is a sturdy linen especially woven for the purpose. Since it is difficult to find (and expensive) in the United States, we just substituted rug burlap which is available in many needlework departments.

The pile in the early rya was made of wool plucked directly from the sheep so the colors were usually just the natural color of wool with an occasional cross or simple design worked in the wool from (can you believe it?) a black sheep! Later on the wool (linen and rags, too) were dyed. Although modern ryas can be very colorful, the most traditional ones use the muted colors obtained when wools were dyed with natural materials such as berries or bark. To get this effect it is suggested that you use yarn of worsted weight in what the manufacturers call heather tones.

EQUIPMENT

The only special item you need is a rug needle with a large eye. No frame is used.

METHOD

Cut burlap to size of rug desired, allowing for 2″ to 4″ margins all around. If you can leave selvages for the time being, so much the better. Whip raw edges to prevent fraying.

Thread 1 or 2 strands of yarn cut 25″ to 1 yard long and practice the rya knot on scrap burlap (see diagrams). Work row of knots from left to right as follows: Leaving 2″ end of yarn on right side of fabric, take needle from right to left behind 2 threads of burlap. Insert needle behind 2 new threads of

burlap and pull up yarn (rya knot formed). You will note that the knot goes over 4 threads of burlap. Make stitch behind 2 new threads of burlap but pull up yarn only far enough to leave loop of desired length. Diagram shows how each new knot anchors a loop in place. Make these loops desired length by using 2 or 3 fingers of left hand as a gauge or cut a cardboard gauge 5″ long by desired width.

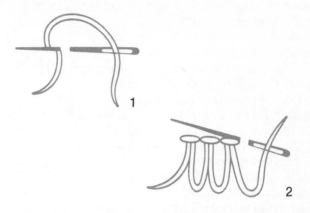

When a row of knots has been completed, cut off yarn, leaving end on right side of work as at beginning. Now cut loops to form pile. Each row of knots is worked above the preceding row. Leave 6 horizontal threads of burlap between rows. When entire rug is finished, clip the pile again to even it up as necessary.

FINISHING

Cut off margins, leaving 2″ all around. Turn under raw edges and hem or line entire rug.

RYA RUG

The handsome rug on page 117 has many of the basic characteristics of the traditional rya. The colors are soft and muted. The design is simple and geometric. And it does make you want to dig your toes into the luxurious warm pile! Make it following the chart on the next page.

SIZE: About 32″ x 38″.
MATERIALS: 39″-40″ rug burlap, 1¼ yards; knitting worsted in heather tones, 10 ozs. medium blue, 10 ozs. oxford gray, 12 ozs. golden brown, 24 ozs. dark brown.
EQUIPMENT: 3 large-eyed rug needles.
PREPARING BURLAP: Leave selvages on side edges. Cut burlap 42″ long. Whip raw ends. Centering it, mark an area 32″ x 38″ on burlap.

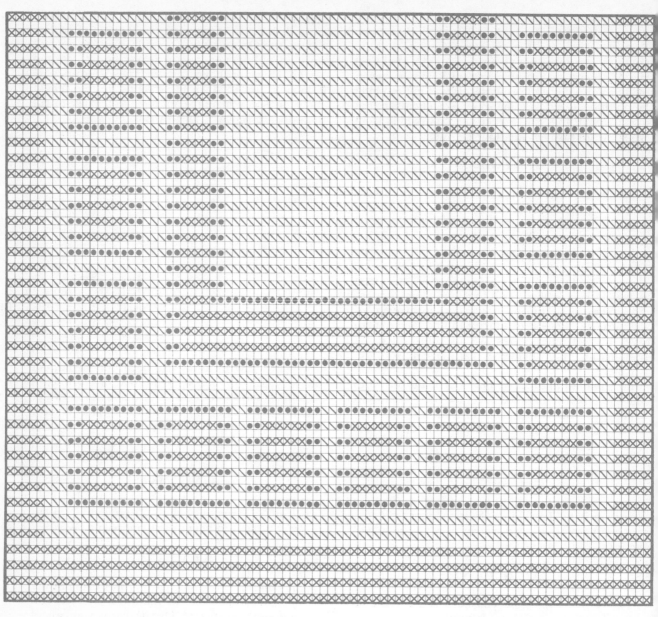

⊡ GOLDEN BROWN   ⊠ DARK BROWN   ☐ BLUE AND GRAY

KNOTTING RUG: Thread 1 needle with 4 strands of dark brown yarn, 1 needle with 4 strands of golden brown and 1 needle with 2 strands of blue and 2 strands of gray. Narrow end toward you, place burlap on a table. Start at this end with dark brown. Inside left edge of marked area begin first row of knots (bottom row of chart). Each symbol on chart indicates 1 knot in the color indicated by the key. Gauge length of loops by working over 3 fingers. Work 1 complete row before going on to the next. **Note:** On the chart there is a row of empty squares between each row of symbols. This indicates 6 horizontal threads of burlap skipped between rows of knots. Continue to top of chart; omit row marked Center and follow chart back to bottom.

FINISHING: Follow general directions for finishing rya rugs at beginning of this section. Rug binding may be sewn on over hem.

The cool blue of Northern lakes, the rough bark of tall pines and the pale gold light of a winter sun have been the inspiration for this rug made by the rya method.

116

LATCH HOOK RUGS

For centuries, the most beautiful rugs in the world have been made in the Middle East and the Orient. Unfortunately those areas, too, have succumbed to industrialization. Only a few rugs are still made by hand with the Oriental knot that is the basic method of producing them. On the other hand, we who have been released from drudgery by just such industrialization now have the leisure to pick up where the Persians left off.

The knot produced by a latch hook is very similar to the knot used in Oriental rugs. Although a few ardent needleworkers made knotted rugs down through the years, it is only in the last few years that latch hook rugs have become popular and are even outstripping the traditional hooked rug in popularity in parts of the United States.

The technique is easy and the results are ensured since the evenness of the pile and regularity of the knots is not dependent on skill. Each knot is made of a measured length of yarn pulled through an open-meshed canvas. You will learn to make the knot in a minute and can have a rug under way in no time.

MATERIALS

The backing is always a heavy double-thread rug canvas (sometimes called Smyrna canvas). It comes 28" or 30", 36" and 40" wide. Buy the most economical width for the rug you are planning. The most popular rug canvas has 4 meshes to 1". The filling is usually wool rug yarn which you may buy by the ounce and cut as needed. However, convenient ready-cut lengths of rug yarn may be purchased in bundles of one color to use in this type of rug. The illustration at the beginning of this chapter shows a section of a latch hook rug and the materials needed.

EQUIPMENT

No frame is needed for latch hooked rugs. You will need a latch hook (sometimes called a latchet hook). If you are not using ready-cut yarn, you may find a commercial yarn cutter handy, although it is not a necessity. A rug needle may be needed to hem and bind the rug.

METHOD

Preparing Canvas: Many latch hook rug kits are readily available by mail order or in needlework departments. To work out your own rug design make a full-size pattern. Lay the canvas over it, allowing sufficient canvas outside pattern for hems. With a felt-tipped pen draw the outlines of the pattern which will show through the meshes of the canvas. If you want to indicate colors to follow, paint them with acrylic paints as described in the Needlepoint section or rough them in with crayon. Each portion of the design is filled in with the color indicated. **Note:** Since each knot is a separate entity, patterns can also be worked out from charts as for the rug on page 113, chart opposite.

To prevent the raw ends of canvas from fraying, bind with masking tape. Keep selvages on canvas until rug is finished.

Knotting: If you are not using ready-cut yarn, prepare at least 50 pieces of each color needed by cutting 2½" lengths (or use a yarn cutter).

Place canvas on table with narrow end toward you. Start at the right edge of marked area and work first knot as follows: Fold piece of yarn in half over shank of hook (Diagram 1). Insert hook into first hole, go under double horizontal threads and come up through hole directly above (Diagram 2). Draw hook back, catching the 2 loose ends of yarn (Diagram 3). Let go of ends of yarn and draw hook toward you until loose ends have been pulled through looped yarn. Tighten knot by pulling ends firmly (Diagram 4). Continue knots across row. Work each row from right to left. Roll up completed work in your lap.

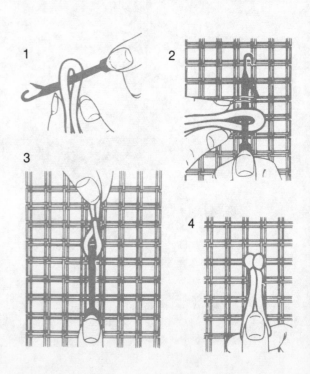

FINISHING

Brush rug to remove fuzz and lint. Clip off uneven ends of yarn. Cut off any extra canvas, leaving 1″ hem allowances. Fold to wrong side; baste. Cover with rug binding sewn around edges. Rug may also be lined or treated with non-skid liquid.

Note: Hem allowances may be folded to front of rug and basted in place *before* any knotting is done. The knots are then worked through the double thickness as the rug is made.

GEOMETRIC RUG

Bold colors and a bold design join in this horizontally striped latch hook rug (page 113) that could easily be the most decorative feature of any room. The design was carefully developed so that you can extend the size of the rug to fit any of your decorating needs. If you would like to make a hall runner, great! Just make it the width you need and keep adding stripes until the runner is as long as required. In fact, this versatile rug will fit in almost anywhere —unless you have an octagonal room!

SIZE: As desired.

MATERIALS: Double-thread canvas, 4 meshes to 1″ (amount depends on size rug desired); 1-oz. bundles ready-cut wool rug yarn, 1½ orange, 1½ medium blue, ½ skipper blue, 1 dark brown (amounts indicate a generous quantity for an area worked the size of chart); masking tape; rug binding; heavy thread.

EQUIPMENT: Latch hook; rug needle.

PREPARING CANVAS: Plan size of rug carefully. Area shown on chart is about 5½″ x 13¼″. Cut canvas allowing 2″ all around for hems. Leave selvages if possible. Bind all raw edges with masking tape.

KNOTTING: Follow chart for design. Each symbol on chart indicates 1 knot in the color specified. Start at right side and bottom row of chart and work each row across, repeating as many times as necessary for the width of your rug. When you reach the top of chart, repeat stripes as necessary for the length of your rug. For example, a small rug might have a *total* of stripes A - B - C - D - C - E - C - D - C - E - C - D - C - B - A.

FINISHING: Cut off selvages and trim hem allowances to 1″. Finish with rug binding or in any way given in the general directions.

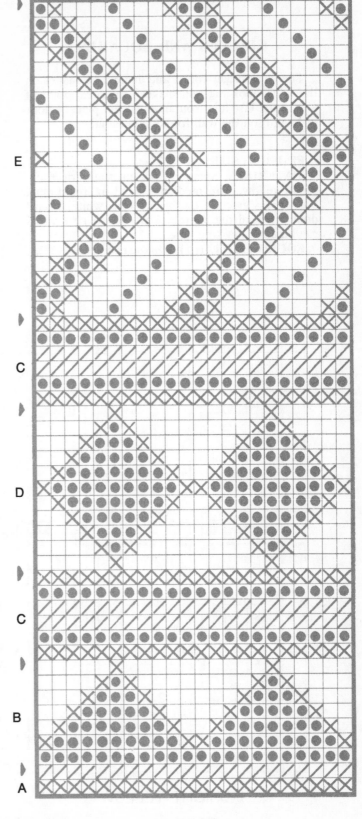

 SKIPPER BLUE    DARK BROWN   ORANGE    MEDIUM BLUE

119

CIRCLES AND SQUARES

The clear bright colors and distinctive shapes on the latch hook rug will make it the focal point of any room. Use it in front of an accent piece, a door or hang it on the wall for added drama!

FINISHED SIZE: 20" x 27".

MATERIALS: Spinnerin pre-cut rug yarn, 6 oz. bright yellow, 5 oz. medium blue, 3 oz. royal blue, 5 oz. grass green, 4 oz. black, 4 oz. white; 1 yard double thread rug canvas, 4 meshes to 1"; 3 yards rug binding; masking tape.

EQUIPMENT: Latch hook, rug needle.

PREPARING CANVAS: Cut canvas 24" x 31", allowing 2 inches all around for hems. Bind all raw edges with masking tape. Copy the diagram below using the method explained on page 118, or you may order a pre-stamped canvas (#198) from Spinnerin Yarn Co.

KNOTTING: Follow chart for colors, filling in the meshes as indicated by outline.

FINISHING: Trim hem allowance to 1" and turn under, mitering corners. Sew securely to back of rug with whip stitch along all 4 sides and corners. Sew rug binding over hems for a clean finish. Apply a non-skid rug backing liquid if desired. If canvas is to be used as a wall hanging, follow general directions on page 247.

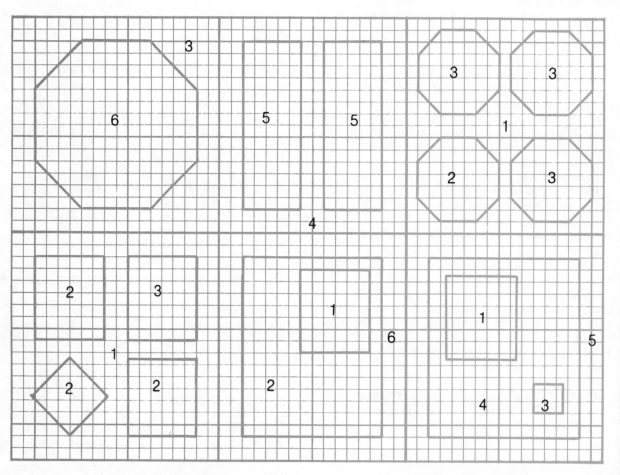

1 BRIGHT YELLOW

2 MEDIUM BLUE

3 ROYAL BLUE

4 GRASS GREEN

5 BLACK

6 WHITE

LAZY DAISY

These not so "lazy" daisies bloom all year long, bringing a breath of spring wherever you choose.

FINISHED SIZE: 40″ x 72″.
MATERIALS: Spinnerin pre-cut yarn, 27 oz. white, 37 oz. bright yellow, 3 oz. orange, 26 oz. spring green, 33 oz. forest green; 2⅛ yds. double thread rug canvas, 4 meshes to 1″; 7 yds. rug binding; masking tape.
EQUIPMENT: Latch hook, rug needle.

PREPARING CANVAS: Cut canvas 44″ x 76″ allowing 2″ all around for hems. Bind all edges with masking tape. Copy the diagram which follows using the method explained on page 118, or you may purchase Spinnerin pre-stamped canvas #101.
KNOTTING: Follow chart for colors filling in the meshes as indicated by outline.
FINISHING: Trim hem allowances to 1″ and turn under, mitering corners. Sew securely to back of rug with whip stitch along all 4 sides and mitered corners. Sew rug binding over canvas hems for a clean finish. Apply a non-skid rug-backing liquid if desired.

Row 45

Row 1

5

3

1

2

4

5

3

1

3

1

3

1

1

WHITE

2 BRIGHT YELLOW

3 ORANGE

4 SPRING GREEN

5 FOREST GREEN
(OUTLINE DAISIES IN THIS COLOR.)

123

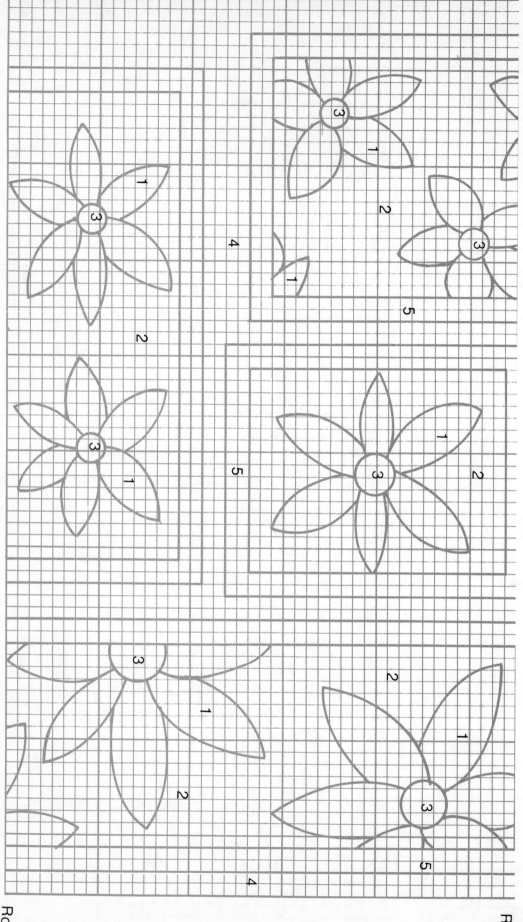

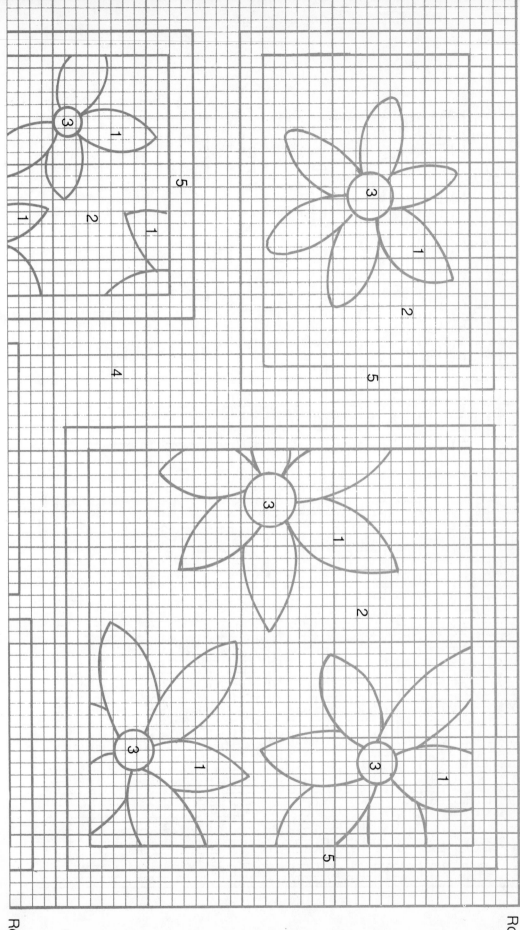

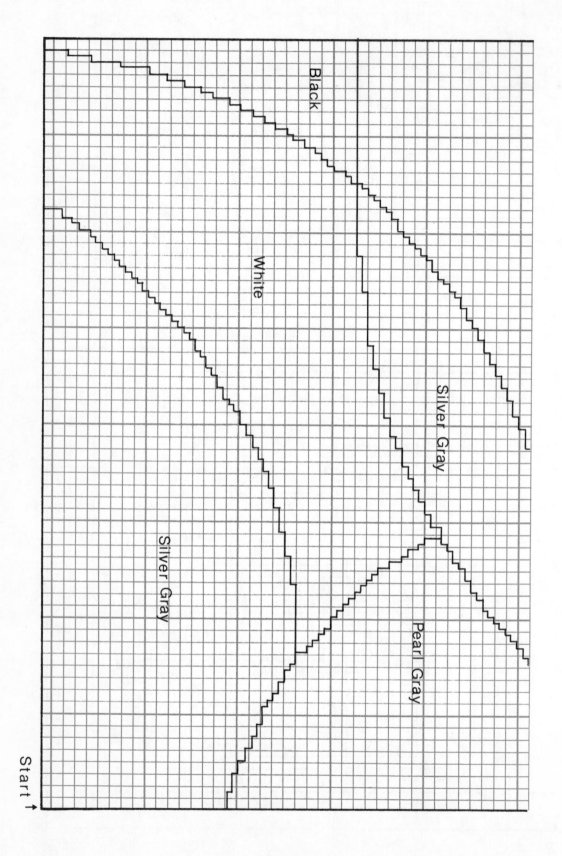

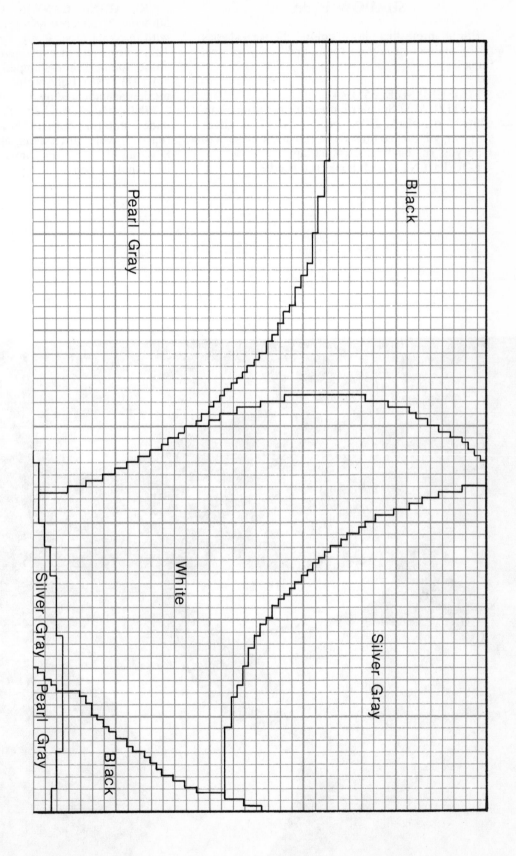

SHADOW PLAY

For an interesting play of colors, choose 4 shades of the main color in your room, and "do your own thing!"

FINISHED SIZE: 35" x 44".

MATERIALS: Spinnerin pre-cut rug yarn, 16 oz. white, 5 oz. black, 23 oz. pearl gray, 15 oz. silver gray; 1¼ yd. double thread rug canvas, 4 meshes to 1"; 5 yds. rug binding; masking tape.

EQUIPMENT: Latch hook, rug needle.

PREPARING CANVAS: Cut canvas 39" x 48" allowing 2" all around for hems. Bind raw edges with masking tape. Copy diagram, pages 126 and 127, using method explained on page 118, or purchase Spinnerin pre-stamped canvas #DG-9.

KNOTTING: Follow chart for colors filling in the meshes as indicated by the outline.

FINISHING: Trim hem allowances to 1" and turn under, mitering corners. Sew securely to back of rug with whip stitch along all 4 sides and corners. Sew rug binding over canvas hems for a clean finish. Apply a non-skid rug-backing liquid if desired.

CHECKERS-IN-THE-WIND

This lush rug made with rya yarn lends itself beautifully to modern decor. The use of rya yarn instead of the regular rug yarn results in a rug of higher pile and shaggier texture.

FINISHED SIZE: 34″ x 48″.

MATERIALS: Spinnerin pre-cut rya yarn, 36 pkgs. deep gold, 37 pkgs. white/smoke; 1½ yd. double thread rug canvas, 4 meshes to 1″; 6 yds. rug binding; masking tape.

EQUIPMENT: Latch hook, rug needle.

PREPARING CANVAS: Cut canvas 38″ x 52″ allowing 2″ all around for hems. Bind all raw edges with masking tape. Copy diagram, pages 130 and 131, using transfer method explained on page 118, or order Spinnerin pre-stamped canvas #228.

KNOTTING: Each pre-cut 4″ length of rya is actually 3 strands of wool, color-blended and fused together. You hook these 3 pieces all at once. You need hook only every other row on your canvas. Follow chart for colors filling in meshes on every other row as indicated by outline.

FINISHING: Trim hem allowances to 1″ and turn under, mitering corners. Sew securely to back of rug with whip stitch along all 4 sides and mitered corners. Sew rug binding over canvas hems for a clean finish. Apply a non-skid rug-backing liquid if desired.

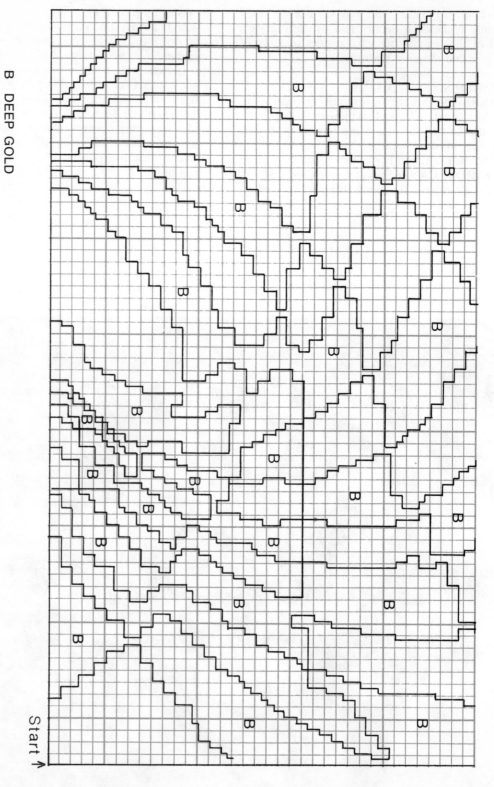

B DEEP GOLD

☐ WHITE SMOKE

RUG IS WORKED FROM LOWER EDGE TO UPPER EDGE.
EACH SQUARE ON GRAPH CORRESPONDS TO 1 MESH ON CANVAS.

Start →

130

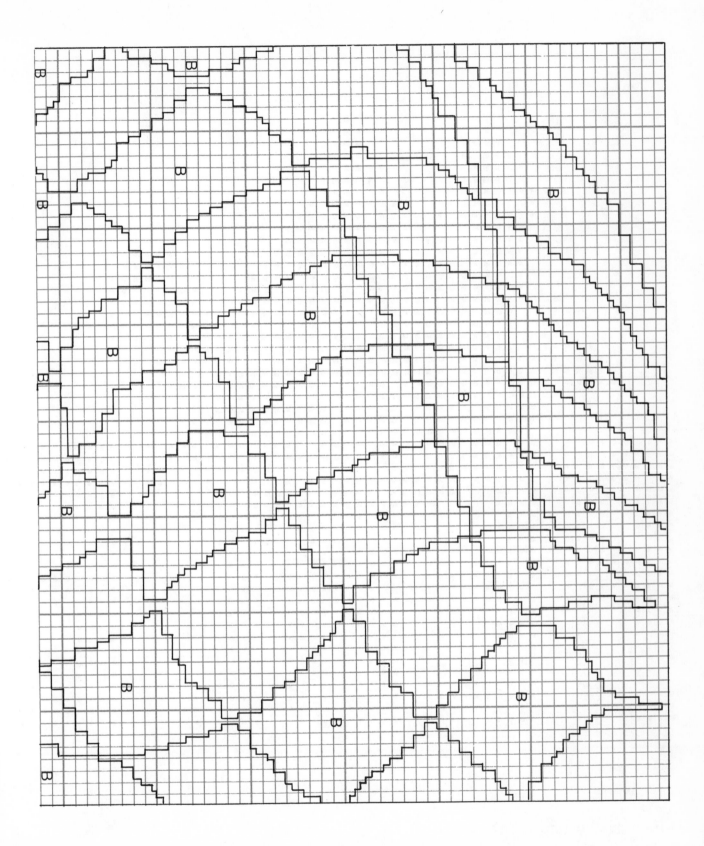

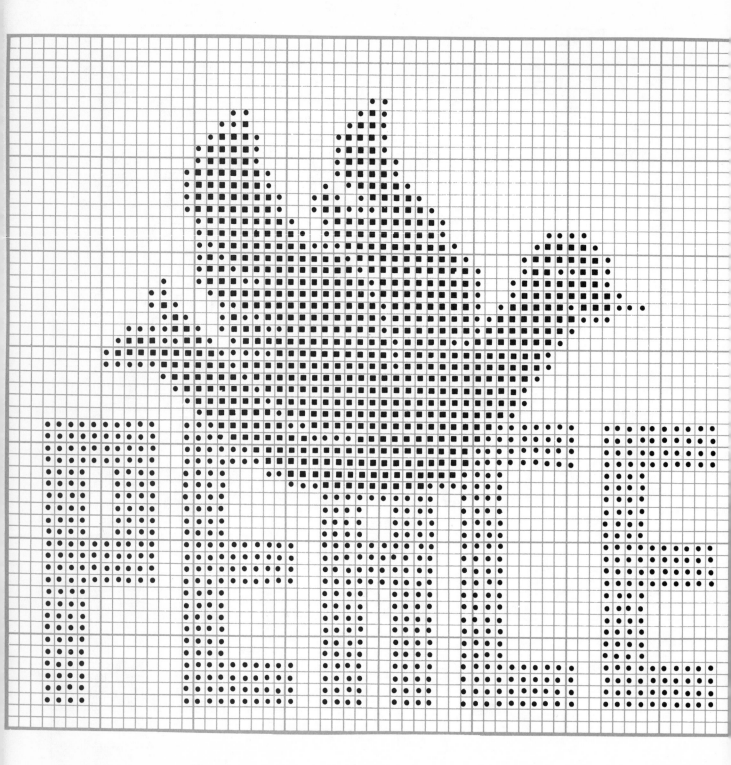

■ WHITE

◨ ROYAL BLUE

☐ MEDIUM BLUE

PEACE DOVE

Peace—in the world, —of mind, —and quiet. Whatever form peace takes it is always welcome, as is the dove, symbol of peace. You will find pleasure in the making of a wall hanging or a pillow, and added pleasure in the viewing and using of it.

FINISHED SIZE: 14″ x 16″.
MATERIALS: Spinnerin pre-cut rug yarn, 6 oz. medium blue, 6 oz. royal blue, 4 oz. white; ½ yd. double thread rug canvas, 4 meshes to 1″; masking tape.
EQUIPMENT: Latch hook, rug needle.
PREPARING CANVAS: Cut canvas 18″ x 20″ allowing 2″ all around for hems. Bind raw edges with masking tape. Copy diagram on page 132, using transfer method explained on page 118, or order Spinnerin Kit #9209.
KNOTTING: Follow chart for colors filling in the meshes as indicated.
FINISHING: Follow general directions for finishing a hooked-rug wall hanging or pillow, below.

RAIN DANCER

In the mode of folk art, this design is aptly named *Rain Dancer*. Shown on page 135 as a pillow, it will also make a very attractive wall hanging.

FINISHED SIZE: 15″ x 15″.
MATERIALS: Spinnerin pre-cut rug yarn, 6 oz. royal blue, 6 oz. black, 2 oz. white; ½ yd. rug canvas, 4 meshes to 1″; masking tape; ½ yd. muslin, 36″ wide for inner pillow; square of cotton, wool or velveteen, 16″ x 16″ for back of pillow; bag of shredded foam rubber or ready-made pillow form.
EQUIPMENT: Latch hook; rug needle.
PREPARING CANVAS: Cut canvas 19″ x 19″ allowing 2″ all around for seams. Bind raw edges with masking tape. Copy diagram on page 136 using transfer method described on page 118, or order Spinnerin Kit #9210.
KNOTTING: Follow chart for colors filling in meshes as indicated.
FINISHING: Follow general directions for finishing a hooked-rug pillow or wall hanging below.

MAKING A HOOKED-RUG WALL HANGING

Small rug canvasses like the Peace Dove are especially effective when used as wall hangings. They can be mounted on a larger piece of plywood paneling (as illustrated on page 133) giving the effect of a framed picture. Or they can be hung on decorative brass curtain rods.

To prepare the finished canvas for a wall hanging or pillow, trim hem allowance to 1″ and turn under, mitering corners. Sew to back of canvas with whip stitch along all 4 sides and corners.

To mount on plywood, center finished piece on plywood board and attach with small carpet tacks inserted between the pile. Regular picture wire and screw eyes can be attached to back of plywood for hanging on a picture hook.

If you prefer using a brass curtain rod or a wooden dowel, the process is very similar. First, turn under hem allowances and finish as above. Cut several 4″ or 5″ strips of rug binding, fold to form loops and sew securely along top edge of canvas hem. Space the loops evenly across the top. Slide rod through the loops and affix rod brackets to the wall.

MAKING A HOOKED-RUG PILLOW

Pillows made from small rug canvases like the Rain Dancer are soft and plush and add a different texture to a sofa or chair. After the design has been completed, finish back of canvas in the same manner as for a wall hanging. Cut 2 squares of muslin ½″ wider than canvas all around. Machine stitch ½″ seam on 3 sides, leaving approximately 3 or 4 inches open on the fourth side. Stuff this lining with shredded foam and hand sew the opening closed. Cut 2 squares of heavy cotton, wool or velveteen ⅝″ wider than canvas for pillow back. With right sides together, machine stitch ½″ seam along 3 sides. Insert foam-filled lining and blind stitch open side together. Pin canvas securely to front of pillow and whip stitch in place.

⊡ BLACK

▲ WHITE

☐ BLUE

MINI SHAG BAGS

Mini shag bags are fun to make and comfortable to carry. They are easily kept bright and fresh, too. When they become soiled, just wash them along with your woolen sweaters.

The shag bags may be purchased as kits. The striped bag is Spinnerin Kit #9229, and the flower bag is Spinnerin Kit #9231. Or, you can 'do-it-yourself' following the directions below.

FINISHED SIZE: $10\frac{1}{2}$" x $10\frac{3}{4}$".

MATERIALS: Striped Bag: Spinnerin pre-cut rug yarn, 5 oz. white, 3 oz. medium purple, 2 oz. lavender, 2 oz. dark purple; $\frac{5}{8}$ yd. double mesh rug canvas, 4 meshes to 1"; $\frac{1}{2}$ yd. 40-inch lining fabric and matching sewing thread.

Flower Bag: Spinnerin pre-cut rug yarn, 8 oz. white, 2 oz. red, 2 oz. black; $\frac{5}{8}$ yd. double mesh rug canvas, 4 meshes to 1"; $\frac{1}{2}$ yd. 40-inch lining fabric and matching sewing thread.

EQUIPMENT: Latch hook; rug needle; sewing needle.

PREPARING CANVAS: Cut section of canvas 15" x 24" for bag, and strip 5" x 36" for strap. With a magic marker, center a rectangle $10\frac{3}{4}$" x $20\frac{1}{2}$" on canvas. Starting at short end of rectangle, copy diagram of your choice on first half of canvas, invert diagram and copy on second half of canvas. Use transfer method explained on page 118.

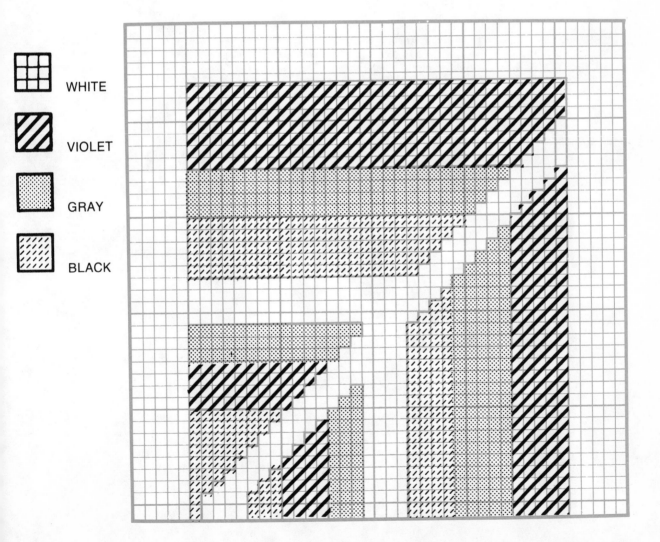

WHITE

VIOLET

GRAY

BLACK

KNOTTING: Follow chart for colors filling in meshes as indicated by outline. For strap, starting approximately 1″ from short end, hook 5 center meshes until strap measures approximately 27 or 28 inches.

FINISHING: Fold excess canvas on the sides of the bag to wrong side on the weave of the last mesh hooked. Baste to wrong side and cut canvas 4 meshes from fold. Trim excess canvas on strap 3 meshes from last hooked row. Fold and baste to wrong side so that no canvas shows on right side. Join sides: Fold bag in half with right sides out. Starting at top edge on right side, hook together the first corner mesh of the back and the front. Skip the next mesh on the back and front, and hook together the next 2 meshes. Continue in this manner, hooking every other mesh of back and front together to the bottom fold of the bag. Turn piece around and work back up to the top edge, hooking every 2 skipped meshes. Join other side in the same manner. Fold under canvas around top of bag on last row and baste in place. Trim excess canvas to 4 meshes from turn. Lining: Cut a 3″ crosswise strip of lining fabric. Turn under raw edges so that strip is equal to the width of the strap, and sew to strap on wrong side. Whip the edges of the fabric to the knots of the yarn so that no canvas shows. Center the ends of the strap at seam stitches of the bag and sew strap firmly to the hooked row of the bag. Fold remaining lining fabric in half and cut to measure 12″ x 12″. Sew side seams so the lining is 10¾″ wide. Turn top hem to wrong side to give a depth of 10¼″. Insert lining in bag and whip stitch in place along last row of hooking.

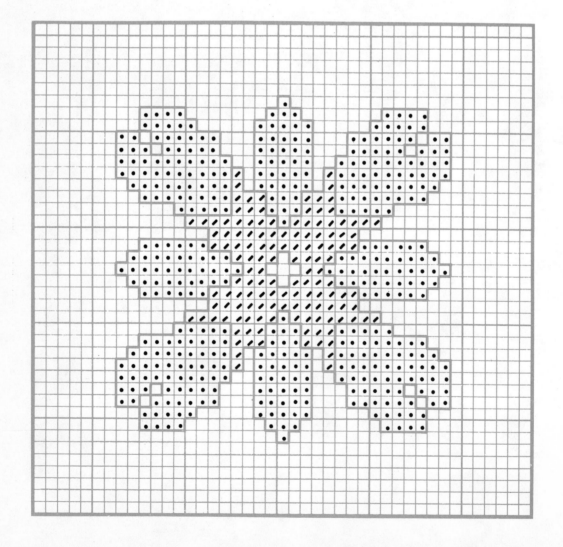

□ WHITE

☑ NAVY

⊡ RED

Knitting

Knitting

tions. Only the expert knitter should attempt substitutions. Purchase all the yarn needed for your project at one time. Later dye lots may differ slightly in color and weight and produce perceptible variations in your work.

No one can say that the art of knitting goes back quite as far as Adam and Eve — but if there hadn't been fig trees in the Garden of Eden, it's possible that mankind would have begun to knit even earlier! As it is, the history of knitting is one of the most fascinating of all the hand arts.

Supposedly Arabic in origin, knitting found its way into many parts of the world long before Columbus set sail on that fateful voyage. Bits of knitting found their way into Egyptian tombs.

Perhaps the most inspiring legend about knitting is that Christ's famous seamless garment worn on His way to Calvary was a knitted one. If it had been woven, the Roman soldiers quite possibly might have cut it up and meted out the precious pieces. Instead, since cutting a knitted garment would have raveled it, they cast lots for it, so the Bible tells us.

No matter what the history and background of knitting may be, it is still second only to basic sewing as a useful needlecraft to know. If you had lived in an earlier era, you would have learned to knit before you learned your ABC's. Unfortunately mothers are often unable to impart this practical skill to their young daughters and grandmothers today may be off waterskiing in Acapulco. So let the following pages take the place of a kindly grandmother and give you the knitting skills that will provide you endless hours of relaxation as well as a source for beautiful sweaters, baby garments, afghans and a supply of wonderful gifts.

Hand knitting is the technique of drawing loops of yarn through loops already on a knitting needle to form a webbing or fabric. This fabric has greater elasticity than a woven one. By manipulating the basic stitches in various yarns and threads one can produce an infinite variety of patterns from cobwebby lace to heavy rugs.

MATERIALS

Although we usually think of wool yarn when we think of knitting, any type of thread or yarn may be used. Fine cotton thread is used for knitting lace, heavier cottons for bedspreads and rugs. Wool in its great variety is used for sweaters, suits, coats, afghans. Now fascinating synthetics are available so that many garments may be machine washable.

In any case, use the yarn specified in the direc-

EQUIPMENT

Knitting needles vary in size from a little thicker than a straight pin to a giant 1″ in diameter. They may be made of aluminum, steel, plastic or wood. The small number indicates a fine needle; the large number indicates a large needle. Directions will always specify the needles to use.

Single-pointed needles come in pairs and are used to knit back and forth in rows. They are readily available in 10″ and 14″ lengths. Other lengths may be found, however. Sizes run 0, 1, 2, 3, 4, 5, 6, 7, 8, 9, 10, 10½, 11, 13, 15, 17, 19, 35 and 50. These are American sizes. If you have an old collection of needles, they may indicate English sizes. Be sure that you determine their size by comparing them with some needles in a knitting shop or department store, or using a purchased needle gauge (a piece of plastic punched with needle holes numbered according to size).

Double-pointed needles come in sets of four and are used to knit in the round such things as socks, mittens and neckbands on sweaters. They come in various lengths. Sizes run from 0 to 8 in aluminum and from 1 to 15 in plastic.

Circular needles are used to knit skirts and other comparatively wide items in the round. They are also used to hold a great number of stitches — more than would fit on a straight needle — and may be used for knitting back and forth. They are readily available in 11″, 16″, 24″, 29″ and 36″ lengths and are occasionally found in very short lengths. The 11″, 16″ and 24″ lengths go up to size 10½; the 29″ and 36″ lengths go up to size 15.

Jumper needles are flexible needles used when a great many stitches are being knitted and are easier to handle than a circular needle.

Many other knitting accessories are available and may be convenient to use. For the beginner simple household items can be substituted, however. Safety pins make good stitch holders. Instead of commercial point guards, rubber bands can be twisted around the points of your needles to prevent the stitches from sliding off when you put away your work. Bobbins can be made of stiff cardboard.

142

METHOD

How To Cast On

For a practice piece, use knitting worsted and No. 6 needles. Make a slip loop and insert point of needle through it. Tighten loop. Hold needle in left hand. Hold second needle in right hand, with yarn in working position. Insert point of right needle into loop on left needle from left to right, shown above. With index finger bring the yarn over the point of right needle. Draw the yarn through the loop. Insert left needle through new loop and remove right needle. You now have 2 stitches cast on. Make the third and all succeeding stitches the same way. For a stronger edge, insert right needle between stitches just below left needle instead of through loops. Cast on 15 stitches for a practice swatch. You are now ready to begin knitting.

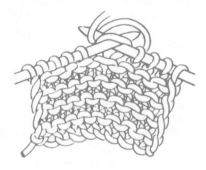

The Knit Stitch

Hold needle with cast-on stitches in your left hand. Insert right needle into front of first stitch on left needle from left to right. With right hand bring yarn under and over the point of right needle and draw the yarn through the stitch; slip the stitch just worked in off the left needle. This completes first stitch of row. Repeat in each stitch.

Always push work along left needle so that stitch to be worked is near tip. When all the stitches have been knitted off left needle, you should have 15 sts on right needle, as you had on the left originally. Count stitches occasionally to make sure that you keep the same number. At the end of row, turn work so needle with stitches is in your left hand. Continue working rows in this manner until you are making the stitches all the same size and you feel familiar with the stitch. When you knit each stitch in each row, it is called **garter stitch.**

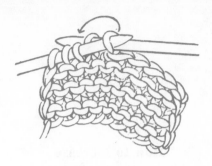

To Bind Off

You are now ready to finish off your practice piece. This process is called binding off.

Loosely knit 2 stitches. With point of left needle pick up first stitch and slide it over the second; slip it off needle.* Knit next stitch and slip preceding one over it. Repeat from * across all the stitches.

When you come to your last stitch, cut yarn about 3″ from the needle. Bring loose end through last stitch and pull tightly. Darn in end with tapestry needle so that it will not show.

The Purl Stitch

To make this stitch the yarn is in front of work instead of back, and needle is inserted into stitch from the right instead of left. The wrong side of a purl stitch is a knit stitch. The purl stitch is rarely used alone, so to practice the stitch proceed with stockinette stitch.

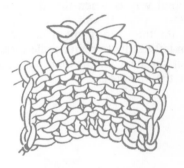

Stockinette Stitch

Cast on 15 stitches for a practice swatch. Knit first row. Turn work. Insert right needle into front of first stitch on left needle from right to left. With right hand bring yarn over the point of right needle and draw yarn through the stitch; slip the stitch just worked into off left needle. This completes the first purl stitch. Keeping yarn in front of work, repeat in each stitch across.

Knit next row, purl next row. Repeat these 2 rows until you are making the stitches all the same size and you feel familiar with the purl stitch. Bind off. (If you bind off on a purl row, purl the stitches instead of knitting them.)

How to Increase

Increases are usually used to shape garments. First work knit (or purl) stitch as usual into front of stitch but leave stitch on left needle. Then knit (or purl) into back of this same stitch.

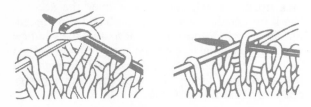

How to Decrease

There are two ways of decreasing and directions will tell you which one to use.

The first, and most often used way, is when the directions say "dec 1" and specify where to do it. To dec 1, simply knit (or purl) two stitches together as one stitch. This is also what is meant when directions say "k 2 tog (or p 2 tog)."

The second way is when the directions say "sl 1, k 1, psso." (Slip 1, knit 1, pass slipped stitch over.) To do this, slip 1 stitch (simply pass the stitch from left needle to right needle without working it), knit the next stitch, then pass the slipped stitch over the knit stitch.

To Make A Yarn Over

Yarn over automatically increases a stitch and is used mostly in lace patterns, since it produces a hole in the work.

On a knit row, bring yarn under tip of right needle, up and over needle, then work the next stitch.

On a purl row, bring yarn over right needle, around and to front again, then work the next stitch.

A yarn over forms an extra loop on right needle. On the next row, work it as a regular stitch.

144

How To Attach A New Yarn

Plan to attach new yarn at beginning of a row. Tie a single knot around old yarn, then knit several stitches with new yarn. Pull up old yarn so first stitch is same length as other stitches and knot again. When work is completed, weave both ends into the back of knitting.

How to Pick Up Dropped Stitches

Beginners and even advanced knitters often drop a stitch or stitches. They must be picked up or they will "run" just like a stocking.

Use a crochet hook. Catch the loose stitch and draw the horizontal thread of the row above through it. When picking up a knit stitch, insert hook through first stitch from front to back.

To pick up a purl stitch, insert hook through first stitch from back to front.

Repeat until you reach the row on which you are working, then place stitch on needle.

How to Pick Up Stitches Along an Edge

With right side of work facing you, tie yarn to spot where picking up is to start. Work with yarn and only one needle. Insert point of needle through knitting a short distance from the edge, wrap yarn around needle as if to knit and draw loop through. Continue in this manner across edge, spacing stitches evenly.

Weaving or Kitchener Stitch

This is a method of joining two pieces of knitting together, such as the tip of a mitten or the toe of a sock. The effect is one of a continuous piece of knitting.

Divide the stitches equally between two needles. Break off yarn leaving about a 15″ end (depending, of course, on the number of stitches to be woven). Thread end into a tapestry needle and work as follows: Hold the 2 needles even and parallel, having the yarn come from the right end of the back needle. Draw tapestry needle through first stitch of front needle as if to purl.

Draw yarn through leaving stitch on needle; draw tapestry needle through first stitch of back needle as if to purl leaving stitch on needle; * draw tapestry needle through first stitch of front needle as if to knit and slip stitch off needle; draw tapestry needle through next stitch on front needle as if to purl but leave stitch on needle; draw tapestry needle through first stitch of back needle as if to purl and slip stitch off needle; draw tapestry needle through next stitch on back needle as if to knit but leave stitch on needle. Repeat from * until all stitches are worked off. Draw end through one remaining stitch and fasten.

You may wish to tighten the woven stitches for a neater finish. Be sure to start with the first woven stitch and work across to the last.

Gauge

It is most important that you knit to the gauge specified in the directions so that your finished article will be the correct size. Gauge means the number of stitches to 1″, and may also include the number of rows to 1″.

Make a practice piece at least 4″ square, using the needles and yarn specified in the direction. With a ruler measure the number of stitches you have to 1″. If your stitches do not correspond to the gauge given, experiment with needles of different size.

Abbreviations

beg	beginning
dec	decrease
dp	double pointed
inc	increase
k	knit
p	purl
pat	pattern
psso	pass slipped stitch over
rnd	round
sk	skip
sl	slip
st	stitch
sts	stitches
tog	together
yo	yarn over

Knitting Terminology

Multiple of stitches: A pattern often requires an exact number of stitches, to be worked properly. When the directions say, for example, "multiple of 6 sts," it means the number of stitches must be divisible by 6 — 12, 18, 24, etc. "Multiple of 6 sts plus 3″ would be 15, 21, 27, etc.

Place a marker in work: This phrase means to mark with a safety pin a certain point in the work itself to use as a guide in taking future measurements.

Place a marker on needle: This means to place a safety pin, paper clip or purchased plastic stitch marker on the needle between the stitches at the point specified. It is slipped from one needle to the other on subsequent rows.

Slip a stitch: Sometimes also "sl 1", this means that you are to insert the right needle in stitch to be slipped as if to purl and pass it from left to right needle without working it.

Work even: This means to continue working without increasing or decreasing, always keeping the pattern as it has been established.

Repeat from *: This means that all instructions following the * are to be repeated as many times as specified in the directions.

Parentheses ( ): This is used in two ways: To enclose directions for larger sizes as listed at the start of each set of directions, and to indicate that the instructions which they enclose are to be repeated the number of times stated immediately after. For example, (k 2, p 1) twice means that you should knit 2, purl 1, knit 2, and purl 1.

How To Read Charts

Charts are sometimes given to clarify directions as given or as a substitute for what would be very involved directions. They are generally used when a design is to be worked with more than one color, less frequently when the design is worked in one color but with a change of stitch. In either case, simply think of each little square on the chart as one stitch in your work. Usually, the first row of the chart is read from right to left, the second from left to right, and so on.

Working Designs In Color

There are two methods of achieving color patterns on a background. One, sometimes referred to as "Fair Isle knitting," involves using two or more colors of yarn and changing colors every few stitches while knitting. The other is to work a design on top of a piece of knitting in Duplicate Stitch.

When knitting with more than one color of yarn, always carry the yarn not in use at the back of the work. If the unused strand is to be carried more than 3 stitches, twist it with the yarn in use every 3 stitches to avoid having long loops at the back. When changing colors, pick up the strand to be used from under the dropped strand. Be careful not to draw yarn too tightly, or work will pucker.

To work a design on top of a knit piece, thread a tapestry needle with the desired contrasting color. Draw yarn from wrong to right side through center of lower point of stitch. Insert needle at top right-hand side of same stitch. Then, holding needle in horizontal position, draw through to top left side of stitch. Insert again into base of same stitch. Keep yarn loose enough so it completely covers the knit stitch being worked over.

How to Block

To ensure a smooth, professional look, block the knit pieces before sewing them together. Blocking is the process of steaming and shaping a garment. Two similar pieces (sleeves, for example) may be blocked together at the same time. With wrong side up (or right sides together, if working with two pieces), pin to padded board with rustproof pins or thumbtacks placed at ¼″ to ½″ intervals. Pin to desired measurements. Place a damp cloth over knit piece and press with hot iron, raising it as you move it rather than sliding it back and forth. Don't press down too hard, especially on patterned pieces. Allow to dry thoroughly before unpinning.

Boys' Classic Sweaters

Anyone of the classic sweaters with set-in sleeves (pictured on page 141) or with raglan sleeves (pictured on page 152) will be an important addition to your youngster's wardrobe. Sweaters include set-in and raglan sleeved slipons and cardigans and a sleeveless slipon.

Directions are given for 3 weights of Spinnerin yarns in small, medium and large sizes.

MATERIALS GROUP A
LIGHT WEIGHT

SPINNERIN Wintuk Fingering (1-oz. skeins)

For **Slipons** 4 (6–8)
For **Cardigans** 5 (7–9)
For **Sleeveless** 3 (5–7)

OR Mona (50-gr. balls)
For **Slipons** 5 (7–8)
For **Cardigan** 6 (8–9)
For **Sleeveless** 4 (6–8)

MATERIALS GROUP B
MEDIUM WEIGHT

SPINNERIN Allround or Wintuk Sport (2-oz. skeins)

For **Slipons** 4 (5–6)
For **Cardigans** 5 (6–7)
For **Sleeveless** 3 (4–4)

OR Mona (50-gr. balls)
For **Slipons** 4 (6–8)
For **Cardigans** 5 (7–9)
For **Sleeveless** 3 (5–7)

OR Wintuk Featherlon (2-oz. skeins)
For **Slipons** 4 (5–6)
For **Cardigans** 5 (6–7)
For **Sleeveless** 3 (4–5)

MATERIALS GROUP C
HEAVY WEIGHT

SPINNERIN Marvel Twist Wash Fit® Germantown Deluxe or Deluxe Knitting Worsted (4-oz. skeins)
For **Slipons** 3 (3–4)
For **Cardigans** 3 (4–4)
For **Sleeveless** 2 (2–3)

Needles: No.2 and No.3 **OR SIZE TO GIVE GAUGE**

For Round or V-Neck Slipons 1 set dp No. 2
For Turtleneck *add* 1 set dp No. 3

Needles: No.4 and No.5 **OR SIZE TO GIVE GAUGE**

For Round Neck of V-Neck Slipons 1 set dp No. 4
For Turtleneck *add* 1 set dp No. 5

Needles: No.6 and No.7 **OR SIZE TO GIVE GAUGE**

For Round or V-Neck Slipons 1 set dp No. 6
For Turtleneck *add* 1 set dp No. 7

GAUGE: 7 sts = 1 inch
10 rows = 1 inch

GAUGE: 6 sts = 1 inch
8 rows = 1 inch

GAUGE: 5 sts = 1 inch
6 rows = 1 inch

FINISHED CHEST MEASUREMENTS
For All Slipons 28 (32–36) inches
For All Cardigans (buttoned) 27 (33–37) inches

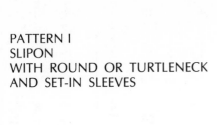

PATTERN I
SLIPON
WITH ROUND OR TURTLENECK
AND SET-IN SLEEVES

Note: Bands are worked in K 1, P 1 ribbing.
Body is worked in stockinette st (K 1 row, P 1 row).

SIZES	GROUP A			GROUP B			GROUP C		
	S	M	L	S	M	L	S	M	L
BACK: With smaller needles, cast on ....sts	98	112	126	84	96	108	70	80	90
Work band for ....inches	1	1½	2	SAME AS GROUP A					
Change to larger needles.									
Work body to ....inches	10	12	14	SAME AS GROUP A					
from beg, or desired length to underarms.									
Armholes: At beg of next 2 rows, bind off ....sts	7	7	7	6	6	6	5	5	5
Dec 1 st each side every 2nd row ....times	5	5	5	5	5	5	4	4	4
Work on ....sts	74	88	102	62	74	86	52	62	72
until armholes are.........................inches	5	6	8	SAME AS GROUP A					
Shoulders: At beg of next ....rows	4	4	4	2	2	2	2	2	2
bind off ....sts	8	10	12	10	12	14	9	10	12
At beg of next 2 rows, bind off.........................sts	8	9	10	10	12	14	8	10	12
Place on holder remaining ....sts	26	30	34	22	26	30	18	22	24
FRONT: Work same as back until armholes are.......inches	3	4	6	SAME AS GROUP A					
There are on needle.........................sts	74	88	102	62	74	86	52	62	72
Neck: Work.........................sts	29	34	39	24	28	32	20	23	27
place on holder center.........................sts	16	20	24	14	18	22	12	16	18
tie in another ball of yarn, work last.........................sts	29	34	39	24	28	32	20	23	27
Work each side with separate yarn. Dec 1 st at neck edges every 2nd row.........................times	5	5	5	4	4	4	3	3	3
Work on.........................sts	24	29	34	20	24	28	17	20	24
to same length as back to shoulders.									
Shoulders: Shape as on back.									
SLEEVES (Shaped): With smaller needles, cast on........sts	48	52	56	40	44	48	36	38	40
Rib as on back, inc across last row ....sts	8	8	8	6	6	6	4	4	4
Change to larger needles. Work stockinette st, inc 1 st each side every.........................inches	1½	1½	1	1½	1½	1	1½	1½	1½
.........................times	5	8	11	5	8	11	4	7	9
Work on.........................sts	66	76	86	56	66	76	48	56	62
to ....inches	11	13½	16½	SAME AS GROUP A					
from beg, or desired length to underarm.									

SIZES	GROUP A			GROUP B			GROUP C		
	S	M	L	S	M	L	S	M	L
Shape Cap: At beg of next 2 rows, bind off..................sts	7	7	7	6	6	6	5	5	5
Dec 1 st each side every 2nd row ....times	7	12	23	4	7	18	2	4	13
every row...times	6	6	0	8	10	4	8	10	4
At beg of next ....rows	4	4	4	4	4	4	2	2	2
bind off ....sts	3	3	3	2	2	2	4	4	4
Bind off remaining..sts	14	14	14	12	12	12	10	10	10
SLEEVES (Full): With smaller needles, cast on ....sts	40	44	48	36	40	44	34	36	38
Rib as on back.									
Next row: K᾿...sts	7	6	5	8	7	6	10	8	7
inc 1 st in each of next...sts	26	32	38	20	26	32	14	20	24
K ....sts	7	6	5	8	7	6	10	8	7
Change to larger needles.									
Work on ....sts	66	76	86	56	66	76	48	56	62
to ....inches	11	13½	16½	SAME AS GROUP A					

Shape Cap: Same as shaped sleeve.

FINISHING: Block pieces to measurements. Assemble.

Neckband: With dp needles, from right side and beg at right shoulder seam, pick up around neck (including sts on holders)...sts	86	98	110	76	84	92	64	72	80

Join and work around in ribbing.
For single neckband, work ³/₄ inch.
For double neckband, work 1½ inches.
For turtleneck, work 2 inches. Change to larger dp needles, work 4 inches, or desired depth.
Bind off loosely in ribbing.
For double neckband, turn ribbing in half to wrong side and sew bound-off edge loosely to neck edge.

PATTERN II
SLIPON
WITH BOAT NECK OR V NECK
AND SET-IN SLEEVES

SIZES
BOAT NECK

	GROUP A			GROUP B			GROUP C		
	S	M	L	S	M	L	S	M	L
BACK AND FRONT: Work same as Pattern I, page 147, until armholes are................................inches	4	5	7		SAME AS GROUP A				
Shoulders: Rib in K 1, P 1 for 1 inch. Continue ribbing and at beg of next ....rows	6	6	6	4	4	4	4	4	4
bind off ....sts	5	6	7	6	7	9	4	6	8

Bind off remaining sts in ribbing.

V NECK

BACK: Same as Pattern I.

FRONT: Work same as back to 1 row less than back to armholes, ending with a K row.

	GROUP A			GROUP B			GROUP C		
Neck and Armholes: P...................................sts	49	56	63	42	48	54	35	40	45
join another ball of yarn, P to end. Work each side with separate yarn. Shape armholes as on back **AND AT SAME TIME** dec 1 st at neck edges on next row and rep dec at neck edges every 6th row ....times	0	0	6	0	0	0	0	0	0
every 4th row ....times	12	14	10	10	12	14	8	10	11

shaping shoulder as on back when armholes are same length.

SLEEVES: Same as Pattern I, page 147.

FINISHING: Block pieces to measurements and assemble.

	GROUP A			GROUP B			GROUP C		
Single Neckband for V Neck: With dp needles from right side and beg at left shoulder seam, pick up on left front neck edge ....sts	40	48	64	36	42	56	30	36	48
pick up 1 st at center and mark st, pick up on right front neck edge ....sts	39	47	63	35	41	55	29	35	47

K across sts at back of neck. Join. **Rnd 1:** K 1, P 1 to center st, K center st, P 1, K 1 to end. **Rnd 2:** Rib to 2 sts before center st, sl 1 as to K, K 1, psso, K center st, K 2 tog, rib to end. **Rnd 3:** Rib to center st, K center st, rib to end. Rep last 2 rnds for 1 inch, ending with Rnd 3. Bind off loosely in ribbing, dec as before.

Double Neckband for V Neck: Work same as single neckband; do *not* bind off. Continue ribbing, inc 1 st each side of center st on next rnd and rep incs every 2nd rnd until same number of inc rnds as dec rnds. Bind off loosely in ribbing. Turn neckband in half to wrong side and sew bound-off edge loosely to neck edge.

PATTERN III
SLEEVELESS V NECK SLIPON

SIZES	GROUP A			GROUP B			GROUP C		
	S	M	L	S	M	L	S	M	L

BACK: Work same as back of Pattern 1, page 147, to armholes.

	GROUP A			GROUP B			GROUP C		
Armholes: At beg of next 2 rows, bind off ....sts	7	7	7	6	6	6	5	5	5
At beg of next 2 rows, bind off................................sts	5	5	5	4	4	4	3	3	3
Dec 1 st each side every 2nd row ....times	5	5	5	5	5	5	4	4	4
Work on...sts	64	78	92	54	66	78	46	56	66
until armholes are...inches	6	7	8½	SAME AS GROUP A					
Shoulders: At beg of next ....rows	4	4	4	2	2	2	2	2	2
bind off...sts	6	8	10	8	10	12	7	9	11
At beg of next 2 rows, bind off................................sts	7	8	9	8	10	12	7	8	10
Place on holder..sts	26	30	34	22	26	30	18	22	24

FRONT: Work same as back to 1 inch less than back to armholes, ending with a K row.

	GROUP A			GROUP B			GROUP C		
Neck and Armholes: P..sts	49	56	63	42	48	54	35	40	45
join another ball yarn, P to end. Work each side with separate yarn. Dec 1 st at neck edges on next row and rep dec every 6th row ....times	11	12	16	7	7	10	4	3	5
AND AT SAME TIME, when same length as back to armholes, shape armholes as on back. Dec 1 st at neck edges every 4th row ....times	1	2	0	3	5	4	4	7	6

shaping shoulders as on back when armholes are same length.

FINISHING: Block pieces to measurements and assemble.

	GROUP A			GROUP B			GROUP C		
Single or Double Neckband: With dp needles from right side and beg at left shoulder seam, pick up on left front neck edge..sts	48	56	72	42	50	62	36	42	56
pick up 1 st at center and mark st, pick up on right front neck edge ....sts	47	55	71	41	49	61	35	41	53

K across sts at back of neck. Join and work same as single or double neckband of Pattern II above.

	GROUP A			GROUP B			GROUP C		
Single Armhole Bands: With dp needles from right side and beg at underarm edge, pick up on bound-off sts of back ....sts	10	10	10	10	10	10	8	8	8
on armhole edge ....sts	88	102	122	74	86	104	62	72	86
on bound-off sts of front..sts	10	10	10	10	10	10	8	8	8

Join and rib for 1 inch. Bind off loosely in ribbing.
Double Armhole Bands: Rib in K 1, P 1 for 2 inches. Bind off loosely in ribbing. Turn bands in half to wrong side and sew bound-off edge loosely to picked-up row.

PATTERN IV
CARDIGAN
WITH V NECK AND SET-IN SLEEVES

	GROUP A S	M	L	GROUP B S	M	L	GROUP C S	M	L
SIZES									
BACK: Same as Pattern 1, page 147, except bind off sts for back of neck; do *not* place on holder.									
RIGHT FRONT: With smaller needles, cast on............sts	65	72	79	56	62	68	49	54	59
Row 1: * K...sts	7	7	7	6	6	6	5	5	5
sl 1 as to P; rep from * once, P 1, K 1 to end.									
Row 2: Rib to last ....sts	16	16	16	14	14	14	12	12	12
P to end.									
Rep these 2 rows for ....inches	1	1½	2		SAME AS GROUP A				
ending with Row 2.									
Change to larger needles.									
Next row: * K...sts	7	7	7	6	6	6	5	5	5

sl 1; rep from * once, K to end.

Next row: Purl.

Rep last 2 rows to 1 inch less than back to armholes, ending with a P row at front edge. Continue to sl same 2 sts at front until neckband is completed.

Neck, Armhole and Shoulder:

	GROUP A S	M	L	GROUP B S	M	L	GROUP C S	M	L
Work ....sts	16	16	16	14	14	14	12	12	12
K 2 tog thru *back* loops (neck dec) K to end.									
Continue to dec 1 st after 2nd sl st every 6th row.....times	0	0	6	0	0	0	0	0	0
every 4th row...times	13	15	11	11	13	15	7	8	12
every 2nd row..times	0	0	0	0	0	0	4	5	2

AND AT SAME TIME, when same length as back to armholes, shape armhole as on back, **AND,** when same length as back to shoulder, shape shoulder as on back.

	GROUP A S	M	L	GROUP B S	M	L	GROUP C S	M	L
Back Neckband: Continue on......................................sts	15	15	15	13	13	13	11	11	11
for ....inches	1¾	2¼	2¾		SAME AS GROUP A				

Place sts on a holder.

Mark place for 5 buttons on front band, having first marker ½ inch above lower edge, 5th marker just below first neck dec and other 3 spaced evenly between.

LEFT FRONT: Work to correspond to right front, reversing all shaping and forming double buttonholes opposite markers as follows:

	GROUP A S	M	L	GROUP B S	M	L	GROUP C S	M	L
Beg at underarm edge, work to last ....sts	16	16	16	14	14	14	12	12	12
sl 1, K 2, bind off next...sts	3	3	3	2	2	2	1	1	1
K to next sl st, sl 1, K 2, bind off next.........................sts	3	3	3	2	2	2	1	1	1
On next row, cast on ....sts	3	3	3	2	2	2	1	1	1

over each set of bound-off sts.

SLEEVES: Same as Pattern 1, page 147.

FINISHING: Block pieces to measurements and assemble. Weave ends of neckband tog. Turn front borders and back neckband to wrong side at sl st (turning ridge) and sew in place along inner sl st. Sew free edge of back neckband to right side of neck edge. Overcast double buttonholes. Sew on buttons.

PATTERN V
SLIPON
WITH ROUND OR TURTLENECK
AND RAGLAN SLEEVES

	GROUP A			GROUP B			GROUP C		
SIZES	S	M	L	S	M	L	S	M	L
BACK: Work same as Pattern I, page 147, to armholes.									
Raglan Armholes: At beg of next 2 rows, bind off.........sts	6	7	8	5	6	7	5	6	7
Row 3: K 2, K 2 tog, K to last 4 sts, sl 1 as to K, K 1, psso, K 2.									
Row 4: Purl.									
Rep last 2 rows...times	25	28	29	23	25	27	17	20	24
Dec 1 st each side as before every 4th row.............times	2	3	6	0	1	3	0	0	0
Place on holder...sts	30	34	38	26	30	32	24	26	26
FRONT: Work same as back until...............armhole decs	20	25	31	16	20	26	12	15	19
and on needle..sts	46	48	48	42	44	42	36	38	38
On next P row, work...sts	16	15	13	14	13	11	12	12	12
place on holder center..sts	14	18	22	14	18	20	12	14	14
join 2nd ball yarn, work to end. Work each side with separate yarn. Continue to shape armholes as on back									
AND AT SAME TIME bind off at neck edges 2 sts ... times	3	3	3	2	2	2	2	2	2
Work remaining 2 sts at each side tog and fasten off.									
SLEEVES: Same as Pattern I, page 147, to cap shaping.									
Raglan Cap: At beg of next 2 rows, bind off ....sts	6	7	8	5	6	7	5	6	7
Dec 1 st each side (as on back) every 2nd row.........times	16	19	20	16	20	22	16	19	19
every 4th row ....times	7	8	11	4	4	6	1	1	3
Place on holder..sts	8	8	8	6	6	6	4	4	4

FINISHING: Block pieces to measurements. Weave sleeve caps to back and front armholes. Sew underarm and sleeve seams.

	GROUP A			GROUP B			GROUP C		
Neckband: With smaller dp needles from right side and beg at right back raglan seam, K across sts of back and sleeve, pick up on left front neck edge ....sts	14	14	14	12	12	14	11	11	13
K across sts of front, pick up on right front neck edge ....sts	14	14	14	12	12	14	11	11	13
K across sts of 2nd sleeve. There are on needles..........sts	88	96	104	76	84	92	66	70	74

Work single or double neckband for round neck, or work turtleneck, same as Pattern I.

PATTERN VI
SLIPON
WITH BOAT OR V NECK
AND RAGLAN SLEEVES

	GROUP A			GROUP B			GROUP C		
SIZES	S	M	L	S	M	L	S	M	L

BOAT NECK

BACK AND FRONT: Work same as back of Pattern V,

	S	M	L	S	M	L	S	M	L
above, until there are ....armhole decs	20	25	31	16	20	26	12	15	19
and on needle ....sts	46	48	48	42	44	42	36	38	38

Work in K 1, P 1 ribbing, continuing to dec armholes as on back of Pattern V. Bind off remaining sts loosely in ribbing.

SLEEVES: Work same as Pattern V until there are...........

	S	M	L	S	M	L	S	M	L
....dec rows	18	22	26	16	20	24	12	15	19
and on needles..sts	18	18	18	14	14	14	14	14	10

Work in K 1, P 1 ribbing, continuing to dec armholes as on sleeves of Pattern V. Bind off remaining sts loosely in ribbing.
FINISHING: Weave sleeve caps to back and front armholes. Sew seams.

V NECK

BACK: Work same as Pattern V, page 153.

FRONT: Work same as back to 1 row less than back to armholes, ending with a K row.

	S	M	L	S	M	L	S	M	L
Neck and Armholes: P ....sts	49	56	63	42	48	54	35	40	45
tie in 2nd ball yarn, P last..............................sts	49	56	63	42	48	54	35	40	45

Work each side with separate yarn. Shape armholes as on
back **AND AT SAME TIME** dec 1 st at neck edges on next

	S	M	L	S	M	L	S	M	L
row and rep decs every 4th row ....times	2	1	6	0	0	3	0	0	0
every 2nd row...times	11	14	11	11	13	11	10	11	11

K last 2 tog. Fasten off.

SLEEVES: Same as Pattern I, page 147, to cap shaping.

Raglan Cap: Same as Pattern V.

Neckband: With dp needles from right side and beg at right
front raglan seam, K across sts of sleeve; K across sts of

	S	M	L	S	M	L	S	M	L
back neck, dec at even spaces ....sts	6	6	4	4	4	2	6	4	2
pick up on left front neck edge ....sts	48	56	66	42	48	58	34	40	48

pick up and mark 1 st at center, pick up on right front

	S	M	L	S	M	L	S	M	L
neck edge ....sts	47	55	65	41	47	57	33	39	47

K across sts of sleeve. Join. Work and finish single or double neckband same as Pattern II, page 149.

CARDIGAN
WITH V NECK AND RAGLAN SLEEVES

	GROUP A			GROUP B			GROUP C		
SIZES	**S**	**M**	**L**	**S**	**M**	**L**	**S**	**M**	**L**
BACK: Same as Pattern V, page 153, except bind off for back of neck, dec at even spaces across row...............sts	6	6	4	4	4	2	6	4	2
RIGHT FRONT: Work same as Pattern IV, page 157, to beg of neck, ending at underarm edge.									
Neck and Armhole: Work...sts	16	16	16	14	14	14	12	12	12
K 2 tog thru *back* loops (neck dec), K to end. Continue to dec 1 st after 2nd sl st every 4th row ....times	13	16	19	9	11	16	2	4	7
every 2nd row..times	2	1	0	4	4	0	12	11	8

AND AT SAME TIME, when same length as back to raglan armholes, shape armhole same as left side of back.

Neckband: Same as Pattern IV. Mark places for buttons as Pattern IV.

LEFT FRONT: Same as Pattern IV to armhole. Complete to correspond to right front, reversing shaping and forming double buttonholes same as on right front of Pattern IV.

SLEEVES: Same as Pattern I, page 147, to cap shaping.

Raglan Cap: Same as Pattern V, page 153.

FINISHING: Block pieces to measurements. Weave sleeve caps to back and front armholes. Complete same as Pattern IV.

Girls' Classic Sweaters

Classic sweaters are important for girls too. They go with skirts, slacks and even look good over dresses. The patterns include set-in sleeves and raglan sleeves with a variety of neck finishes. Directions are for 3 weights of Spinnerin yarns in sizes 4, 6, 8, 10 and 12.

Sweaters with set-in sleeves are pictured on page 157, raglan sleeved sweaters are on page 164.

MATERIALS GROUP A
LIGHT WEIGHT

SPINNERIN Wintuk Fingering (1-oz. skeins
for sleeveless slipons 3 (4–4–5–5)
for slipons with sleeves 5 (6–7–8–8)
for cardigans 6 (7–8–8–9)

OR Mona (50-gr. balls)
for sleeveless slipons 4 (5–5–6–6)
for slipons with sleeves 6 (7–7–8–9)
for cardigans 6 (7–8–9–9)

MATERIALS GROUP B
MEDIUM WEIGHT

SPINNERIN Allround or Wintuk Sport (2-oz. skeins)
for sleeveless slipons 3 (3–3–4–4)
for slipons with sleeves 4 (5–6–7–7)
for cardigans 4 (5–6–7–8)

OR Wintuk Featherlon (2-oz. skeins)
for sleeveless slipons 3 (3–4–4–5)
for slipons with sleeves 4 (5–5–6–6)
for cardigans 5 (5–6–6–7)

OR Mona (50-gr. balls)
for sleeveless slipons 3 (4–4–5–5)
for slipons with sleeves 5 (6–7–7–8)
for cardigans 5 (6–7–8–8)

MATERIALS GROUP C
HEAVY WEIGHT

SPINNERIN Marvel Twist Wash Fit® or Germantown Deluxe (4-oz. skeins)
for sleeveless slipons 2 (2–2–3–3)
for slipons with sleeves 2 (3–3–4–4)
for cardigans 3 (3–4–4–4)

Needles: No. 2 and No. 3 **OR SIZE TO GIVE GAUGE**
For Round or V-neck slipons, 1 set dp No. 2
For Turtleneck, add 1 set dp No. 3

Needles: No. 3 and No. 5 **OR SIZE TO GIVE GAUGE**
For Round or V-neck slipons, 1 set dp No. 3
For Turtleneck, add 1 set dp No. 5

Needles: No. 5 and No. 7 **OR SIZE TO GIVE GAUGE**
For Round or V-neck slipons, 1 set dp No. 5
For Turtleneck, add 1 set dp No. 7

GAUGE: 7 sts = 1 inch
10 rows = 1 inch

GAUGE: 6 sts = 1 inch
8 rows = 1 inch

GAUGE: 5 sts = 1 inch
6 rows = 1 inch

FINISHED MEASUREMENTS

Chest for all slipons 26 (28–30–32–34) inches
Chest for all cardigans (buttoned) 27 (29–31–33–35) inches
Sleeves at underarm 9 (9½–10–11–11½) inches

PATTERN I
SLIPON
ROUND OR TURTLENECK
WITH SET-IN SLEEVES,
LONG OR SHORT

SIZES	GROUP A					GROUP B					GROUP C				
	4	6	8	10	12	4	6	8	10	12	4	6	8	10	12
BACK: With smaller needles, cast on ....sts	90	98	104	112	118	78	84	90	96	102	64	70	74	80	84
Rib in K 1, P 1 for ....inches	1½	1½	2	2	2	SAME AS GROUP A									
inc on last row.........................sts	1	0	1	0	1	0	0	0	0	0	1	0	1	0	1
Change to larger needles. Work stockinette st (K 1 row, P 1 row) to ....inches from beg, or desired length to underarm.	9	9½	10	11	12	SAME AS GROUP A									
Armholes: At beg of next 2 rows bind off...................................sts	5	6	7	7	7	4	5	6	6	6	4	5	5	5	5
Dec 1 st each side every 2nd row ....times	5	6	7	7	7	5	5	5	6	6	4	4	5	5	5
Work even on..........................sts	71	74	77	84	91	60	64	68	72	78	49	52	55	60	65
until armholes are...............inches	4½	5	5½	6	6½	SAME AS GROUP A									
Shoulders: Bind off...................sts	6	8	6	7	7	6	6	7	7	8	5	5	5	6	6
at beg of next ....rows	2	2	8	4	8	6	2	4	2	6	6	4	2	4	2
Bind off................................sts	5	5	0	6	0	0	7	8	8	0	0	6	6	7	7
at beg of next ....rows	6	6	0	4	0	0	4	2	4	0	0	2	4	2	4
Place on holder......................sts	29	28	29	32	35	24	24	24	26	30	19	20	21	22	25
FRONT: Work same as back until armholes are.......................inches ending with a P row.	3½	4	4½	5	5½	SAME AS GROUP A									
Neck: Knit ....sts	28	30	31	34	37	24	26	28	29	31	19	21	22	24	25
place on holder center..............sts	15	14	15	16	17	12	12	12	14	16	11	10	11	12	15
join another ball of yarn, work to end. Working each side with separate yarn, dec 1 st at neck edges every 2nd row ....times	7	7	7	8	9	6	6	6	6	7	4	5	5	5	5
AND AT SAME TIME, shape shoulders as on back when armholes are same length															
LONG SLEEVES: With smaller needles, cast on ....sts	44	48	50	54	56	40	42	44	46	48	32	34	36	38	40
Rib in K 1, P 1 for 2 inches. Change to larger needles. Work stockinette st, inc 1 st each side every ....rows	8	8	8	8	8	8	8	8	8	8	6	6	6	6	6
....times	9	9	10	11	12	7	8	8	10	11	7	7	7	8	8
Work even on..........................sts	62	66	70	76	80	54	58	60	66	70	46	48	50	54	56
to ....inches from beg, or desired length to underarm.	10	11	12	13½	15	SAME AS GROUP A									

SIZES	GROUP A					GROUP B					GROUP C				
	4	6	8	10	12	4	6	8	10	12	4	6	8	10	12
Shape Cap: At beg of next 2 rows, bind off..................................sts	5	6	7	7	7	4	5	6	6	6	4	5	5	5	5
Dec 1 st each side every 2nd row ....times	7	12	15	18	20	3	6	10	11	13	2	6	7	9	10
every row ....times	6	2	0	0	0	10	8	4	6	6	8	4	4	4	4
Bind off 2 sts at beg of next......rows	6	6	6	6	6	4	4	4	4	4	4	4	4	4	4
Bind off remaining..................sts	14	14	14	14	14	12	12	12	12	12	10	10	10	10	10
SHORT SLEEVES: With smaller needles, cast on ....sts Rib in K 1, P 1 for 1 inch. Change to larger needles. Work stockinette st,	54	58	62	68	72	48	52	54	60	64	42	44	44	48	48

SIZES	GROUP A					GROUP B					GROUP C				
inc 1 st each side every 2nd row ....times	4	4	4	4	4	3	3	3	3	3	2	2	3	3	4
Work even on.........................sts	62	66	70	76	80	54	58	60	66	70	46	48	50	54	56
to ....inches from beg, or desired length to underarm.	2	2	2½	2½	3			SAME AS GROUP A							

Shape Cap: Same as for long sleeve.

FINISHING: Block pieces to measurements and assemble.
Neckband: With smaller dp needles and beg at left shoulder seam, from right side pick up around neck edge, including sts on holders............sts

	GROUP A					GROUP B					GROUP C				
	82	86	90	96	102	70	74	78	82	86	60	64	68	72	76

For Round Neck: Join and work around in K 1, P 1 rib for 1 inch (for single neckband) or 2 inches (for double neckband). Bind off loosely in rib. For double neckband, turn to wrong side and sew bound-off sts to neck edge.

For Turtleneck: Work same as for round neck for ½ desired depth. Change to larger dp needles to complete. Bind off loosely in rib.

PATTERN II
SLIPON
WITH V NECK AND SET-IN SLEEVES

	GROUP A					GROUP B					GROUP C				
SIZES	4	6	8	10	12	4	6	8	10	12	4	6	8	10	12

BACK: Same as Pattern I, page 158.

FRONT: Work same as back to 1 row less to armholes, ending with a K row.

Neck and Armholes:

Next Row: P ....sts	45	49	52	56	59	39	42	45	48	51	32	35	37	40	42
place on holder center ....st	1	0	1	0	1	0	0	0	0	0	1	0	1	0	1
join another ball of yarn, P ....sts	45	49	52	56	59	39	42	45	48	51	32	35	37	40	42

Working each side with separate yarn, shape armholes as on back **AND AT SAME TIME,** dec 1 st at

neck edges every 2nd row.....times	8	5	3	4	4	8	6	4	4	7	6	6	5	6	6
every 4th row ....times	6	9	11	12	13	4	6	8	9	8	3	4	5	5	6

shaping shoulders as on back when armholes are same length.

SLEEVES: Same as Pattern I.

FINISHING: Block pieces to measurements and assemble.

Single Neckband: With smaller dp needles, from right side and beg at left shoulder seam, pick up on left

front neck edge.......................sts	50	56	62	66	72	40	44	48	52	56	30	34	38	40	44

K from holder or pick up a st at center and mark, pick up on right

front neck edge.......................sts	50	56	62	66	72	40	44	48	52	56	30	34	38	40	44
across sts at back of neck, inc .....sts	0	1	0	1	0	1	1	1	1	1	0	1	0	1	0

Mark for beg of rnds and join.

Rnd 1: Rib in K 1, P 1 to 2 sts before center st, K 2 tog thru back loops, K center st, K 2 tog thru front loops, rib in P 1, K 1 to end of rnd. **Rnd 2:** Rib to center 3 sts, K 3, rib to end. Rep these 2 rnds until band is 1 inch, ending with first rnd. Bind off loosely in ribbing, dec as before.

Double Neckband: Work same as single neckband for 1 inch. Continue ribbing, inc 1 st each side of center st on next rnd and rep incs every 2nd rnd until same number of inc rnds as dec rnds. Bind off loosely in ribbing. Turn neckband in half and sew bound-off edge loosely to neck edge.

PATTERN III
SLEEVELESS SLIPON
WITH ROUND OR V NECK

		GROUP A					GROUP B					GROUP C			
SIZES	4	6	8	10	12	4	6	8	10	12	4	6	8	10	12
BACK: Same as Pattern I, page 158 to underarm.															
Armholes: At beg of next 2 rows, bind off.................sts	8	9	10	10	10	7	8	9	9	9	6	7	7	7	7
Dec 1 st each side every 2nd row..........................times	8	9	10	10	10	7	7	8	8	8	6	6	7	7	7
Work on......................sts	59	62	65	72	79	50	54	56	62	68	41	44	47	52	57
until armholes are.............inches	4½	5	5½	6	6½			SAME AS GROUP A							
Shoulders: Bind off.................sts	5	5	6	6	7	5	5	5	6	6	5	6	6	7	8
at beg of next ....rows	6	2	6	2	4	2	6	4	6	4	2	4	2	2	4
Bind off.............................sts	0	6	0	7	8	4	0	6	0	7	6	0	7	8	0
at beg of next ....rows	0	4	0	4	2	4	0	2	0	2	2	0	2	2	0
Place on holder......................sts	29	28	29	32	35	24	24	24	26	30	19	20	21	22	25

FOR ROUND NECK

FRONT: Work same as back until armholes are....................inches	3	4	4½	5	5½			SAME AS GROUP A							

Shape neck same as Pattern I, shaping shoulders as on back when armholes are same length.

FOR V NECK

FRONT: Work same as back, shaping V-neck as for Pattern II, page 160.

FINISHING: Block pieces to measurements and assemble.

Neckband: For **Round Neck,** work same as Pattern I, page 158. **For V Neck,** work same as Pattern II, page 160.

Armhole Bands: With smaller dp needles and beg at underarm seam, from right side pick up around armholes.....................................sts	70	80	88	96	102	60	68	76	82	88	50	58	62	68	72

Place marker to indicate beg of rnds. Rib in K 1, P 1, dec 1 st at each side of marker every 2nd rnd for 1 inch for single band. Bind off loosely in ribbing. For double band, continue rib for 1 inch, inc 1 st each side of marker every 2nd rnd. Bind off loosely in ribbing, turn to wrong side and sew in place.

PATTERN IV
ROUND NECK
WITH SET-IN SLEEVES

	GROUP A					GROUP B					GROUP C				
SIZES	4	6	8	10	12	4	6	8	10	12	4	6	8	10	12

BACK: Same as Pattern I, page 158.

LEFT FRONT: With smaller needles, cast on ....sts

	4	6	8	10	12	4	6	8	10	12	4	6	8	10	12
cast on sts	50	54	58	62	66	44	48	52	54	58	38	40	44	46	48
Row 1: K 1, P 1 to last......sts Knit last sts.	7	7	7	7	7	7	7	7	7	7	5	5	5	5	5
Row 2: Knit...........sts rib to end.	7	7	7	7	7	7	7	7	7	7	5	5	5	5	5
Rep these 2 rows for......inches	1½	1½	2	2	2		SAME AS GROUP A								

Change to larger needles. Keeping sts for front border in garter st (K every row), remaining sts in stockinette st (K 1 row, P 1 row) work to same length as back to underarm, ending with a P row.

	4	6	8	10	12	4	6	8	10	12	4	6	8	10	12
Armhole: Bind off..........sts	5	6	7	7	7	4	5	6	6	6	4	5	5	5	5
Dec at armhole edge every 2nd row ......times	5	6	7	7	7	5	5	6	6	6	4	4	5	5	5
Work on ....sts	40	42	44	48	52	35	38	40	42	46	30	31	34	36	38
until armhole is ....inches ending with a P row.	3½	4	4½	5	5½		SAME AS GROUP A								

Neck: K to front border and place border sts on holder.

	4	6	8	10	12	4	6	8	10	12	4	6	8	10	12
Next row: Bind off.........sts P to end. Dec 1 st at neck edge every	4	4	5	7	9	4	5	5	6	9	5	5	7	7	8
2nd row ....times	8	8	8	8	8	6	6	6	6	6	5	5	5	5	5

AND AT SAME TIME, shape shoulder as on back when armhole is same length.

For Buttonholes: Mark place for 4 buttons on front band, having first marker ½ inch above lower edge (5th marker to be at center of a 1 inch neckband), the other 3 spaced evenly between.

	4	6	8	10	12	4	6	8	10	12	4	6	8	10	12
RIGHT FRONT: Work to correspond to Left Front, reversing border and all shaping and working buttonholes opposite markers as follows: Beg at front edge K ....sts K 2 tog, yo, work to end of row. On next row, work yo as a stitch.	2	2	2	2	2	2	2	2	2	2	1	1	1	1	1

SLEEVES: Same as Pattern I.

FINISHING: Block pieces to measurements and assemble.

	4	6	8	10	12	4	6	8	10	12	4	6	8	10	12
Neckband: Slip border sts for right front to needle. Join yarn and including sts for back of neck, pick up around neck ....sts	72	76	82	86	90	60	62	68	72	80	52	54	58	60	66
K across sts of left front border. Knit every row for 1 inch on.......sts ending at left front. Bind off as to K.	86	90	96	100	104	74	76	82	86	94	62	64	68	70	76

PATTERN V
V-NECK CARDIGAN
WITH SET-IN SLEEVES

	GROUP A					GROUP B					GROUP C				
SIZES	4	6	8	10	12	4	6	8	10	12	4	6	8	10	12

BACK: Same as Pattern I, page 158.

LEFT FRONT: Same as Left Front of Pattern IV, page 162, to underarm.

Armhole and Neck shaping: (Started on same row.) Bind off ....sts — A: 5 6 7 7 7 | B: 4 5 6 6 6 | C: 4 5 5 5 5

K to within 2 sts of front border, K 2 tog, K to end. Dec 1 st at armhole every 2nd row......................times — A: 5 6 7 7 7 | B: 5 5 6 6 6 | C: 4 4 5 5 5

AND AT SAME TIME, rep dec before front border every

2nd row ....times — A: 0 0 0 0 0 | B: 0 0 0 0 2 | C: 5 3 6 9 5

every 4th row ....times — A: 11 8 9 12 16 | B: 9 8 10 9 12 | C: 4 6 5 2 7

every 6th row ....times — A: 0 3 3 2 0 | B: 0 2 0 2 0 | C: 0 0 0 0 0

and shape shoulder as on back when armhole is same length. Continue to K remaining border sts for .....inches — A: 2½ 2½ 2½ 2¾ 3 | **SAME AS GROUP A**

Bind off...................................sts — A: 7 7 7 7 7 | B: 7 7 7 7 7 | C: 5 5 5 5 5

Mark place for 5 buttons on front band, having first marker ½ inch above lower edge, 5th marker ½ inch below first neck dec and other 3 evenly spaced between.

RIGHT FRONT: Work to correspond to Left Front reversing border and all shaping and working buttonholes as follows: Beg at front edge, K...........................sts — A: 2 2 2 2 2 | B: 2 2 2 2 2 | C: 1 1 1 1 1

K 2 tog, yo, work to end. On next row, work yo as a st.

SLEEVES: Same as Pattern I.

FINISHING: Block pieces to measurements and assemble. Sew bands to back of neck, seaming short ends at center. Sew on buttons.

PATTERN VI
SLIPON
WITH ROUND OR TURTLENECK
AND RAGLAN SLEEVES

SIZES	GROUP A					GROUP B					GROUP C				
	4	6	8	10	12	4	6	8	10	12	4	6	8	10	12

BACK: Same as Pattern I, page 158, to underarm.

Raglan armholes: At beg of next 2 rows, bind off ....sts

	5	6	7	7	7	4	5	6	6	6	4	4	5	5	5

Note: Raglan decreases may be made on K rows in either of two ways, as desired.

Method 1: K 2 tog, K to last 2 sts, K 2 tog thru back loops.

Method 2: K 2, sl 1 as to K, K 1, psso, K to last 4 sts, K 2 tog, K 2.
Dec 1 st each side every

4th row ....times	2	1	2	2	3	0	0	0	0	0	0	0	0	0	0
every 2nd row ....times	24	28	29	31	32	22	24	26	28	30	16	18	20	21	23
Place on holder remaining..........sts	29	28	29	32	35	26	26	26	28	30	25	26	25	28	29

FRONT: Same as back until there are.........................armhole decs ending with a dec row and on needle

	21	23	26	28	31	16	18	20	22	24	11	13	15	16	18
.... sts	39	40	39	42	43	38	38	38	40	42	35	36	35	38	39
On next row, P ....sts	14	15	14	14	13	13	13	13	13	13	12	12	12	12	12

Join a 2nd ball of yarn and bind off the center ....sts

	11	10	11	14	17	12	12	12	14	16	11	12	11	14	15

P to end. Working each side with separate yarn, continue to dec at armhole **AND AT SAME TIME,** at neck edges, bind off 2 sts every 2nd row ....times

	4	4	4	4	4	3	3	3	3	3	3	3	3	3	3

Fasten off last st.

SLEEVES: Same as Pattern I, page 158, to sleeve cap.

Raglan Cap: At beg of next 2 rows, bind off...................................sts

	5	6	7	7	7	4	5	6	6	6	4	5	5	5	5

Dec as on back every

4th row ....times	7	8	10	9	10	3	4	6	5	5	0	2	3	2	3
every 2nd row ....times	14	14	13	17	18	16	16	14	18	20	16	14	14	17	17
Place on holder remaining..........sts	10	10	10	10	10	8	8	8	8	8	6	6	6	6	6

FINISHING: Block pieces to measurements and assemble.

Neckband: With smaller dp needles, from right side and beg at right back raglan seam, K across sts of back and of sleeve, pick up on left front neck edge ....sts

	11	14	16	15	15	8	10	12	12	14	6	8	10	9	10

K across center sts of front, pick up on right front neck edge ....sts

	11	14	16	15	15	8	10	12	12	14	6	8	10	9	10

K across sleeve. There are........sts

	82	86	92	96	102	70	74	78	82	90	60	66	68	72	76

Work desired neck rib same as Pattern I.

PATTERN VII
SLIPON WITH V NECK
AND RAGLAN SLEEVES

SIZES

BACK: Same as Pattern VI, page 165.

FRONT: Same as back to 1 row less to armholes, ending with a K row.

	GROUP A					GROUP B					GROUP C				
	4	6	8	10	12	4	6	8	10	12	4	6	8	10	12
Neck and Armholes: P ....sts	45	49	52	56	59	39	42	45	48	51	32	35	37	40	42
place on holder center..............sts	1	0	1	0	1	0	0	0	0	0	1	0	1	0	1
neck edges every 2nd row ......times	0	0	0	0	0	3	1	0	0	0	7	7	3	6	6
every 4th row ....times	12	9	8	11	10	8	10	11	12	13	3	4	7	6	6
every 6th row ....times	0	3	4	3	5	0	0	0	0	0	0	0	0	0	0

join a 2nd ball of yarn, P to end. Working each side with separate yarn, shape armholes as on back **AND AT SAME TIME,** dec 1 st at neck edges every 2nd row ...

Fasten off.

SLEEVES: Same as Pattern VI, page 165.

FINISHING: Block pieces to measurements. Assemble. Place sts for back of neck on needle. With smaller dp needles, from right side K across back of neck, dec evenly ....sts

	GROUP A					GROUP B					GROUP C				
back of neck, dec evenly ....sts	6	3	4	3	4	3	3	3	3	5	4	3	4	5	6
K across sleeve, dec ....sts	0	1	0	1	0	3	3	3	3	4	2	2	2	2	2
pick up on left neck edge.........sts	46	50	58	60	66	36	40	44	48	52	26	30	34	36	42
neck edge ....sts	46	50	58	60	66	36	40	44	48	52	26	30	34	36	42

K from holder or pick up a st at center and mark, pick up on right neck edge ....sts
Place marker to indicate beg of rnds.

Rnd 1: Rib in P 1, K 1 to 2 sts before center st, K 2 tog thru back loops, K center st, K 2 tog thru front loops, rib in P 1, K 1 to end of rnd. **Rnd 2:** Rib to center 3 sts, K 3, rib to end. Rep these 2 rnds.

For single neckband, work 1 inch, bind off loosely in ribbing.

For double neckband, Same as Pattern II, page 160.

PATTERN VIII
CARDIGAN WITH ROUND NECK
AND RAGLAN SLEEVES

	GROUP A					GROUP B					GROUP C				
SIZES	4	6	8	10	12	4	6	8	10	12	4	6	8	10	12

BACK: Same as Pattern VI, page 165.

LEFT FRONT: Same as Pattern IV, page 162 to underarm, ending with a P row.

Armhole: Bind off.................sts	5	6	7	7	7	4	5	6	6	6	4	4	5	5	5
Dec as on back until there are a total of..............................dec rows	21	23	26	28	31	16	18	20	22	24	11	13	15	16	18
ending with a K row. There are on needle...................................sts	24	25	25	27	28	24	25	26	26	28	23	23	24	25	25

Neck: Work across................sts	7	7	7	7	7	7	7	7	7	7	5	5	5	5	5

and place these sts on holder, P to end. Continue to dec at armhole edge **AND AT SAME TIME,** at

neck edge, bind off.................sts	5	5	4	6	6	4	5	6	6	5	6	6	4	5	5
once. Then bind off.................sts	3	3	4	4	5	2	2	2	2	3	3	3	3	3	3
every 2nd row......................times	2	2	2	2	2	3	3	3	3	3	2	2	3	3	3

When armhole decs are completed, fasten off last st.
Refer to Pattern IV for marking and making buttonholes.
RIGHT FRONT: Same as Left Front, reversing border, all shaping and working buttonholes.

SLEEVES: Same as Pattern VI, page 165.

FINISHING: Block pieces to measurements and assemble.

Neckband: Slip border sts for right front to needle. Join yarn and including sts on holders, around neck edge to left front border.

Pick up ....sts	73	76	83	86	91	60	62	68	72	80	53	54	59	60	67

Rib for 1 inch, working buttonhole after ½ inch.

PATTERN IX
CARDIGAN WITH V NECK
AND RAGLAN SLEEVES

SIZES	GROUP A					GROUP B					GROUP C				
	4	6	8	10	12	4	6	8	10	12	4	6	8	10	12

BACK: Same as Pattern VI, page 165.

LEFT FRONT: Same as Pattern IV, page 162 to underarm, ending with a P row.

Armhole and Neck: Bind off ......sts K to within 2 sts of front border, K 2 tog, K to end.	5	6	7	7	7	4	5	6	6	6	4	4	5	5	5

Next row: Knit border, P to end. Continuing to dec at armhole edge same as back, rep dec before front border

every 6th row ....times	2	5	5	3	1	0	0	0	2	0	0	0	0	0	0
every 4th row ....times	9	6	7	11	15	10	11	12	10	14	2	4	5	5	7
every 2nd row...................times	0	0	0	0	0	0	0	0	0	0	10	8	8	9	7

After completing last armhole dec, work on remaining border sts for

......................................inches	2½	2½	2½	2¾	3			SAME AS GROUP A							

Bind off.
Refer to Pattern IV, for marking and making buttonholes.

RIGHT FRONT: Same as Left Front, reversing border and all shaping and working buttonholes.

SLEEVES: Same as Pattern VI and after last dec, bind off.............sts	10	10	10	10	10	8	8	8	8	8	6	6	6	6	6

FINISHING: Block pieces to measurements and assemble. Sew borders to back of neck, seaming short ends at center back. Sew on buttons.

CABLE V-NECK SLIPON
AND CARDIGAN

Patterns in knitted garments are fun to do and enhance the beauty of the finished product. Cables are an old favorite and are not at all difficult. Shown on page 169 are v-neck slipon and cardigan using the identical cable pattern.

Directions are for size 38. Changes for sizes 40-42-44-46-48 are in parentheses. Material requirements and gauge are the same for both sweaters.

MATERIALS:

Spinnerin Marvel Twist Wash Fit® or Germantown Deluxe (4-oz. skeins) 5 (5-6-6-6-7) skeins
1 pair each needles No. 5 and No. 7
1 set double-pointed (dp) needles No. 5

GAUGE: Stockinette st on No. 7 needles:

5 sts = 1 inch, 6 rows = 1 inch
Cable pat worked on 23 sts = 4 inches

FINISHED MEASUREMENTS:

Chest 38(40-42-44-46-48) inches
Width of back or front at underarms 19(20-21-22-23-24) inches
Width of back at shoulders 16½(17-17½-18-18½-18½) inches
Width of sleeve at underarm 15(15-16-16-17-17) inches

PATTERN STITCH: Worked on 23 sts.

Row 1 (right side): P 1, K 1, P 1; K 6, P 1, K 1, P 1, K 1, P 1, K 6; P 1, K 1, P 1. **Row 2:** P 1, K 1, P 1; P 6, P 1, K 1, P 1, K 1, P 1, P 6, P 1, K 1, P 1. **Rows 3 and 4:** Rep Rows 1 and 2. **Row 5:** P 1, K 1, P 1; slip next 3 sts to a dp needle, hold at *front* of work, K next 3 sts, K 3 sts from dp needle, P 1, K 1, P 1, K 1, P 1, slip next 3 sts to a dp needle, hold at *back* of work, K next 3 sts, K 3 sts from dp needle; P 1, K 1, P 1. **Rows 6 and 8:** Rep Row 2. **Row 7:** Rep Row 1. Rep these 8 rows for pat.

BACK: With No. 5 needles, cast on 101 (107-111-117-121-127) sts. **Row 1:** K 1, * P 1, K 1, rep from * to end. **Row 2:** P 1, * K 1, P 1, rep from * to end. Rep these 2 rows for 2-inches. Change to No. 7 needles. **Beg pat— Row 1:** K 14 (16-18-20-22-24) sts; work Pat Row 1 over next 23 sts; K 27 (29-29-31-31-33) sts; work Pat Row 1 over next 23 sts; K 14 (16-18-20-22-24) sts.

Row 2: P 14 (16-18-20-22-24) sts, work Pat Row 2 over next 23 sts, P 27 (29-29-31-31-33) sts; work Pat Row 2 over next 23 sts; P 14 (16-18-20-22-24). Continue in this way, working the 23 sts at each side in pat as established and remaining sts in stockinette st to 16 inches from beg, or desired length to underarms, ending on wrong side.

Armholes: Bind off 3 (3-4-4-5-5) sts at beg of next 2 rows. **Row 3:** K 2 tog thru *back* loops, work to last 2 sts, K 2 tog thru *front* loops. **Row 4:** Work even. Rep last 2 rows 2 (4-4-5-5-8) times. Work even on 89 (91-93-97-99-99) sts until armholes are 9 (9-9½-9½-10-10) inches.

Shoulders: Bind off 10 sts at beg of next 4 rows, then 9 (10-10-11-12-12) sts at beg of next 2 rows. Place 31 (31-33-35-35-35) sts on holder.

FRONT: Work same as back for 1 row less than back to beg of armholes.

Neck and Armholes: Work 50 (53-55-58-60-63) sts, place center st on a holder, tie in another ball of yarn, work last 50 (53-55-58-60-63) sts. Working on each side with a separate ball of yarn, shape armholes as on back **AND AT THE SAME TIME** dec 1 st at neck edges every 4th row. Keeping armhole edges even, continue to dec at neck edges every 4th row until there are 12 (12-14-14-14-14) decs, then dec every 2nd row 3 (3-2-3-3-3) times **AND AT THE SAME TIME,** when same length as back to shoulders, bind off 10 sts from armhole edges every 2nd row twice, then 9 (10-10-11-12-12) sts once

SLEEVES: With No. 5 needles, cast on 41 (41-43-43-45-45) sts. Rib K 1, P 1 for 2½ inches, inc 6 (6-8-8-10-10) sts evenly spaced across last row. There are 47 (47-51-51-55-55) sts on needle. Change to No. 7 needles. Work stockinette st, inc 1 st each side every 1 inch 14 (14-15-15-15-15) times. Work even on 75 (75-81-81-85-85) sts to 18 inches from beg, or desired length to underarms. **Shape Cap:** Bind off 3 (3-4-4-5-5) at beg of next 2 rows. Dec 1 st each side every 2nd row 13 (13-15-15-16-16) times. Bind off 3 sts at beg of next 4 rows. Bind off remaining sts.

FINISHING: Block pieces to measurements and assemble.

Neckband: With dp needles and beg at right shoulder seam, K across the 31 (31-33-35-35-35) sts on holder at back of neck, pick up 60 (60-64-64-66-66) sts on left front neck edge, K st from holder and mark for center st, pick up 60 (60-64-64-66-66) sts on right front neck edge. Join—**Rnd 1:** K 1, P 1 to within 2 sts of center st, K 2 tog, K center st, slip 1, K 1 psso, K 1, P 1 to end. Rep Rnd 1 for 1½ inches. Bind off in ribbing, dec each side of center st as before.

CABLE CARDIGAN

FINISHED MEASUREMENTS:

Chest (buttoned) 39(41–43–45–47–49) inches
Width of back at underarms 19(20–21–22–23–24) inches
Width of back at shoulders 16½(17–17½–18–18½–18½) inches
Width of each front at underarm without band 9½(10–10½–11–11½–12) inches
Width of sleeve at underarm 15(15–16–16–17–17) inches
Back and sleeves are same as for slipon.

POCKET LININGS: Make 2. With No. 7 needles cast on 25 sts. Work stockinette for 22 rows ending with a P row; place on holder.

LEFT FRONT: With No. 5 needles cast on 51(53–55–59–61–63) sts. Rib as on back. Change to No. 7 needles and beg pattern. **Row 1:** (Right side) K 14(16–18–20–22–24); work Pat Row 1 over next 23 sts, K last 14(14–14–16–16–16) sts. **Row 2:** P 14(14–14–16–16–16) sts; work Pat Row 2 over next 23 sts, P 14(16–18–20–22–24) sts. Keeping 23 sts in pat as established and remaining sts in stockinette, work even to 24 rows above ribbing ending on wrong side.

Pocket Opening: Beg at underarm edge, K 13(15–17–19–21–23) sts, slip next 25 sts to a holder; working across sts of 1 pocket lining K 1, work Pat Row 1 over 23 sts, K 1, K to end of row. Continue to work in established pattern to under arm ending on wrong side.

Armhole and Neck: Bind off 6(6–7–7–8–8) sts from armhole edge once. Dec 1 st at armhole edge (by K 2 tog thru back loops) every 2nd row 4(6–6–7–7–10) times AND AT THE SAME TIME dec 1 st at neck edge (K 2 tog thru back loops) every 4th row. Keeping armhole edge even, continue to dec 1 st at neck edge every 4th row until there are 14(13–14–16–15–15) decs at neck edge AND AT THE SAME TIME, when same length as back to shoulders, shape shoulders as on back.

RIGHT FRONT: Work same as left reversing shaping.

POCKET BORDERS: Slip 25 sts from holder to No. 5 needle; work K 1, P 1 ribbing for 1 inch and bind off in ribbing.

FRONT BAND: With No. 5 needles cast on 9 sts and work K 1, P 1 ribbing until sufficient length to fit along fronts and around neck when slightly stretched; do not bind off, hold sts on holder for final adjustment.

FINISHING: Block pieces and assemble. With cast on edge of front band at lower edge of left front, sew band to fronts and back neck edges adjusting length at lower right front. Weave ends of pocket borders neatly to fronts. Sew pocket linings in place. Work machine buttonholes on left front.

SLEEVELESS SLIPON
WITH CHAIN CABLE

After you have mastered the cable stitch, you will surely want to try variations of it. One interesting pattern is the chain cable shown on the sleeveless sweater opposite.

Directions are for size 38. Changes for sizes 42–46–50 are in parentheses.

MATERIALS:

SPINNERIN Mona (50-gram balls)—7 (8–10–11) balls
OR SPINNERIN Wintuk Fingering (1-oz. skeins)—7 (8–10–11) skeins
1 pair each needles No. 3 and No. 5
1 double-pointed or cable needle

GAUGE: Pattern Stitch on No. 5 needles (blocked)—15 sts = 2 inches, 10 rows = 1 inch

FINISHED MEASUREMENTS:

Chest—39 (43–46–50) inches
Width of back and front at underarms—19½ (21½–23–25) inches
Width of back at shoulders (without armhole bands)—16 (16½–17–17½) inches

PATTERN STITCH: Multiple of 14 sts plus 6

Note 1: Cable Pattern will shift from center to each side of center in different sizes.

Note 2: Slip sts as to K unless otherwise specified.

Row 1 (right side): P 2, slip 2, *(P 2, slip 1, P 1, slip 1) twice, P 2, slip 2, rep from *, ending P 2. **Row 2:** K 2, P 2, *(K 2, P 1, K 1, P 1) twice, K 2, P 2, rep from *, ending K 2. **Rows 3 thru 6:** Rep Rows 1 and 2 twice. **Row 7:** P 2, slip 2, *P 2, slip 1, P 1, slip next 3 sts to dp needle as if to P, hold at *back* of work, K next st, place the 2 P sts back on left needle, bring dp needle and 1 st to *front* of work, P 2 sts on left needle, K st from dp needle, P 1, slip 1, P 2, slip 2, rep from *, ending P 2. **Row 8:** Same as Row 2. **Rows 9 and 10:** Rep Rows 1 and 2. **Row 11:** P 2, slip 2, *P 2, (slip next 2 sts to dp needle as if to P and hold at *front* of work, K next st, place P st back on left needle and P the st, slip st from dp needle, P 2) twice, slip 2, rep from *, ending P 2. **Row 12:** Same as Row 2. **Rows 13 and 14:** Rep Rows 1 and 2. **Rows 15**

and 16: Rep Rows 7 and 8. **Rows 17 thru 24:** Rep Rows 1 and 2 four times.
Rep Rows 1 thru 24 for pat.

BACK: With No. 3 needles, cast on 146 (160–174–188) sts. Rib in K 1, P 1 for 3 inches. Change to No. 5 needles. P 1 row. Work in pat st to 15½ inches from beg, or desired length to underarms.

Armholes: Keeping continuity of pat bind off 7 (9–12–15) sts at beg of next 2 rows. Dec 1 st each side every 2nd row 6 (9–11–13) times. Work even on 120 (124–128–132) sts until armholes are 10½ (11–11½–12) inches.

Shoulders: Bind off 14 sts at beg of next 4 rows, then 12 (14–14–16) sts at beg of next 2 rows. Bind off remaining 40 (40–44–44) sts.

FRONT: Work same as back until armhole shaping is completed, ending on wrong side. There are 120 (124–128–132) sts on needle.

Next row: Work 59 (61–63–65) sts, place 2 center sts on holder, join another ball of yarn, work last 59 (61–63–65) sts. Continue working on each side with a separate ball of yarn. Dec 1 st at neck edges every 4th row 19 (19–21–21) times. Work even on 40 (42–42–44) sts of each side to same length as back to shoulders.

Shoulders: Shape as on back.

FINISHING: Block pieces lightly to measurements. Sew left shoulder seam.

Neckband: With No. 3 needles from right side, pick up 40 (40–44–44) sts across back of neck, 60 sts on left front neck edge, P 2 sts from holder, pick up 60 sts on right front neck edge.

Row 1 (wrong side): K 1, P 1 to 2 center sts, K 2 tog and mark, P 1, K 1, to end. **Row 2:** Rib to 2 sts before marked st, work 2 sts tog, P center st, work 2 sts tog, rib to end. Always K center st on wrong side, P center st on right side, and dec 1 st each side of center st *every* row until there are 7 dec rows. Dec as before, bind off loosely in ribbing. Sew right shoulder seam, including neck band.

Armhole Bands: With No. 3 needles from right side, pick up 140 (150–160–170) sts around armhole. Rib in K 1, P 1, dec 1 st each side *every* row 8 times. Bind off loosely in ribbing.

Sew underarm seams, including armhole bands.

Men's Classic Sweaters

Classic sweaters are basic to every sweater you will want to make. Men's classics are offered in three different weights of Spinnerin yarns and in sizes 38–40–42–44–46–48. Like the other classic sweaters in this book, directions are given for a variety of necklines and set-in and raglan sleeves.

The materials and measurements below are for all the classic sweaters which follow.

MATERIALS FOR GROUP A—LIGHT WEIGHT

SPINNERIN Wintuk Fingering Yarn (1-oz. skeins) 10 (11–11–12–12–13)

1 pair each needles No. 2 and No. 3
1 set double-pointed (dp) needles No. 2

GAUGE: 7 sts = 1 inch, 9 rows = 1 inch

MATERIALS FOR GROUP B—MEDIUM WEIGHT

SPINNERIN Wintuk Sport (2-oz. skeins) 8 (8–9–9–10–10)
OR SPINNERIN Allround (2-oz. skeins) 8 (8–9–9–10–10)

1 pair each needles No. 4 and No. 5
1 set double-pointed (dp) needles No. 4

GAUGE: 6 sts = 1 inch, 8 rows = 1 inch

MATERIALS FOR GROUP C—HEAVY WEIGHT

SPINNERIN Marvel Twist Wash Fit®
or Germantown Deluxe or Deluxe Knitting Worsted (4-oz. skeins) 5 (5–6–6–6–7)
OR SPINNERIN Wintuk Featherlon (2-oz. skeins) 7 (7–8–8–9–9)

1 pair each needles No. 6 and No. 7
1 set double-pointed (dp) needles No. 6

GAUGE: 5 sts = 1 inch, 6 rows = 1 inch

FINISHED MEASUREMENTS

Chest ....inches	38	40	42	44	46	48
Width of back and front at underarms...............inches	19	20	21	22	23	24
Width of back at shoulders ....inches	16½	17	17½	18	18½	18½
Width of sleeve at underarm ....inches	15	15	16	16	17	17

PATTERN I
SLIPON
WITH ROUND OR TURTLENECK
AND SET-IN SLEEVES

	GROUP A						GROUP B						GROUP C					
	38	40	42	44	46	48	38	40	42	44	46	48	38	40	42	44	46	48
BACK: With smaller needles, cast on ....sts	133	141	147	153	161	167	113	119	125	131	137	143	95	101	105	111	115	121
Row 1: K 1, * P 1, K 1; rep from * to end. **Row 2:** P 1, * K 1, P 1; rep from * to end. Rep these 2 rows for 3 inches. Change to larger needles. Work stockinette st (K 1 row, P 1 row) to 16 inches from beg, or desired length to underarms, ending with a P row.																		
Armholes: At beg of next 2 rows, bind off...............sts	5	5	5	5	6	7	4	4	5	5	6	6	3	3	4	4	5	5
Dec 1 st at beg of next .... rows	8	12	14	18	20	24	6	10	10	14	14	20	6	10	10	12	12	18
Work even on.................sts	115	119	123	125	129	129	99	101	105	107	111	111	83	85	87	91	93	93
until armholes are.......inches	9	9	9½	9½	10	10	9	9	9½	9½	10	10	9	9	9½	9½	10	10
Shoulders: At beg of next .... rows	6	6	6	8	8	8	4	4	4	4	6	6	4	4	4	4	4	4
bind off.........................sts	8	8	8	8	8	8	8	8	9	9	9	9	9	9	9	10	10	10
At beg of next ....rows	4	4	4	2	2	2	4	4	4	4	2	2	2	2	2	2	2	2
bind off.........................sts	7	8	8	9	10	10	9	9	9	9	10	10	9	10	10	10	11	11
Slip on holder.................sts	39	39	43	43	45	45	31	33	33	35	37	37	29	29	31	31	31	31
FRONT: Work same as back until armholes are.. ....inches	6	6	6½	6½	7	7	6	6	6½	6½	7	7	6	6	6½	6½	7	7
ending with a P row. There are................................sts	115	119	123	125	129	129	99	101	105	107	111	111	83	85	87	91	93	93
Neck: Work.....................sts	44	46	47	47	49	49	38	39	40	41	42	42	31	32	33	34	35	35
place center.....................sts	27	27	29	31	31	31	23	23	25	25	27	27	21	21	21	23	23	23
on a holder, tie in another ball of yarn, work last ......sts	44	46	47	47	49	49	38	39	40	41	42	42	31	32	33	34	35	35

	GROUP A						GROUP B						GROUP C					
	38	40	42	44	46	48	38	40	42	44	46	48	38	40	42	44	46	48

Continue to work each side with a separate ball of yarn.

Dec 1 st at neck edges every 4th row....................times

Work even on.................sts at each side until armholes are same length as on back.

	GROUP A						GROUP B						GROUP C					
times	6	6	7	6	7	7	4	5	4	5	5	5	4	4	5	4	4	4
sts	38	40	40	41	42	42	34	34	36	36	37	37	27	28	28	30	31	31

Shoulders: Shape to correspond to back.

SLEEVES (Shaped): With smaller needles, cast on ....sts

	60	60	64	64	68	68	50	50	54	54	56	56	40	40	44	44	48	48

Rib K 1, P 1 for 4 inches. Change to larger needles. P 1 row, inc 15 sts evenly spaced across row. Work in stockinette st, inc 1 st each side every ....inches

.... times

Work even on................sts to 18 inches from beg, or desired length to underarms.

inches	3/4	3/4	3/4	3/4	3/4	3/4	1	1	1	1	1	1	1 1/4	1 1/4	1 1/4	1 1/4	1 1/4	1 1/4
times	15	15	16	16	18	18	13	13	13	13	15	15	10	10	10	10	11	11
sts	105	105	111	111	119	119	91	91	95	95	101	101	75	75	79	79	85	85

Shape Cap: At beg of next 2 rows, bind off...............sts

Dec 1 st at beg of next ....rows

Bind off 3 sts at beg of next 4 rows. Bind off sts.

sts	5	5	5	5	6	6	4	4	5	5	6	6	3	3	4	4	5	5
rows	50	50	54	54	58	58	44	44	46	46	50	50	32	32	34	34	38	38

SLEEVES (Full or Golf): With smaller needles, cast on...................................sts

Rib in K 1, P 1 as on back for 4 inches. Change to larger needles. Knit, inc 1 st in each st.

Work even on.................sts to 18 inches from beg.

sts	53	53	56	56	60	60	46	46	48	48	52	52	38	38	40	40	43	43
sts	106	106	112	112	120	120	92	92	96	96	104	104	76	76	80	80	86	86

Shape Cap: Same as cap of shaped sleeve.

FINISHING: Block pieces to measurements and assemble.

Neckband: With dp needles from right side and beg at right shoulder seam, pick up around neck, including sts on holders................sts

sts	120	124	128	132	136	140	96	100	104	106	110	114	82	86	88	90	94	96

Join and work around in K 1, P 1 ribbing.

For single neckband, work 1 inch.

For double neckband, work 2 inches.

For turtleneck, work 6 inches.

Bind off loosely in ribbing. For double neckband, turn ribbing in half to wrong side and sew bound-off edge to neck edge, taking care to hem loosely.

PATTERN II
SLIPON
WITH BOAT OR V NECK
AND SET-IN SLEEVES

V-neck sweater is pictured on page 173.

	GROUP A						GROUP B						GROUP C					
BOAT NECK	**38**	**40**	**42**	**44**	**46**	**48**	**38**	**40**	**42**	**44**	**46**	**48**	**38**	**40**	**42**	**44**	**46**	**48**

BACK AND FRONT: Work same as back of Pattern I, page 175, until armholes are ....inches $\quad$ 7 $\quad$ 7 $\quad$ 7½ $\quad$ 7½ $\quad$ 8 $\quad$ 8 $\qquad$ 7 $\quad$ 7 $\quad$ 7½ $\quad$ 7½ $\quad$ 8 $\quad$ 8 $\qquad$ 7 $\quad$ 7 $\quad$ 7½ $\quad$ 7½ $\quad$ 8 $\quad$ 8
Rib K 1, P 1 for 2 inches, ending on wrong side.

Shoulders: Continue ribbing, shaping same as Pattern I, page 175.

V NECK

BACK: as Pattern I

FRONT (V Neck): Work same as back with 1 row less to armhole, ending with a K row.

Neck and Armholes—Next row: P ....sts $\quad$ 66 $\quad$ 70 $\quad$ 73 $\quad$ 76 $\quad$ 80 $\quad$ 83 $\qquad$ 56 $\quad$ 59 $\quad$ 62 $\quad$ 65 $\quad$ 68 $\quad$ 71 $\qquad$ 47 $\quad$ 50 $\quad$ 52 $\quad$ 55 $\quad$ 57 $\quad$ 60
place center st on a holder, tie in another ball of yarn.
P last ....sts $\quad$ 66 $\quad$ 70 $\quad$ 73 $\quad$ 76 $\quad$ 80 $\quad$ 83 $\qquad$ 56 $\quad$ 59 $\quad$ 62 $\quad$ 65 $\quad$ 68 $\quad$ 71 $\qquad$ 47 $\quad$ 50 $\quad$ 52 $\quad$ 55 $\quad$ 57 $\quad$ 60
Continue to work each side with a separate ball of yarn.
Shape armholes as on back
AND AT THE SAME TIME
dec 1 st at neck edges on next row and rep decs every 4th row ....times $\quad$ 18 $\quad$ 18 $\quad$ 20 $\quad$ 20 $\quad$ 21 $\quad$ 21 $\qquad$ 14 $\quad$ 15 $\quad$ 15 $\quad$ 16 $\quad$ 17 $\quad$ 17 $\qquad$ 13 $\quad$ 13 $\quad$ 14 $\quad$ 14 $\quad$ 14 $\quad$ 14
Work even on..................sts $\quad$ 38 $\quad$ 40 $\quad$ 40 $\quad$ 41 $\quad$ 42 $\quad$ 42 $\qquad$ 34 $\quad$ 34 $\quad$ 36 $\quad$ 36 $\quad$ 37 $\quad$ 37 $\qquad$ 27 $\quad$ 28 $\quad$ 28 $\quad$ 30 $\quad$ 31 $\quad$ 31
of each side to same length as back to shoulders. Shape shoulders as on back.

	GROUP A						GROUP B						GROUP C					
	38	40	42	44	46	48	38	40	42	44	46	48	38	40	42	44	46	48

SLEEVES: Work shaped or full sleeves as for Pattern I, page 176.

FINISHING: Block pieces to measurements and assemble.

Single Neckband for V Neck: With dp needles from right side and beg at left shoulder seam, pick up on left front neck edge ....sts

	74	74	78	78	82	82	62	62	66	66	70	70	56	56	58	58	62	62

K center st from holder and mark st, pick up on right front neck edge...............sts

	74	74	78	78	82	82	62	62	66	66	70	70	56	56	58	58	62	62

K across sts at back of neck. Join. **Rnd 1:** K 1, P 1 to center st, K center st, P 1, K 1, to end. **Rnd 2:** Rib to 2 sts before center st, sl 1 as to K, K 1, psso, K center st, K 2 tog, rib to end. **Rnd 3:** Rib to center st, K center st, rib to end. Rep last 2 rnds for 1 inch, ending with Rnd 3. Bind off loosely in ribbing, dec as before.

Double Neckband for V Neck: Work same as single neckband; do not bind off.

Facing: Continue ribbing, inc 1 st each side of center st on next rnd and rep inc every 2nd rnd until same number of rnds as on neck ribbing. Bind off loosely in ribbing. Turn neckband in half to wrong side and sew bound-off edge loosely to neck edge.

PATTERN III
SLIPON
WITH ROUND OR TURTLENECK
AND RAGLAN SLEEVES

	GROUP A						GROUP B						GROUP C					
	38	40	42	44	46	48	38	40	42	44	46	48	38	40	42	44	46	48
BACK: Work same as back of Pattern I, page 175, to same length as back to armholes, ending with P row. There are ....sts	133	141	147	153	161	167	113	119	125	131	137	143	95	101	105	111	115	121
Raglan Armholes: At beg of next 2 rows, bind off ....sts	5	5	6	6	7	7	3	3	4	4	5	5	4	4	5	5	6	6
Row 3: K 2, K 2 tog, K to last 4 sts, slip 1 as if to K, K 1, psso, K 2. **Row 4:** Purl. Rep last 2 rows ....times	44	44	46	46	49	49	39	39	41	41	43	43	29	29	31	31	32	32
Place on a holder ....sts	33	41	41	47	47	53	27	33	33	39	39	45	27	33	31	37	37	43
FRONT: Work same as back until there are armhole ....decs	32	32	34	34	37	37	28	28	30	30	32	32	21	21	23	23	24	24
and on needle ....sts ending with a K row.	59	67	67	73	73	79	51	57	57	63	63	69	45	51	49	55	55	61
Neck: P ....sts	22	24	24	25	25	26	19	20	20	20	20	22	14	15	15	16	16	16
place on holder center.......sts	15	19	19	23	23	27	13	17	17	23	23	25	17	21	19	23	23	29
tie in another ball of yarn, P last ....sts	22	24	24	25	25	26	19	20	20	20	20	22	14	15	15	16	16	16
Continue to work each side with a separate ball of yarn. Continue to dec 1 st at armhole edges every K row ....times	13	13	13	13	13	13	12	12	12	12	12	12	9	9	9	9	9	9
more **AND AT THE SAME TIME** dec 1 st at neck edge (each side) every K row ....times	8	10	10	11	11	12	6	7	7	7	7	9	4	5	5	6	6	6
Fasten off last st.																		

	GROUP A						GROUP B						GROUP C					
	38	40	42	44	46	48	38	40	42	44	46	48	38	40	42	44	46	48

SLEEVES (Shaped): Work same as shaped sleeves of Pattern I, page 176, to cap shaping.

SLEEVES (Full or Golf): Work same as full or golf sleeves of Pattern I, page 176, to cap shaping.

Raglan Cap: Shape same as raglan armholes on back. Place on a holder ....sts

	38	40	42	44	46	48	38	40	42	44	46	48	38	40	42	44	46	48
Raglan Cap sts	5	5	5	5	5	5	5	5	3	3	3	3	7	7	5	5	7	7

FINISHING: Block pieces to measurements. Weave sleeve caps to back and front armholes. Sew underarm and sleeve seams.

Neckband: With dp needles from right side beg at right front raglan seam K 2 sts tog across sts of sleeves; knit across sts of back dec evenly spaced...........................sts K 2 sts tog across sts of 2nd sleeve. Count sts on needle, then pick up around entire neck edge, including sts on needle and holder.............sts Work single or double neckband for round or turtle neck same as Pattern I, page 176.

	38	40	42	44	46	48	38	40	42	44	46	48	38	40	42	44	46	48
dec sts	0	0	0	0	0	0	0	0	0	0	0	0	5	5	3	5	5	8
total sts	120	124	128	132	136	140	96	100	104	106	110	114	82	86	88	90	94	96

PATTERN IV
SLIPON
WITH V NECK
AND RAGLAN SLEEVES

BACK: Work same as Pattern III, page 179.

FRONT: Work same as back to 1 row less to armholes, ending with a K row.

Neck and Armholes—Next row: P...........................sts place center st on holder, tie in another ball of yarn, P last ....sts Continue working each side with a separate ball of yarn. Shape armholes as on back **AND AT THE SAME TIME** dec 1 st at neck edge (each side) every...................row .... times Fasten off last st.

SLEEVES: Work shaped or full sleeves as for Pattern I, page 176, to cap shaping.

Raglan Cap: Same as Raglan Cap for Pattern III, page 180.

FINISHING: Block pieces to measurements. Weave sleeve caps to back and front armholes. Sew underarm and sleeve seams.

	GROUP A						GROUP B						GROUP C					
	38	40	42	44	46	48	38	40	42	44	46	48	38	40	42	44	46	48
	66	70	73	76	80	83	56	59	62	65	68	71	47	50	52	55	57	60
	66	70	73	76	80	83	56	59	62	65	68	71	47	50	52	55	57	60
	6th	4th	4th	4th	4th	4th	6th	4th	4th	4th	4th	4th	4th	4th	4th	3rd	3rd	3rd
	15	19	19	22	22	25	12	15	15	18	18	21	12	15	14	17	17	20

	GROUP A						GROUP B						GROUP C					
	38	40	42	44	46	48	38	40	42	44	46	48	38	40	42	44	46	48

Neckband: With dp needles from right side and beg at right front raglan seam, K across sts of sleeve, dec to .... sts

K across sts of back neck, dec evenly .... sts

pick up on left front neck edge .... sts

K center st from holder and mark, pick up on right front neck edge .... sts

K across sts of sleeve, dec to .... sts

Join, work and finish single or double neckband same as Pattern II, page 178.

	GROUP A						GROUP B						GROUP C					
K across sts of sleeve, dec to	4	4	4	4	4	4	4	4	2	2	2	2	4	4	4	4	4	4
K across sts of back neck, dec evenly	0	2	0	4	4	10	0	0	0	4	2	8	0	0	0	1	1	1
pick up on left front neck edge	74	74	78	78	82	82	62	62	66	66	70	70	56	56	58	58	62	62
pick up on right front neck edge	74	74	78	78	82	82	62	62	66	66	70	70	56	56	58	58	62	62
K across sts of sleeve, dec to	4	4	4	4	4	4	4	4	2	2	2	2	4	4	4	4	4	4

PATTERN V
SLEEVELESS SLIPON
WITH V NECK

FINISHED MEASUREMENTS

Chest	inches	38	40	42	44	46	48	
Width of back and front at underarms	inches	19	20	21	22	23	24	
Width of back at shoulders (without armhole bands)	inches	13½	14	14½	15	15½	15½	

	GROUP A						GROUP B						GROUP C					
	38	40	42	44	46	48	38	40	42	44	46	48	38	40	42	44	46	48
BACK: Work same as Pattern I, page 175 to armholes.																		
Armholes: At beg of next ...... rows	6	6	6	6	6	6	6	6	6	6	6	6	4	4	4	4	4	4
Bind off .... sts	5	5	5	5	5	5	4	4	4	5	5	5	6	6	6	6	6	6
Dec 1 st at beg of next ...... rows	8	14	16	18	22	28	8	12	14	12	14	20	4	8	8	12	14	20
Work even on .... sts	95	97	101	105	109	109	81	83	87	89	93	93	67	69	73	75	77	77
until armholes are ...... inches	10	10	10½	10½	11	11	10	10	10½	10½	11	11	10	10	10½	10½	11	11
Shoulders: At beg of next ...... rows	6	8	8	8	8	8	6	6	6	6	6	6	4	2	4	2	4	4
bind off .... sts	6	6	6	6	6	6	7	7	7	7	7	7	6	6	6	6	6	6
then at beg of next ...... rows	4	2	2	2	2	2	2	2	2	2	2	2	2	4	2	4	2	2
bind off .... sts	5	5	5	7	7	7	4	4	4	6	7	7	7	7	9	8	11	11
Slip to holder .... sts	39	39	43	43	47	47	31	33	37	35	37	37	29	29	31	31	31	31
FRONT (V Neck): Work same as back with 1 row less to armhole, ending with a K row.																		
Neck and Armholes—Next row: P .... sts	66	70	73	76	80	83	56	59	62	65	68	71	47	50	52	55	57	60
place center st on a holder, tie in another ball of yarn, P last .... sts	66	70	73	76	80	83	56	59	62	65	68	71	47	50	52	55	57	60

Continue to work each side with a separate ball of yarn. **Shape armholes** as on back **AND AT THE SAME TIME** dec 1 st at neck edges on next row and rep decs every 4th row ....times

Group A						Group B						Group C					
18	18	20	20	22	22	14	15	17	16	17	17	13	13	14	14	14	14

Work even on.................sts

Group A						Group B						Group C					
28	29	29	31	31	31	25	25	25	27	28	28	19	20	21	22	23	23

until same length as back to shoulders. Shape shoulders as on back.

FINISHING: Block pieces to measurements and assemble. Work single or double V Neckband same as Pattern II, page 178.

Single Armhole Bands: With dp needle from right side and beg at underarm edge, pick up on bound-off sts of back ....sts

Group A						Group B						Group C					
14	14	14	14	14	14	12	12	12	12	12	12	10	10	10	10	10	10

on armhole edge..............sts

Group A						Group B						Group C					
150	150	156	156	162	162	130	130	134	134	138	138	110	110	114	114	118	118

on bound-off sts of front ....sts

Group A						Group B						Group C					
14	14	14	14	14	14	12	12	12	12	12	12	10	10	10	10	10	10

Join and rib in K 1, P 1 for 1 inch. Bind off loosely in ribbing.

Double Armhole Bands: Work in K 1, P 1 ribbing for 2 inches. Bind off loosely in ribbing. Turn bands in half to wrong side and sew loosely to picked up row.

CARILLON

Striking stripes of sharply contrasting colors, worked from side to side in stockinette without bobbins—the secret is a round needle!

MATERIALS:

Spinnerin Marvel Twist Wash Fit® or Germantown Deluxe or Deluxe Knitting Worsted (4-oz.) 6 MC and 1 each B, C, D, E, F

OR Wintuk (2-oz.) 12 MC and 2 each B, C, D, E, F

OR Frostlon Petite (1-oz.) 18 MC and 4 each B, C, D, E, F

OR Featherlon (1-oz.) 16 MC and 3 each B, C, D, E, F

Needles: Circular No. 10 **OR SIZE TO GIVE GAUGE**

Crochet Hook: Size H Aluminum

GAUGE: 4 sts = 1 inch
          5 rows = 1 inch

FINISHED SIZE: Approx. 58″ x 63″.

Afghan is worked vertically in stockinette stitch (K 1 row, P 1 row) following striped pattern given below. Break off color when stripe is complete.

STRIPED PATTERN:

30 rows MC;

2 rows B, 8 rows C, 2 rows B, 8 rows D, 2 rows B; 30 rows MC;

2 rows B, 8 rows E, 2 rows B, 8 rows F, 2 rows B (104 rows in pat).

AFGHAN

Cast on 252 sts for 1 side edge.

Work striped pat until there are 2 complete pats (208 rows).

Work first 82 rows again (290 rows).

Bind off; do **not** break yarn.

FINISHING: Beg from right side, work 3 rows sc along each long side, spacing sts to keep edge flat.

Ch 1 and turn at ends of rows 1 and 2. Fasten off at end of 3rd row.

Along each end, work 2 rows sc.

FRINGE: Fringe matches color stripes of afghans and is tied as follows: 20 in each outer MC panel, 1 in each 2-row stripe, 4 in each 8-row stripe, 15 in other MC stripes. Wrap yarn around a 9-inch cardboard. Cut at one end. Using 2 strands, fringe (see page 208), **completely covering the 2 rows of sc across ends.** Tie in Triple Knot Fringe.

Fisherman Knitting

The traditional Irish fisherman patterns are both beautiful and timeless. Although they appear to be intricate work requiring the skill of expert knitters, the patterns are really quite simple once the individual stitches are mastered. Fisherman knitting needs only light steaming when finished because the puffy, raised effect of the patterns is its true character. It must never be pressed flat.

The patterns evolve from the repetition of basic stitches (twists, popcorn, cable) which are worked in specified sequence across a row. It is important to mark the beginning and end of each pattern group with yarn markers that are slipped from one needle to the other as you proceed. Once you have worked a few rows, you will be amazed at how quickly you pick up the routine of the patterns.

In each set of instructions for a garment or an afghan full details are given as to how each stitch is worked in that particular pattern. To understand how to work some of these stitches study the diagrams below. They show how to make some of the stitches. We suggest that you take needles and wool in hand and practice before you undertake a project in fisherman knit.

THE TWIST STITCHES

There are many different ways of doing "Right" and "Left Twists," but the same abbreviations (RT and LT) are always used, regardless of the number of stitches being twisted. (Twist stitches are not the same as Cable stitches.)

RIGHT TWIST—A

Sk 1 st, K next st thru front loop and leave on left needle (arrow shows how right needle is inserted —and note that right needle remains on **top** of left needle).

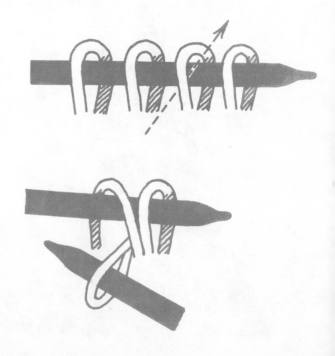

Shows yarn drawn thru st. K the skipped st (instructions will specify whether thru front or back loop) and drop 2 from left needle. (As you K the skipped st, pull both original sts from left needle and the 2 twisted sts are now on the right needle.)

RIGHT TWIST—B

Sk 1 st, K next st and leave on left needle (right needle is inserted thru st to back of work, remaining **under** the left needle) K skipped st and drop 2 from needle (see Right Twist—A).

Diagram shows how a Right Twist looks when completed.

LEFT TWIST

Sk 1 st, K next st thru back loop (right needle is kept behind left needle).

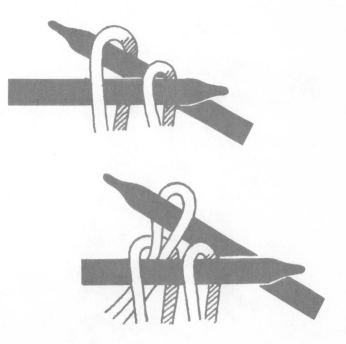

Shows st drawn thru. Bring right needle back to the front and K the skipped st (thru front or back loop as specified in instructions) and drop 2 from left needle. A Left Twist is just the reverse of a Right Twist, slanting toward the left.

PURL THRU BACK LOOP

This is the one that has puzzled many knitters — yet it is quite easy to do. Arrow in diagram shows direction right needle is inserted thru stitch. Keep yarn in front of work and just twist your right needle to go thru st as shown, bringing point of right needle back to the front and **below** the left needle. Purl the stitch.

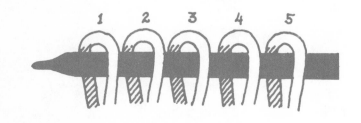

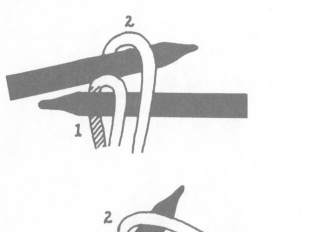

POPCORN OR BOBBLE

There are many different ways of working these, but the principle is the same for many. An increase of several sts is made in 1 st (5 in our example) and several rows are worked on just these sts. The extra sts are then passed one at a time (beg with 2nd as shown, then 3rd, 4th and 5th) over the first st and off the needle. One st remains.

FISHERMAN AFGHAN

This lovely afghan is knitted in simple squares and trimmed with an unusual knotted fringe. It is certain to become a treasured family heirloom.

MATERIALS:
Spinnerin Irish Fisherman Yarn (4-oz.) 12 skeins

NEEDLES: No. 10 **OR SIZE TO GIVE GAUGE**
1 dp or cable needle

HOOK: Size F Aluminum
Large Eye Tapestry Needle

GAUGE: Each motif is 8½ inches square

FINISHED SIZE: Approx. 52″ x 68″.
Afghan is worked in 48 squares.

STITCHES

BACK CABLE (BC): Sl next 2 sts to dp needle and hold at *back,* K next 2 sts, K 2 from dp.

FRONT CABLE (FC): Sl next 2 sts to dp needle and hold at *front,* K next 2 sts, K 2 from dp.

TWIST 2 (T2): Sk 1 st, K next st thru *front* loop and leave on left needle, K skipped st, drop 2 sts from left needle.

LEFT TWIST (LT): Sk 1 st, P next st thru *back* loop and leave on left needle, K skipped st, drop 2 sts from left needle.

RIGHT TWIST (RT): Sk 1 st, K next st, P the skipped st.

BOBBLE (BO): K next st, leave on left needle, yo, pass last st on right needle over the yo, (K the worked st on left needle, leave on left needle, yo, pass last st on right needle over yo) twice, K in back

loop of worked st on left needle, drop st from left needle, pass 3 sts on right needle over the last st on right needle.

MOTIF (Make 48): Cast on 41 sts. K 2 rows. **Row 1 (right side):** K 1, P 1, K 8, P 2, **T2,** P 3, K 1, P 5, K 1, P 3, P 12, K 2. **Row 2:** K 2, place a marker on needle; (on front loop of next st K 1, P 1, K 1; P next 3 sts tog) 3 times; place a marker on needle, K 3, P 1, K 5, P 1, K 3, P 2, K 2, P 8, K 2. Sl markers every row. **Row 3:** K 1, P 1, (**BC**) twice, P 2, **T2,** P 3, K 1, P 5, K 1, P 3, P 12, K 2. **Row 4:** K 2, (P 3 tog, work 3 sts in next st) 3 times, K 3, P 1, K 5, P 1, K 3, P 2, K 2, P 8, K 2. **Row 5:** K 1, P 1, K 8, P 2, **T2,** P 3, **LT,** P 3, **RT,** P 3, P 12, K 2. **Row 6:** K 2; rep between markers of Row 2, K 4, P 1, K 3, P 1, K 4, P 2, K 2, P 8, K 2. **Row 7:** K 1, P 1, K 2, **FC,** K 2, P 2, **T2,** P 4, **LT,** P 1, **RT,** P 4, P 12, K 2. **Row 8:** K 2, rep between markers of Row 4, K 5, P 1, K 1, P 1, K 5, P 2, K 2, P 8, K 2. **Row 9:** K 1, P 1, K 8, P 2, **T2,** P 2, **BO,** P 2, sl next st to dp needle, hold at *front,* **RT,** K st from dp, P 2, **BO,** P 2, P 12, K 2. **Row 10:** K 2; rep between markers of Row 2, K 2, P 1, K 2, P 3, K 2, P 1, K 2, P 2, K 2, P 8, K 2. Rep these 10 rows (taking care to alternate sts between markers on every wrong side row) until there are 40 rows in pat. P 1 row on right side. Bind off.

FINISHING: Block each square lightly to measure 8½ inches square. Check photograph for the position of squares, and weave together from the right side. Join 6 squares in width, 8 squares in length.

KNITTED FRINGE (Make 2 strips): With 2 strands of yarn held tog, cast on 8 sts. **Row 1:** Yo (wrap yarn around right needle), P 2 tog, (yo, P 2 tog) 3 times. Rep Row 1 until same length as lower edge of afghan. **Next Row:** Work 6 sts and drop last 2 sts from left needle without working (to form loops when raveled). Turn and bind off 6 sts loosely. Pin long side (opposite fringe) to edge of afghan and weave in same manner as with squares. Ravel fringe and steam lightly. Do not cut.

MOTHER AND DAUGHTER JUMPERS

A deceptively simple jumper for the lucky little miss and her talented mother.

Instructions for mother in sizes 8, 10, 12 and 14 are in parentheses; instructions for daughter in sizes 4, 6, 8 and 10 are in brackets.

MATERIALS:
Spinnerin Irish Fisherman Yarn (4-oz.) (5-5-5-6) [2-3-4-4] skeins

NEEDLES: No. 6 and No. 9 **OR SIZE TO GIVE GAUGE**

1 set each dp No. 6 and No. 9

HOOK: Size G Aluminum

GAUGE: 11 sts = 2 inches
6 rows = 1 inch

FINISHED MEASUREMENTS: Bust or Chest (34-36-38-40) [26-28-30-32] inches. Lower Edge (42-44-46-48) [34-36-38-40] inches.

STITCHES

CABLE FRONT (CF): Sl next 2 sts to dp needle and hold at *front* of work, K next 2 sts, K 2 from dp.

CABLE BACK (CB): Sl next 2 sts to dp and hold at *back* of work, K next 2 sts, K 2 from dp.

CABLE 8 FRONT (C8F): Sl next 4 sts to dp and hold at *front,* K next 4 sts, K 4 from dp.

CABLE 8 BACK (C8B): Sl next 4 sts to dp and hold at *back,* K next 4 sts, K 4 from dp.

PATTERN 1: Worked on an uneven number of sts. **Row 1:** P 1, * K 1, P 1; rep from * to end. **Rows 2 and 3:** K 1, * P 1, K 1; rep from * to end. **Row 4:** Same as Row 1. Rep these 4 rows for Pat 1.

PATTERN 2: Worked on 10 sts. **Row 1:** K 1, P 2, K 4, P 2, K 1. **Row 2:** P 1, K 2, P 4, K 2, P 1. **Row 3:** K 1, P 2, sl next 2 sts to dp needle, hold at *front* of work, K next 2 sts, K 2 from dp, P 2, K 1. **Row 4:** Same as Row 2. Rep these 4 rows for Pat 2.

PATTERN 3: Worked on 36 sts. **Row 1:** K 1, P 2, K 4, P 2, (K 8, P 2) twice, K 4, P 2, K 1. **Row 2 and All Even-Numbered Rows:** Knit the K sts and purl the P sts. **Row 3:** K 1, P 2, **CF,** P 2, (K 8, P 2) twice, **CB,** P 2, K 1. **Row 5:** Rep Row 1. **Row 7:** K 1, P 2, **CF,** P 2, **C8B,** P 2, **C8F,** P 2, **CB,** P 2, K 1. **Rows 9, 11 and 13:** Rep Rows 1, 3 and 1. **Row 15:** Rep Row 7. **Row 16:** Knit the K sts and purl the P sts. **Rows 17 thru 24:** Rep Rows 1 thru 4 twice. Rep these 24 rows for Pat 3.

JUMPER

BACK: With No. 9 needles, cast on (116-120-124-128) [96-100-104-108] sts. P 1 row. **Row 1 (right side):** Work first rows of Pat 1 over (17-19-19-19) [13-15-17-19] sts, Pat 2 over (10-10-10-10) [10-10-10-10], Pat 1 over (13-13-15-17) [7-7-7-7], Pat 3 over (36-36-36-36) [36-36-36-36], Pat 1 over (13-13-15-17) [7-7-7-7], Pat 2 over (10-10-10-10) [10-10-10-10], Pat 1 over (17-19-19-19) [13-15-17-19]. Work pats as established to (4) [1½] inches from beg. Keeping continuity of pats when shaping, dec 1 st each side of next row and rep decs every (2-2-2½-2½) [1-1-1½-1½] inches (10-10-9-8) [11-11-9-9] times. Work on (94-98-104-110) [72-76-84-88] to (31-31-31-31) [14-16-18-20] inches from beg, or desired length to underarm.

Armholes: Bind off (6-6-6-6) [4-4-5-5] at beg of next 2 rows. Dec 1 st each side every 2nd row (3-4-5-6) [3-4-5-6] times. Work on (76-78-82-86) [58-60-64-66] until armholes are (7½-7½-8-8) [5-5½-6-6½] inches, ending with a right side row.

Next Row: Work (26-27-29-31) [19-20-22-23] sts, place center (24) [20] on a holder, join 2nd ball yarn, work to end.

Shoulders and Neck: Working each side with separate yarn, bind off (8-8-9-9) [6-6-6-7] sts from armhole edges every 2nd row twice, (8-9-9-11) [5-6-8-7] once, **AND AT SAME TIME** dec 1 st at neck edges every 2nd row twice.

FRONT: Work same as back until armhole shapings are complete and there are (76-78-82-86) [58-60-64-66] sts on needle.

Neck: Work (29-30-32-34) [22-23-25-26] sts, place center (18) [14] on a holder, join 2nd ball yarn, work to end. Work each side with separate yarn, dec 1 st at neck edges every 2nd row (5) [5] times. Work on (24-25-27-29) [17-18-20-21], shaping shoulders as on back when armholes are same length.

Back Neckband: With No. 6 needles from right side, pick up (36) [30] sts across neck edge, including sts on holder. Rib in K 1, P 1, for 1 row. Bind off in ribbing. **Front Neckband:** With No. 6 needles from right side, pick up (110-114-118-122) [78-82-86-90] on neck edge, including sts on holder. Complete same as back neckband.

FINISHING: Sew or weave shoulder seams, including neckband.

Armhole Bands: With No. 6 needles from right side, pick up (94-94-98-98) [64-66-68-70] around armhole. Complete same as other bands. Sew or weave underarm seams. From right side, work 1 row sc around lower edge, spacing sts to keep edge flat. Join with a sl st; fasten off. Block lightly.

STRIPED AFGHAN

This brightly striped afghan is easy to make yet gives the inexperienced knitter excellent practice in changing colors frequently. There is no complicated pattern to remember, however, and you will soon be able to work on your afghan and still watch television out of the corner of your eye.

SIZE: About 40″ x 54″ not including fringe.
MATERIALS: Knitting worsted, 20 ozs. each of bright blue (A) and bright green (B).
EQUIPMENT: Circular knitting needle No. 10 (29″ length); steel crochet hook Size 1/0.
GAUGE: 12 sts = 2″; 11 rows = 2″.
NOTE: When changing colors, always twist one around the other.

Beg at narrow end with A, cast on 244 sts. Attach B. **Row 1:** Sl 1 as if to p, with B, k 2, * with yarn in back of work sl 2 as if to p, k 2, repeat from * across, ending k 3. **Row 2:** Sl 1 as if to p, with B, k 2, * with yarn in front of work sl 2 as if to p, k 2, repeat from * across, ending sl 1 as if to p. **Row 3:** With A, k 1, with yarn in back of work sl 2 as if to p, * k 2, with yarn in back of work sl 2 as if to p, repeat from * across, ending k 1. **Row 4:** With A and yarn in front of work, sl 3 as if to p, * p 2, with yarn in front of work sl 2 as if to p, repeat from * across, ending p 1 with B instead of A. Repeat these 4 rows for pat until piece measures 54″, ending with Row 2. With B, bind off in p.

FRINGE: Cut two 12″ strands A. Double the strands to form a loop. Right side facing, insert crochet hook from back to front through bound-off edge of an A stripe and draw loop through. Draw loose ends through loop and pull up tightly. Matching fringe color to stripe color, tie 2 strands in same way on every stripe across. Trim evenly. Repeat fringe at other end.

KNIT TURTLENECK PULLOVER

A big-boy turtleneck look for a very young man. Pictured to the right, this sweater has the added interest of cable panels. Directions are for 6 months; sizes 1 and 2 are in parentheses.

MATERIALS: Coats & Clark's "Red Heart" Knitting Worsted, 4 ply ("Tangle-Proof Pull-Out Skeins): 5 (5,6) oz. No. 814 Robin Blue.

Circular needle No. 8, 18-inch length.

One set double-pointed No. 8 needles.

GAUGE: 9 sts = 2 inches; 6 rows = 1 inch.

FINISHED MEASUREMENTS: Chest, 20(21½, 23) inches.

Starting at neck edge with circular needle, cast on 36 (40, 42) sts. **Do not join. Turn and work in ROWS as follows: 1st row—wrong side:** P 1 for Front, place a marker on needle; p 8 (9, 9) for Sleeve, place a marker on needle; p 18 (20, 22) for Back, place a marker on needle; p 8 (9, 9) for Sleeve, place a marker on needle; p 1 for Front. **2nd row:** *K in front and back of first st—an inc made;* (slip marker, inc in next st, k across to within one st before next marker, inc in next st) 3 times; slip marker, inc in next st—8 sts increased.

NOTE: Always slip markers. 3rd row: Increasing one st in first and last st, p across. **4th row:** Increasing one st in first and last st, and in the st before and after each marker, k across—10 sts increased. Repeat 3rd and 4th rows alternately until 5 (7, 9) rows in all have been completed. There are 58 (74, 88) sts on needle. **Next row:** Omitting the inc at both ends of row, repeat 4th row. Cast on 10 (8, 6) sts at end of last row—76 (90, 102) sts. Join and work in **RNDS** as follows: **1st rnd:** K around. **2nd rnd:** K around, increasing one st before and after each marker as before—8 sts increased. Repeat last 2 rnds alternately until there are 132 (146, 158) sts on rnd, ending with first rnd. K to within next marker, remove marker and k next st.

Sleeve: Leaving the next 28 (31, 33) sts on the needle, remove markers and place remaining sts on stitch holders to be worked later. On left-hand point of needle, cast on 3 sts for underarm. K the cast-on sts and next 28 (31, 33) sts, cast on 3 sts. Work in stockinette st (p 1 row, k 1 row) over the 34 (37, 39) sts on needle, decreasing one st at both ends of every 8th row until there remain 28 (31, 31) sts. Work even until length from underarm is 6 (6½, 7) inches, decreasing one st at end of last row on Sizes 1 and 2 only. Work in k 1, p 1 ribbing for 1 inch. Bind off in ribbing. Skip 38 (42, 46) sts of Back, slip next 28 (31, 33) sts of other Sleeve on needle and work same as previous Sleeve.

Body: Slip the sts of Back onto the needle, attach yarn to first st, cast on 3 sts for underarm, k across the 3 sts and next 38 (42, 46) sts of Back, cast on 6 sts for underarm, k across remaining 38 (42, 46) sts of Front, cast on 3 sts—88 (96, 104) sts. Place a marker on needle between first and last st and join. K next 44 (48, 52) sts for Back, place another marker on needle, k remaining 44 (48, 52) sts for Front. Slipping markers, k each round for ¾ (1, 1½) inches. On last rnd inc one st in center st of Front.

NOTE: Directions for Aran pattern are to be worked on the Front stitches between markers only. Knit the sts of Back on each rnd.

Work Aran pattern as follows: **1st rnd:** P 2 (4, 6), * k 2, p 3, k 2, p 1, k 2, p 3. Repeat from * twice more, k 2, p 2 (4, 6). **2nd rnd:** P 2 (4, 6), * k 2, p 3, slip next 3 sts onto a double-pointed needle and hold in back of work, k next 2 sts, from double-pointed needle p 1 and k 2; p 3. Repeat from * twice more, k 2, p 2 (4, 6). **3rd rnd:** Repeat first rnd. **4th rnd:** P 2 (4, 6), * k 2, p 2, *slip next st onto a double-pointed needle and hold in back of work, k 2, p the st from double-pointed needle—a right twist made;* p next st, *slip next 2 sts onto a double-pointed needle and hold in front of work, p 1, k the 2 sts from double-pointed needle—a left twist made;* p 2. Repeat from * twice more; k 2, p 2 (4, 6). **5th rnd:** P 2 (4, 6), * k 2, p 2, k 2, p 3, k 2, p 2. Repeat from * twice more; k 2, p 2 (4, 6). **6th rnd:** P 2 (4, 6), * k 2, p 1, make a right twist, p 3, make a left twist, p. 1. Repeat from * twice more, k 2, p 2 (4, 6). **7th rnd:** P 2 (4, 6), * k 2, p 1, k 2, p 5, k 2, p 1. Repeat from * twice more, k 2, p 2 (4, 6). **8th rnd:** P 2 (4, 6), * k 2, p 1, left twist, p 3, right twist, p 1. Repeat from * twice more, k 2, p 2 (4, 6). **9th rnd:** Repeat 5th rnd. **10th rnd:** P 2 (4, 6), * k 2, p 2, left twist, p 1, right twist, p 2. Repeat from * twice more, k 2, p 2 (4, 6). Repeat last 10 rnds twice more; then work first and 2nd rnds once. **Next rnd:** K 1, * p 1, k 1. Repeat from * to within last 24 (26, 28) sts, p 2 tog, k 1. Repeat from * to end of rnd. Removing markers, work in k 1, p 1 ribbing as established until length from underarm is 7 (7¾, 8½) inches. Bind off loosely in ribbing.

Collar: With right side of work facing and using double-pointed needles, pick up and k around entire neck edge 70 (74, 78) sts. Divide sts evenly among 3 dp needles and join. Work in rnds of k 1, p 1 ribbing for 3½ inches. Bind off in ribbing.

Block to measurements. Sew sleeve and underarm seams.

Crocheting

If it is true that familiarity breeds contempt, we are going to have a tough time convincing you of the intrinsic beauty of crochet. We have all seen too many bad examples of handkerchief edgings and limp doilies to view crochet with a completely unjaundiced eye. Do try to forget the bad examples, however, and you will soon see how lovely a really fine piece of crochet can be.

Crochet (as well as many other forms of needlework) is like the well-known prophet—without honor in his own country. Since crochet was always taken for granted, nothing was done to preserve it or to record its history for later generations. As a result we know little about its origins. We do know, however, that even the most primitive people inevitably manipulate a string to make a series of interlocking loops—a chain. This is the foundation of all crocheting. We can imagine that whenever people, especially children, had a string—perhaps a fiber or a sinew—they would loop it through itself using only the fingers as a tool. As they became more adept at this looping technique they sought for a tool more refined than stubby fingers. Finally the first crochet hook was probably developed from a sliver of bone or wood. From that point on there was no stopping the crocheter.

The big impetus for crocheting came in the first half of the nineteenth century when nuns used their delicate products to obtain a bit of money to feed the starving in famine-stricken Ireland. Their crocheted laces copied from the exquisite needle and bobbin laces of France and Italy had quite a vogue in London and other fashion-minded capitals of Europe. With the great emigration of Irish people to the United States at that time, came the women with samples of their favorite crochet patterns, and the skills to make them. American women were eager to learn the new technique and soon produced miles of crochet that, if laid end to end, would stretch from "sea to shining sea."

Today crochet need not be elaborate to be totally acceptable. A functional pot holder is as significant as a glittery crocheted evening bag. They each serve their purpose. The great variety of uses is one of the most interesting things about crochet. Many of us old-time needleworkers learned to crochet by making the inevitable wash cloth. We learned—and the wash cloth did its job. As we become fascinated by the technique we can produce everything from the filmiest laces to the most luxurious suits. Although there is nothing more to crocheting than pulling one loop through another with a little hook, the variations are endless. Learn the basics and you will find a lifetime of pleasure and fulfillment.

MATERIALS

Although we usually think of cotton when we think of crocheting, the thread or yarn can be of any fiber, natural or man-made. Linen thread would make a cool summer blouse. Wool, of course, is ideal for an afghan, a sweater, a baby carriage cover. The synthetics work up beautifully in any of the preceding items and are often machine washable. But we invariably return to cotton when we do any amount of crocheting. Crochet cottons may be as fine as sewing thread or as thick as cord. It may be mercerized and have a smooth silky finish or it may have the matte appearance of some bedspread cottons.

Always buy all the thread or yarn you need at one time to be sure that you have one dye lot. Even white or ecru threads may vary slightly and the variations will show up in your finished work. Also be sure to check yardages when you are switching from the yarn or thread of one manufacturer to a similar product of another manufacturer. The ball or skein may have an entirely different yardage from the amount you need.

EQUIPMENT

Modern production methods produce crochet hooks of fine quality which are lightweight and comfortable to use. Steel crochet hooks 5″ long are usually used for cotton and come in sizes 00, 0, 1 all the way through 14. Size 00 is the largest, 14 the smallest. Bone hooks are available but are rapidly being supplanted by plastic and aluminum hooks. In fact, aluminum hooks 6″ long are the most readily available today. These are used for slightly heavier types of crocheting (sweaters, pot holders, etc.) They are usually designated by letters and run from E through K, K being the largest. The plastic hooks may also be designated by number but these numbers vary from manufacturer to manufacturer.

Afghan hooks are used for a special type of crocheting called afghan stitch. These are plastic or, more commonly today, aluminum. They are 9″ or 14″ long and come in sizes E through K.

Extra large hooks for rugs and jiffy crochet have usually been made of wood and (just to confuse the poor crocheter) are numbered from 10 (the smallest) through 15 (the largest). New jumbo hooks are now available in plastic; Q, for instance, is $5/8$″ in diameter.

METHOD

1

To Begin To Crochet

Make a practice piece of each new stitch and work until you are familiar with it. To practice, use medium-weight thread (a little heavier than bedspread cotton) and a No. 4 steel crochet hook. Make a loop at the end of thread and hold loop in place with thumb and forefinger of left hand. At left is short end of thread; at right is the long or working thread. With right hand, grasp the crochet hook as you would a pencil and put hook through loop, catch working thread and draw it through. Pull short end and working thread in opposite directions to bring loop close around the end of hook. Measure down working thread about 4″ from loop on hook. At this point, insert thread between ring finger and little finger of left hand. Weave thread toward back, under little and ring fingers, over middle finger and under forefinger toward you. Grasp hook and loop with thumb and forefinger of left hand. Gently pull working thread so that it is taut but not tight. Hold hook as you would a pencil, but bring middle finger forward to rest near tip of hook. In order to begin working, adjust fingers of left hand as in Diagram 1. The middle finger is bent so it can control the tension while the ring and little fingers prevent the thread from moving too freely. As you practice, you will become familiar with the correct tension. Now you are ready to begin the chain stitch.

2   3

Chain Stitch (ch)

Pass hook under thread and catch thread with hook (Diagram 2). Draw thread through loop on hook. This makes one chain (Diagram 3).

Repeat these two steps until you have as many chain stitches as you need. One loop always remains on hook. Keep thumb and forefinger of your left hand near stitch on which you are working. Practice making chains until they are uniform.

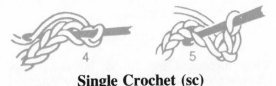

4   5

Single Crochet (sc)

Make a foundation chain of 20 stitches for practice piece. Insert hook from front under 2 top threads of 2nd chain from hook (Diagram 4). Pass hook under thread and catch thread with hook to make "thread over." Draw through stitch. Thread over and draw through two loops on hook. One loop remains on hook. One single crochet is now completed. For next single crochet, insert hook under 2 top threads of next stitch (Diagram 5) and continue to work in this manner in each stitch across. At the end of row of single crochet, chain 1 for "turning chain." Turn work so reverse side is facing you. Insert hook under 2 top threads of first single crochet and work across as before. Continue working single crochet in this manner. On the last row do not make a turning chain. Clip thread about 3″ from work, bring loose end through the loop remaining on hook and pull tight.

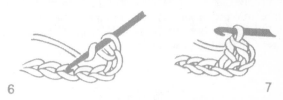

6   7

Double Crochet (dc)

Make a foundation chain of 20 stitches for practice piece. Thread over, insert hook under the 2 top threads of 4th chain from hook (Diagram 6). Thread over, draw through stitch. Thread over and draw through 2 loops. Thread over again and draw through 2 remaining loops. One loop remains on hook. One double crochet is now completed (Diagram 7). For next double crochet, thread over, insert hook under the 2 top threads of next stitch and continue to work in this manner in each stitch. At end of row, chain 3 and turn work. On next row, thread over, skip first double crochet, insert hook under the 2 top threads of 2nd double crochet and work across as before. Continue working double crochet in this manner. On the last row do not make a turning chain. Clip thread about 3″ from work, bring loose end through the loop remaining on hook and pull tight.

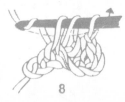

8

Half Double Crochet (hdc)

To make half double crochet, thread over, insert hook under the 2 top threads of 3rd chain from hook. Three loops are on hook. Thread over and draw through all 3 loops at once (Diagram 8). Half double crochet is now completed. At end of rows, chain 2 to turn.

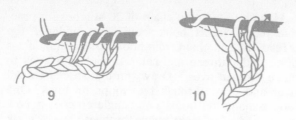

9   10

Treble Crochet (tr)

Make foundation chain of 20 stitches for practice piece. Thread over twice, insert hook under 2 top threads of 5th chain from hook. Thread over and draw a loop through the chain. There are now 4 loops on hook. Thread over again (Diagram 9). Draw through 2 loops on hook. Thread over again and draw through 2 loops. Thread over again (Diagram 10) and draw through 2 remaining loops. One loop remains on hook. One treble crochet is now completed. At end of row, chain 4 to turn. Continue making treble in this manner until you are familiar with the stitch. Finish piece same as for single or double crochet.

11

Double Treble (d tr)

Thread over hook 3 times, insert hook under 2 top threads of 6th chain from hook and draw a loop through the chain. Five loops are on hook. Thread over and draw through 2 loops four times (Diagram 11). A double treble is now completed. At end of row, chain 5 to turn.

12

Triple Treble (tr tr)

Thread over hook 4 times, insert hook under 2 top threads of 7th chain from hook and draw a loop

through the chain. Six loops are on hook. Thread over and draw through 2 loops 5 times (Diagram 12). A triple treble is now completed. At end of row, chain 6 to turn.

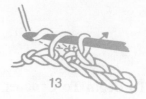

13

Slip Stitch (sl st)

Make a foundation chain of 20 stitches for practice piece. Insert hook under top thread of 2nd chain from hook, thread over. With one motion, draw through stitch and through loop on hook. Insert hook under top thread of next chain, then thread over and draw through stitch and loop on hook (Diagram 13). Repeat until you have made a slip stitch in each chain. When directions say "join," always use a slip stitch. Insert hook through the 2 top threads of stitch, thread over and draw through stitch and loop on hook.

To Decrease Single Crochet

Work one single crochet to point where 2 loops are on hook. Draw up a loop in next stitch. Thread over, draw through 3 loops at one time.

To Decrease Double Crochet

Work one double crochet to point where 2 loops are on hook. Begin another double crochet in next stitch and work until 4 loops are on hook. Thread over, draw through 2 loops. Thread over, draw through 3 loops.

To Increase

When directions call for an increase, work 2 stitches in one stitch to form the extra stitch.

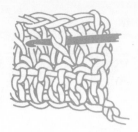

Working Around The Post

The "post" or "bar" is the vertical or upright section of a stitch. When directions say to make a stitch around the post or bar of a stitch in a previous row, insert the hook around the stitch instead of in top of stitch.

ADDITIONAL CROCHET INFORMATION

Gauge

It is most important that you crochet to the gauge specified so that your finished article will be the correct size. Gauge means the number of stitches to 1″ and the number of rows to 1″.

Make a practice piece at least 2″ square, using the hook and materials specified in the directions. With a ruler, measure the number of stitches you have to 1″. If your stitches do not correspond to the gauge, experiment with a hook of a different size.

Crochet Terminology

Multiple of stitches: A pattern often requires an exact number of stitches, to be worked properly. When the directions say, for example, "multiple of 6 sts," it means the number of stitches must be divisible by 6—12, 18, 24, etc. "Multiple of 6 sts plus 3" would be 15, 21, 27, etc.

Work even: This means to continue working without increasing or decreasing.

Repeat from *: This means that all instructions following the * are to be repeated as many times as specified in the directions.

Parentheses ( ): This is used in two ways: To enclose directions for larger sizes as listed at the start of each set of directions, and to indicate that the instructions which they enclose are to be repeated the number of times stated immediately after. For example, (tr, ch 1) twice means that you should make a treble, chain 1, treble, ch 1.

Abbreviations

beg	begin
bl	block
ch	chain
dec	decrease
dc	double crochet
d tr	double treble
h dc	half double crochet
inc	increase
lp	loop
pat	pattern
rnd	round
sc	single crochet
sk	skip
sl	slip
st	stitch
sts	stitches
tog	together
tr	treble
tr tr	triple treble
yo	yarn over

Fastening Ends

After you have completed an article, thread each loose end into a needle and darn it through a solid part of the crochet to fasten it securely. Cut off remaining thread close to the work. Be sure starting ends are long enough to be fastened off.

Blocking

Place article wrong side up on a flat, padded surface. Gently stretch and shape it to the desired measurements. Pin to surface, using rust-proof pins. Place a damp cloth over piece and press with a hot iron, raising it as you move it rather than sliding it back and forth, being careful not to let weight of iron rest on article. Let dry thoroughly before unpinning.

Sewing Edges Together

Pin together edges to be sewed, matching any pattern in rows or stitches. Thread needle with matching thread or yarn. To begin sewing, do not knot thread but take several over and over stitches, darning them, if possible, through a solid part of the crochet. Sew straight even edges with a whipped stitch, placing it at edges of the work. Sew slanting or uneven edges (caused by increasing or decreasing) with a backstitch, placing it just inside edges of work. Leave stitches loose enough to match the elasticity of the crochet. Steam-press seams lightly.

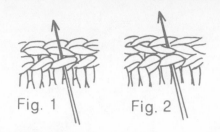

Fig. 1   Fig. 2

CROCHET PULLOVER

This enchanting sweater is decorated with loopy fringe. It will delight any demure young lady.

Directions are given for 6 months size; sizes 1 and 2 are in parentheses.

MATERIALS: Coats & Clark's "Red Heart" Knitting Worsted, 4 ply ("Tangle-Proof" Pull-Out Skeins): 10(11, 12) oz. No. 227 Canary Yellow.

EQUIPMENT: Crochet Hook, size F.

GAUGE: 4 sts = 1 inch; 4 rows = 1½ inches.

FINISHED MEASUREMENTS: Chest, 20(21½, 23) inches.

Back: Starting at lower edge, ch 43 (46, 50) to measure 10½ (11¼, 12) inches, having 4 ch sts to 1 inch. **1st row:** *Insert hook in 2nd ch from hook, with third finger of left hand over the yarn, hold yarn down behind the work, yarn over and draw loop through, yarn over and draw through both loops on hook — loop st made;* make a loop st in each ch across — 42 (45, 49) loop sts. Ch 1, turn. **2nd row — right side:** Sc in each st across. Ch 1, turn. **3rd row:** Make a loop st in each sc across. Ch 2, turn. **4th row:** H dc in each st across — 42 (45, 49) h dc; do not count the turning chain as one st. Ch 2, turn. **5th row:** * Yarn over, insert hook in front loop of next h dc and complete a h dc — 2 loops remain on back of work (Fig. 1). Repeat from * across. There are the same number of sts as on previous row. Ch 2, turn. **6th row:** * Yarn over, insert hook in the 2 front loops of next h dc and complete a h dc — 1 loop remains on back of work. (Fig. 2.) Repeat from * across. Ch 2, turn. Repeat 5th and 6th rows alternately for pattern. Work in pattern until total length is about 7 (7½, 8) inches, ending with a wrong-side row. Ch 1, turn.

Armhole Shaping: 1st row: Sl st in first 2 (2, 3) sts, ch 1, work in pattern across to within last 3 (3, 4) h dc, *yarn over, draw up a loop in each of next 2 sts, yarn over and draw through all loops on hook — 1 h dc decreased over 2 h dc* (do not work in last st). Ch 1, turn. **2nd row:** Sl st in first st, ch 1, work in pattern across to within last 2 h dc, dec 1 h dc over last 2 sts — 36 (39, 41) sts. Ch 2, turn. Work even in pattern for 7 (8, 9) more rows. At end of last row, ch 1, turn.

Shoulder Shaping: 1st row: Sl st in first 5 sts, ch 1, work in pattern across to within last 7 h dc, dec 1 h dc over next 2 sts (do not work over remaining sts). Ch 1, turn. **2nd row:** Sl st in first 3 (4, 4) sts, ch 1, work in pattern across to within last 5 (6, 6) sts, dec 1 h dc over next 2 sts. Break off and fasten. Remaining 18 (19, 21) sts are for back of neck.

Front: Work as for Back until armhole shaping has been completed. Work even on 36 (39, 41) h dc in pattern for 5 (6, 7) rows.

Neck Shaping: 1st row: Work in pattern across first 12 (13, 14) h dc, dec 1 h dc over next 2 sts. Ch 2, turn. **2nd row:** Skip first st, work across. Ch 1, turn. **3rd row:** Sl st in first 5 sts, ch 1, work in pattern across 5 (6, 7) sts, dec 1 h dc over next 2 sts. Ch 2, turn. **4th row:** Skip first st, h dc in next 2 (2, 3) h dc. Break off and fasten. Skip next 8 (9, 9) h dc on last long row, attach yarn to next h dc, ch 2, dec 1 h dc over same st and next st, work in pattern across. Complete as for other side, reversing shapings.

Sleeves: Starting at lower edge, ch 25 (27, 29) to measure 6 (6½, 7) inches. Work as for Back until the first 7 rows have been completed — 24 (26, 28) h dc. Increasing one h dc at both ends of next row and every 3rd row thereafter, work in pattern until there are 30 (34, 36) h dc on row — to inc 1 h dc, make 2 h dc in same st. Work even until total length is about 7 (7½, 8) inches, ending with a wrong-side row. Ch 1, turn.

Top Shaping: 1st row: Repeat first row of armhole shaping of Back. Ch 1, turn. **2nd row:** Sl st in first 2 sts, ch 1, work in pattern across to within last 3 h dc, dec 1 h dc over next 2 h dc — do not work in remaining sts. Ch 1, turn. **Next 4 (5, 6) rows:** Repeat 2nd row of armhole shaping of Back. Break off and fasten.

Block to measurements. Sew shoulder, side and sleeve seams. Sew in sleeves.

Collar: Starting at outer edge, ch 80 (88, 92), having 4 ch sts to 1 inch. Being careful not to twist the chain, join with sl st to first ch. **1st rnd:** Make a loop st in each st around. Join to first st. **2nd rnd:** Sc in each st around. **3rd rnd:** Make a loop st in each st around. Turn. **4th rnd:** Sc in each sc around, decreasing 8 sc evenly spaced — to dec 1 sc — *draw up a loop in each of next 2 sc, yarn over and draw through all loops on hook.* **5th rnd:** Sc in each sc around. Repeat last 2 rnds 2 times more, then work 4th rnd once more. Repeat 5th rnd 3 (4, 5) times more. Break off and fasten. Press. Sew Collar in place.

BABY OUTFIT

Bright as a buttercup! A sacque, bonnet, booties and mittens worked in simple single crochet, adorned with embroidered flowers. Altogether they make a darling outfit for baby's outing.
Directions are given for infant's size 2.

MATERIALS: Coats & Clark's Red Heart Baby Wool, 3 ply (1 oz. "Tangle-Proof Pull-Out Skeins): 6 skeins No. 261, Maize; few yards of fine red and green yarn or embroidery floss.

EQUIPMENT: Steel Crochet Hook No. 1.

GAUGE: 8 sc = 1 inch; 9 rows = 1 inch.

FINISHED MEASUREMENTS: Chest, 20½".

SACQUE

BACK: Starting at lower edge, ch 81 (8 ch sts to 1 inch). **1st row:** Sc in 2nd ch from hook and in each ch across (80 sc). Ch 1, turn. **2nd row:** Picking up **back loop only throughout,** sc in each sc across. Ch 1, turn. Repeat 2nd row for pattern. Work in pattern until total length is 6½ inches. At end of last row ch 46 for sleeve. Drop yarn. Attach another strand of yarn at opposite end of same row and ch 45 for other sleeve. Break off. Pick up dropped yarn, sc in 2nd ch from hook, in each ch, continue across back and other chain. Ch 1, turn. Continue in pattern over these 170 sc's until total length is 10 inches, ending at left sleeve edge.

LEFT FRONT: 1st row: Work across 70 sts. Ch 1, turn. **Next 4 rows:** Working over this set of sts only, work even in pattern. **6th row (Front edge):** 2 sc in first sc—*an inc made*—work across. **Next 2 rows:** Increasing 1 st at front edge, work across. **9th row:** Work across, at end of row ch 16. Turn. **10th row:** Sc in 2nd ch from hook and in each st across. Ch 1, turn. Work even over these 88 sts until length from first row of front is 3½ inches, ending at front edge. **Next row:** Work across 43 sts. Ch 1, turn. Work even over these 43 sts until length from first row of front is 10 inches. Break off and fasten.

RIGHT FRONT: 1st row: Skip next 30 sc of last row of back, attach yarn to next st, sc in same sc and each sc across (70 sc). Work 4 rows even. **Next 3 rows:** Inc 1 st at front edge, work across. **9th row:** Work across. Drop yarn. Attach another strand of yarn to first sc at neck

edge of 9th row and ch 15. Break off. **10th row:** Pick up dropped yarn, sc in each sc and each ch across (88 sc). Ch 1, turn. Complete right front to correspond with left front.

COLLAR: 1st row: With wrong side facing, attach yarn to front edge of neck and work 67 sc around neck edge. Turn. **2nd row:** * Ch 2, 2 dc in same sc, skip next 2 sc, sc in next sc (shell made). Repeat from * across. Break off and fasten. Do not turn. **3rd row:** Attach yarn in the ch-2 space of first shell of previous row, * ch 2, 2 dc in same place, sc in ch-2 space of next shell. Repeat from * across, ending with sc in 2nd dc of last shell. Break off and fasten. Do not turn. **Next 4 rows:** Repeat 3rd row. With right side facing, sc along each front edge. Break off and fasten.

CUFF: 1st rnd: Attach yarn to lower edge of sleeve, sc around. Join. **Next 2 rnds:** Ch 1, sc in each sc around. At end of last round break off and fasten.
With red embroider 3 French Knot flowers, and with green make Lazy-Daisy leaves, evenly spaced along each front edge as illustrated.

BONNET

CROWN: Starting at center, ch 2. **1st rnd:** 6 sc in 2nd ch from hook. **2nd rnd:** 2 sc in each sc around (12 sc). **3rd rnd:** * 2 sc in next sc (1 sc inc), sc in next sc. Repeat from * around (18 sc). Continue to work sc in each sc around, inc 6 sc evenly on each rnd until piece measures 5 inches in diameter.

SIDE PIECE: 1st row: Picking up **back loop only throughout,** sc in each sc to within last 2 inches, having a multiple of 3 plus 1 sts. Ch 1, turn. Repeat last row for 4½ inches, ending with a right side row.

RUFFLE: 1st row: Repeat 2nd row of collar. **2nd row:** Repeat 3rd row of collar, making 3 dc in each shell instead of 2 dc. **3rd row:** Repeat last row making 4 dc in each shell. Fold back last 7 rows for cuff and tack side edges in place. With right side facing, attach yarn to folded edge and sc around entire outer edge including neck edge. Join. Break off and fasten. Embroider 4 flowers and leaves on front of cuff as for Sacque.

STRAP: Make a chain slightly longer than length desired. **1st row.** Sc in 2nd ch from hook and in each ch across. Ch 1, turn. **Next 3 rows:** Work in pattern as for Sacque. At end of last row break off and fasten. Sew one end to Bonnet. Sew snap fastener to opposite side.

BOOTIES

SOLE: Starting at center, ch 21. **1st rnd:** 5 sc in 2nd ch from hook (toe), sc in each ch across, 5 sc in last ch (back), working across opposite side of starting chain, sc in each ch across. Join to first sc. **2nd rnd:** Ch 1, (2 sc in each sc of the 5-sc group, sc in each sc across to next 5-sc group) twice. Join. **3rd rnd:** Ch 1, inc 3 sc evenly across toe and back, sc in each sc around. Join. **Next 3 rnds:** Ch 1, sc in each sc around. Join.

UPPER: 1st rnd: Ch 1, turn. Picking up **front loop only,** sc in each sc around (ridge made). Join. **Next 8 rnds:** Ch 1, turn. Picking up **back loop only throughout,** sc in each sc around. Join. At end of last rnd ch 1, turn.

INSTEP: 1st row: Sc in next 10 sc. Ch 1, turn. **Next 10 rows:** Sc in each sc across. Ch 1, turn. At end of last row break off and fasten. Sew side edges of instep in place.

CUFF: 1st rnd: Attach yarn to last st of instep, ch 3, make 43 dc around last rnd of Upper and Instep. Join to top of ch 1. **2nd rnd (Beading):** Ch 4, * skip next st, dc in next st, ch 1. Repeat from * around. Join to 3rd ch of ch 4 (22 sps). **3rd rnd:** * In next sp make sc, ch 2 and 2 dc (shell), skip next sp. Repeat from * around. Join to first sc. **4th and 5th rnds:** * In ch-2 sp of next shell make sc, ch 2 and 3 dc. Repeat from * around. Join as before. **6th and 7th rnds:** Repeat 4th rnd, making 4 dc in each shell instead of 3 dc. At end of last rnd break off and fasten.

CORD: Ch 80. Sl st in each ch across. Break off and fasten. Tie a knot at each end and lace through beading. Tie in front.

On Instep embroider a flower and leaves as on Sacque.

MITTENS

BACK: Starting at center, ch 17. **1st row:** Sc in 2nd ch from hook and in each ch across, 5 sc in last ch (tip); working across opposite side of starting chain, sc in each ch across. Ch 1, turn. **2nd row:** Picking up **back loop only throughout,** sc in each sc across, making 2 sc in each sc of the 5-sc group at tip. Ch 1, turn. **3rd row:** Sc in each sc across. Ch 1, turn. **4th row:** Sc in each sc across, inc 5 sc evenly spaced across tip. **Next 4 rows:** Repeat last 2 rows alternately. **9th row:** Repeat 3rd row. Break off and fasten.

PALM: Work as for Back.

Holding both pieces together and working through both thicknesses to join, sl st closely around. Break off and fasten.

CUFF: 1st rnd: Attach yarn to wrist edge, work 44 sc around. Join. **Next 4 rnds:** Repeat 2nd to 5th rnds incl of cuff of Bootees. At end of last rnd, break off and fasten.

CORD: Ch 60. Complete as for cord of Bootees. Embroider a flower and leaves in center of back.

CARBON COPIES

(Father and Son Vests)

The youngster is a carbon copy of his dad. Won't he be proud! The gray vests are worked on an afghan hook with a colorful cross-stitch border. Single crochet is quick and easy for the green vests.

SIZES: 4, 8 and 12 for SON — 38, 42, 46 and 50 for FATHER Directions are for Size 4. Changes for sizes 8, 12, 38, 42, 46 and 50 are in parentheses.

FINISHED MEASUREMENTS: Chest 26½(30½, 34½, 39, 43, 47, 51) inches. Back st shoulders 9½(10½, 12½, 16½, 17½, 18½, 19) inches.

MATERIALS: Spinnerin Wintuk (2-oz.) 4(4, 5, 6, 8, 8, 8) or Marvel Twist or Germantown Deluxe or Knitting Worsted (4-oz.) 2(2, 3, 3, 4, 4, 4). 6 buttons, buckle.

EQUIPMENT: Crochet Hooks: Sizes G and J, or size to give gauge.

GAUGE: 3 sts = 1 inch; 4 rows = 1 inch.

BODY: With J Hook, chain 79 (91–103–115–127–139–151) to measure 26 (30–34–38–42–46–50) inches. Work 1 sc in 2nd ch from hook and in each ch to end. Ch 1, turn.

Row 1: Work sc in each sc. Ch 1, turn. Rep Row 1 for pat. Work to 9 (11–13–17–17–17–17) inches from beg. Ch 1, turn.

LEFT FRONT – Armhole – Row 1: Sc in each of 17 (20–22–25–28–31–34). Ch 1, turn. **Row 2:** Draw up a loop in each of 2 sts, yo and thru 3 loops (1 st dec), sc in each sc to end. Ch 1, turn. Dec 1 st at armhole edge on next 4 (4–4–2–4–6–8) rows, ending at front edge.

Neck: Dec 1 st at beg of next row and rep dec at same edge every 2nd row 3 (4–2–3–1–3–5) times, every 4th row 2 (2–4–6–7–6–5) times. Work on 6 (8–10–12–14–14–14) until armhole is 6 (7–8–10–10½–11–11½) inches. End at armhole edge. Ch 1, turn.

Shoulder: Sl st in each of 3 (4–5–6–7–7–7) sts, sc in each sc to end. Fasten off. Skip 5 (5–7–7–7–7–7) to left of last st of left front for underarm. Join yarn in next st. Ch 1.

BACK: Sc in same st with joining and in next 33 (39–43–49–55–61–67). Ch 1, turn. Dec 1 st each side of next 4 (5–5–3–4–6–8) rows. Work on 26 (30–34–44–48–50–52) sts to same number of rows as on left front to shoulder. Ch 1, turn.

Shoulders: Sl st in each of 3 (4–5–6–7–7–7), ch 1, work to last 3 (4–5–6–7–7–7). Ch 1, turn. Sl st in each of 3 (4–5–6–7–7–7), ch 1, work to last 3 (4–5–6–7–7–7). Fasten off. Sk 5 (5–7–7–7–7–7) to left of last st of back for underarm. Join yarn in next st. Ch 1.

RIGHT FRONT: Work to correspond to left front.

POCKETS AND BELT (Make 2): With J hook, chain 15 (15–15–21–25–25–25) to measure 5 (5–5–7–8–8–8) inches. Work sc for 4 (4½–5–6–6–6–6) inches, ch 24 (28–34–40–46–52–58) for belt. Work sc in 2nd ch and each ch, continue sc across pocket. Work 5 (5–5–8–8–8–8) rows of 1 sc in each st. Ch 1, turn at end of each row except last.

Last row (Backward sc): Ch 1, do not turn. With G hook from right side, work sc from left to right around edges of belt and pocket. Fasten off.

FINISHING: Sew shoulder seams. With G hook, join yarn at center back neck. **Row 1:** From right side, work sc in each sc to front edge, sc in end of each row to first neck dec, 2 sc in dec row (mark), continue sc around, working 3 sc at lower front corners and have same number of sc on each front edge, 2 sc at neck dec (mark), sc to first sc, join with a sl st. Ch 1, turn. **Row 2:** Sc in each sc, 3 sc at corners. Join and fasten off. Mark places for buttonholes on left front, first marker 1 inch below marked st, others as desired. **Row 1:** Join yarn at marked st of left front. From right side, *work sc in each sc to buttonhole marker, ch 1 for son's buttonhole, ch 2 for father's buttonhole, sk same number sc; rep from * to lower edge, 3 sc at corner, continue sc to point on right front opposite joining. Ch 1, turn. **Row 2:** Work sc in each sc, 3 sc at corners and sc in each ch. End at first sc of row 1. Fasten off. **Row 3:** Join yarn at center back of neck. From right side, work backward sc (from left to right) around entire vest. Join with a sl st; fasten off. Work 2 rnds sc and 1 rnd backward sc around each armhole. Sew pockets to fronts within front and lower borders of vest. Sew on buttons and belt buckle.

MATERIALS: Wintuk (2-oz.) 3(3, 3, 6, 7, 8, 8)MC. or Marvel Twist, Germantown Deluxe or Knitting Worsted (4-oz.) 2(2, 2, 3, 4, 4, 4)MC. Approx. 4(4, 4, 5, 5, 5, 5)yds. A, 8(8, 8, 12, 12, 12, 12) yds. each B and C.
5 buttons.

EQUIPMENT: Afghan Hook: 14-inch Size H or size to give gauge.

Crochet Hook: Size E.

GAUGE: 4 sts = 1 inch; 13 rows = 4 inches.

Vest is worked with MC in afghan stitch. Design is embroidered with A, B and C in cross-stitch. See pages 207 and 208 for directions in working basic afghan stitch and cross-stitch embroidery. When counting rows, count each vertical bar as one row.

BACK AND FRONTS: With afghan hook, chain 105 (121–137–153–169–185–201) to measure 26 (30–34–38–42–46–50) inches. Work afghan st for 28 (36–42–56–56–56–56) rows. Piece should measure 9 (11–13–17–17–17–17) inches.

Right Front—Armhole and Neck: Pick up until there are 22 (26–30–34–38–42–46) loops on hook. Work off loops. Working on these sts only, dec 1 st at both sides every row 4 times, every 2nd row 1 (3–3–1–4–5–8) times. Keeping armhole edge even, continue to dec at neck edge every 2nd row 3 (1–3–10–7–7–4) times more. Work even on 9 (11–13–14–15–17–18) sts until armhole is 6 (7–8–10–10½–11–11½) inches.

Shoulder: Bind off 4 (5–6–7–7–8–9) from armhole edge once, 5 (6–7–7–8–9–9) once.

Back Armholes: Join yarn to st after right front sts, bind off this st and 7 sts more for underarm, pick up loops until there are 45 (53–61–69–77–85–93) on hook. Work off loops. Working on these sts only, dec 1 st each side on next 5 (7–7–5–8–9–12) rows. Work on 35 (39–47–59–61–67–69) to same number of rows as on right front to shoulder.

Shoulders: Bind off 4 (5–6–7–7–8–9) sts, pick up loops to last 4 (5–6–7–7–8–9) sts. Work off loops. Bind off 5 (6–7–7–8–9–9), pick up loops to last 5 (6–7–7–8–9–9) sts. Work off loops. Bind off 17 (17–21–31–31–33–33) sts for back of neck. Now bind off 9 (11–13–14–15–17–18) sts of left shoulder. Fasten off.

Left Front—Armhole and Neck: Join yarn to st after back sts, bind off this st and 7 sts more, pick up loops to end. Complete to correspond to right front.

FINISHING: Sew shoulder seams.

Armhole Borders: With E hook, join yarn at center of bound-off sts of underarm. From right side, work 1 sc in each bound-off st and in end of each row around. Work 2 rows of 1 sc in each sc.

Front and Neck Border: With E hook, join yarn at center back of neck. From right side, work sc in each bound-off st, sc in end of each row to first neck dec, 3 sc in next row, sc in end of each row to lower edge, 3 sc at corner, sc in each st of foundation ch, continue sc on front and neck, having same number of sts to correspond. Join with a sl st.

For Sizes 38, 42, 46 and 50 only: Work sc in each sc, 3 sc at neck and lower corners.

Mark places on left front for 5 buttonholes, first at first neck dec, last 2 (2–2–3–3–3–3) inches above lower edge, others evenly between.

Next row for all sizes: Work sc to first marker; ch 1 (1–1–2–2–2–2), sk 1 (1–1–2–2–2–2) sts (for buttonhole); continue sc, working buttonholes at markers and 3 sc at corners.

Next row: Work sc in each sc and each ch. **For sizes 38, 42, 46 and 50 only:** Work sc in each sc. Join; fasten off. Follow chart for cross st embroidery. Steam borders. Sew on buttons.

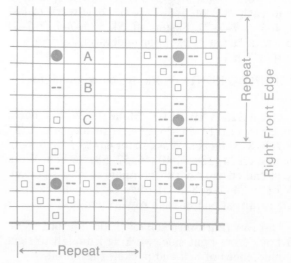

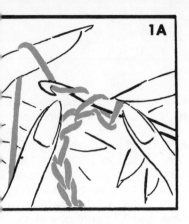
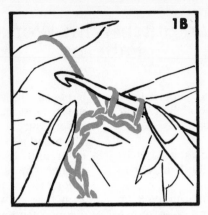
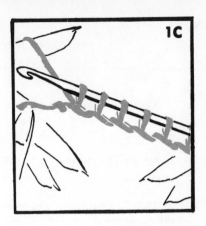

AFGHAN STITCH: ROW 1—FIRST HALF

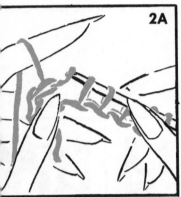
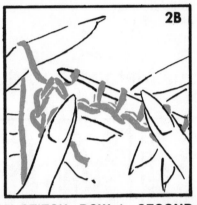
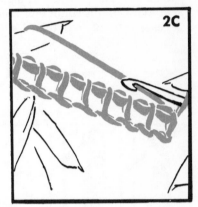

AFGHAN STITCH: ROW 1—SECOND HALF

Basic Afghan Stitch

Work a chain of specified length.

Row 1-First Half: Skip first chain from hook. *Insert hook thru top loop only of next chain. Yarn over hook (1A). Draw yarn thru chain, forming loop on hook. Retain loop on hook (1B). Rep from * across chain (1C). There will be the same number of loops on hook as number of chains.

Row 1-Second Half: Yarn over hook and draw thru first loop (2A). * Yarn over and draw thru 2 loops (2B). Rep from * across row until there is 1 loop on hook (2C). This loop is first st for next row.

Row 2-First Half: Insert hook in 2nd upright st or vertical bar, yarn over hook, draw loop thru bar, forming loop on hook (3A). Retain loop on hook. Continue drawing up a loop thru each bar across row (3B and 3C).

Row 2-Second Half: Same as 2nd half of Row 1. Rep Row 2 for pattern.

TO BIND OFF: Slip st across row as follows: * Draw up loop in bar and thru loop on hook. Rep from * across. Break yarn and draw thru last loop.

AFGHAN STITCH: ROW 2—FIRST HALF

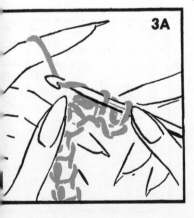
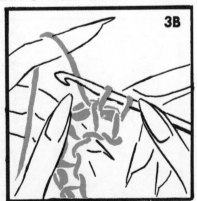
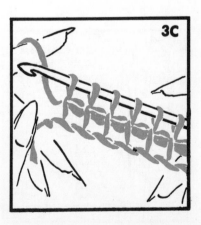

Afghan Stitch With Worked-In Patterns

These Afghans are worked in one piece, following a chart. The stitch used is basic afghan stitch, changing colors according to a chart.

TO FOLLOW CHART: On all rows, read chart from right to left. Remember that both halves of 1 row afghan st = 1 row on chart.
JOINING COLORS: On first half of row pick up the designated number of loops of first color shown on chart, join next color, pick up specified number of loops in this color, etc. When the same color appears with no more than 3 stitches of another color

between, the first ball may be carried across—but **never more than 3 sts.** Join new balls of same color if necessary.

On 2nd half of row, work off loops with matching color until there is one st left of the color, then change colors, picking up yarn to be used under color previously used, thus twisting colors to prevent hole in work. New color will be drawn thru 1 loop of previous color and 1 loop of new color). When a color is no longer needed, break off, leaving an end long enough to be woven in on the wrong side.

Various Methods of Fringing

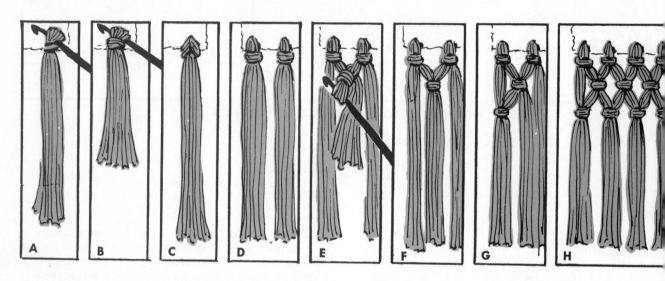

Use specific directions given with each afghan for the length to cut yarn, the number of strands and color to use and how to space.

Fold strands in half. Insert hook from wrong side and draw folds thru. Draw cut ends thru folded loops.

FOR SINGLE KNOT FRINGE: Follow illustrations A thru D.
FOR DOUBLE KNOT FRINGE: Follow illustrations A thru F.
FOR TRIPLE KNOT FRINGE: Follow illustrations A thru H.

Cross Stitch on Afghan Stitch

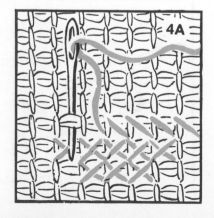
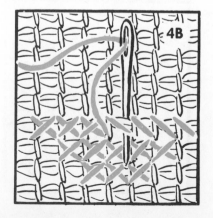
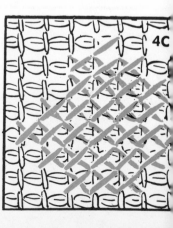

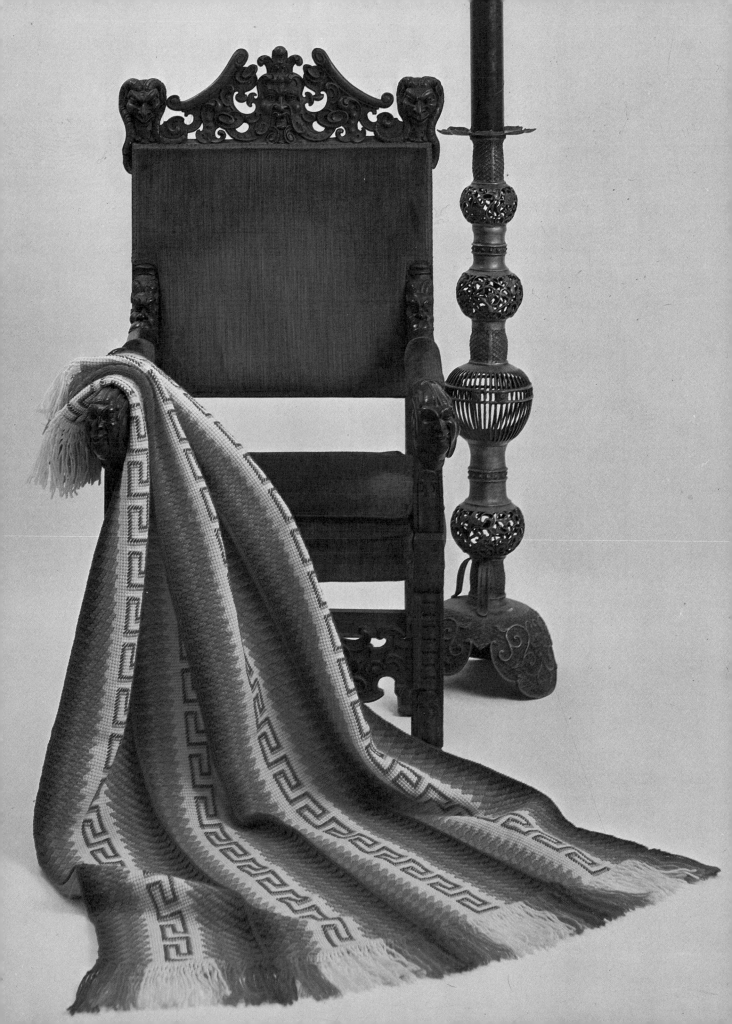

MEDLEY

The classic Greek key design is beautifully adapted to this afghan. It is shown opposite in Marvel Twist No. 137. The name, Medley, is derived from the harmonious blending of five shades of one basic color.

MATERIALS: Spinnerin Marvel Twist or Germantown Deluxe or Deluxe Knitting Worsted (4-oz.) 6 MC, 2 each A, B, C, D, E, shades running from light to dark.

EQUIPMENT: Afghan Hook; Size F or size to give gauge. Crochet Hook: Size F aluminum.

GAUGE: 6 sts = 1 inch; 9 rows = 2 inches.

FINISHED SIZE: Approx. 40″ x 62″.

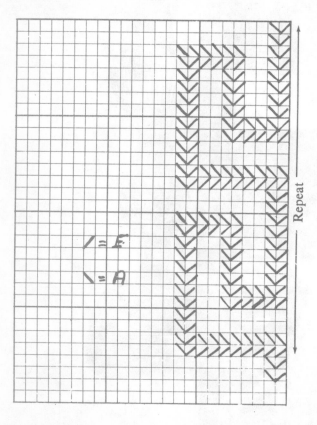

EMBROIDERY: Mark off center 10 sts on a panel. Greek Key design is a diagonal st (like a half cross st) worked over one afghan st. Chart shows how many sts to work over. For the right diagonal st use Color E (darkest color); for left diagonal st use Color A (lightest color). Embroider the other 3 panels the same.

PUFFED DOUBLE CROCHET (PDC) BORDER: Work with crochet hook.

To Work 1 PDC: Yo, insert hook from bottom to top under 3rd bar below in next row, draw yarn thru bar, yo and thru 1 loop, (yo and thru 2 loops) twice.

NOTE: First 3 rows of **PDC's** are worked under bars of afghan panels. Following rows are worked under bars formed by **PDC's.**

First Side—Row 1: With right side of first panel facing, join A (lightest shade) at bound-off row. On side edge, work 1 sc in end of each of 4 rows, *work **PDC** under 3rd bar below in next row, skip row behind **PDC,** 1 sc in end of each of next 3 rows; rep from *, ending 1 sc in each of last 2 rows. Fasten off.

Row 2: With same color and working in **back** loop of each sc, work 1 sc in each of first 3 sc of Row 1, ***PDC** in bar below next st (1 bar above **PDC** of last row), skip st behind **PDC,** 1 sc in each of next 3 sc; rep from * to end. Fasten off. **Row 3:** With same color and in **back** loops, work 1 sc in each of first 2 sc of last row, * **PDC** under bar below next st (1 bar above **PDC** of last row), skip st behind **PDC,** 1 sc in each of next 3 sc; rep from *, ending 1 sc in each of last 4 sc. Fasten off. **Row 4:** Join B (next shade). In **back** loops, work 1 sc in each of 4 sc, **PDC** under bar of first PDC of Row 1, * 1 sc in each of next 3 sc, **PDC** under bar of next **PDC** of Row 1; rep from *, ending sc in each of last 2 sc. Continue in this way, working 3 rows each of the five shades.

Second Side—Row 1: With right side of panel facing, join A at foundation chain. Working on side edge and in **back** loops only, work 1 sc in each of first 2 rows, * **PDC** under bar 4 rows below (**not 3 rows as on first side**), 1 sc in each of 3 rows; rep from *, ending 1 sc in each of last 4 rows. Fasten off. Complete this side to correspond to first side. Work borders on all panels.

JOINING: Hold 2 panels with right sides tog and foundation chains at lower edge. With E (darkest shade) and thru back loops of last row on each panel, work 1 row sl sts from lower edge to bound off edge. Fasten off. Steam seams.

FRINGE: Wind all colors over an 8-inch cardboard. Cut one end. Using 1 strand of color to match crochet, knot fringe (see page 211) in every sc along ends. Tie for Triple Knot Fringe.

GLISSANDO

The pattern in this afghan "glides" in and out as does your afghan hook as you deftly work the design. You will be rewarded with an afghan of heirloom quality.

The afghan shown opposite was worked in Marvel Twist, Nos. 118, 157, 100.

MATERIALS: Spinnerin Marvel Twist Wash Fit® or Deluxe Knitting Worsted or Germantown Deluxe (4-oz.) 5 White (MC), 4 Black, 3 Copper Rose.

EQUIPMENT: Afghan Hook: 14-inch Size I or size to give gauge.
Crochet Hook: Size H aluminum.

GAUGE: 4 sts = 1 inch; 3 rows = 1 inch.

FINISHED SIZE: Approx. 46″ x 67″.

PATTERN STITCH: Afghan st with worked-in pattern. See page 208.

With Black, chain 185 to measure approx 46 inches. Work 1 row basic afghan st. Then follow Chart, working 7 repeats of 29 rows. Work 1 row and bind off with Black.

FINISHING: With Black, from right side, work 1 row sc around afghan, spacing sts to keep edges flat and working 3 sc at each corner. Weave in ends. Block. Trim with giant tassel at each corner.

To Make a Tassel

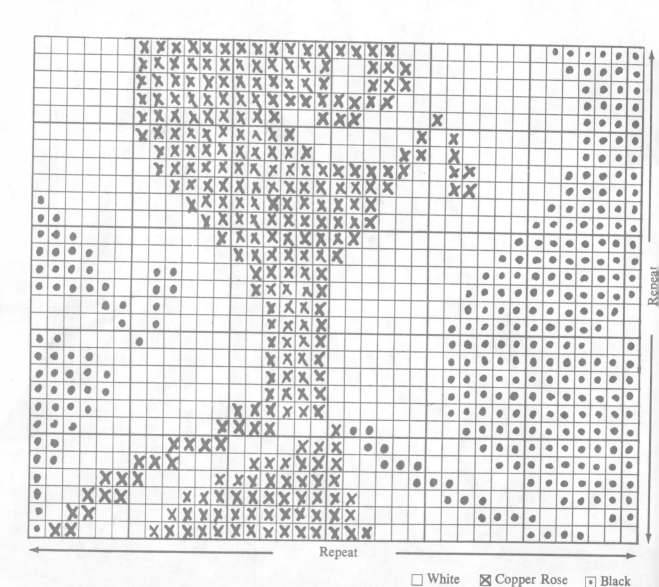

Repeat

□ White   ☒ Copper Rose   ⊡ Black

CAPRICE

Building blocks add charm to this afghan—a colorful addition to a child's room. The blocks are worked in as you crochet. It is shown on page 213 in Marvel Twist No. 131.

MATERIALS: Spinnerin Marvel Twist or Germantown Deluxe or Deluxe Knitting Worsted (4-oz.) 5 skeins MC and 1 skein each red, pink, hot pink, light green, medium green, dark green, light yellow, yellow, orange, white and a few yards of black.

EQUIPMENT: Afghan Hook: 14-inch Size K. **Crochet Hook:** Size J aluminum.

GAUGE: 7 sts = 2 inches; 5 rows = 2 inches.

Note: It is of the utmost importance that you work to the exact gauge given. Use a larger or smaller hook to adjust gauge if necessary. Otherwise afghan will not block to measurements given and the design will be out of proportion.

FINISHED SIZE: Approx. 41″ x 50″.

PATTERN: Afghan stitch with color pattern worked in as on chart. See page 208 for directions on changing colors.

AFGHAN: With main color (MC), chain 136 to measure approximately 39 inches. Entire afghan is 120 rows of afghan stitch. Beginning with the 45th row follow pattern on chart.

FINISHING: Weave in ends. With yellow, from right side, work 1 row sc around afghan, spacing stitches to keep edges flat and working 3 sc at each corner. Join with a slip stitch and fasten off. Work another row in orange the same way. Embroider mouth, whiskers and eyes in cat, and letters A, B, C as shown in photograph. Block.

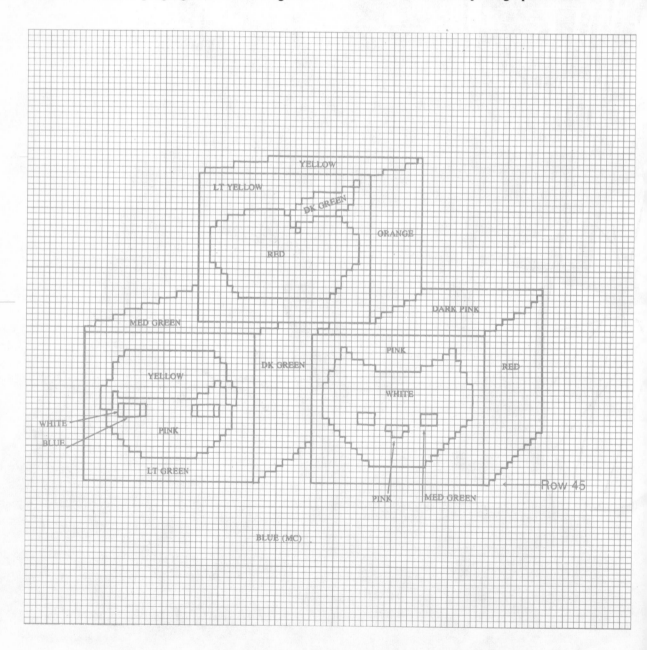

Boutique

Now that you have mastered a variety of needle-work techniques, a whole new world of creative delights lies before you. In this section of the book, we have gathered together a large number of items under the heading "boutique." All are fun to make as well as fun to wear or use, to sell at a bazaar or to give away.

Enjoy!

BAROQUE ACCESSORIES

Hats! Belts! Bags! All pictured on page 215 are crocheted using Spinnerin Baroque yarns in 1-oz. skeins. Baroque is worked to exact measurements, so be sure to change your hook size to get the gauge given for each pattern.

FINISHING: Use steam iron on wrong side to block. **NEVER** let iron come in direct contact with item. Flat pieces can be successfully blocked between towels.

MATERIALS

Item	Yarn (oz.)	Other Materials	Hook Size
Green Pill-Box	3		G
White Brimmed Hat	3		G
Tweed Cloche	2 brown, 1 white		H
Rust Hat	5 rust, 1 green		F & G
Gold Belt	1	buckle	F
Striped Belt	1 ea. red, blue, green		F
Corded Belt	1 pink		F
Granny Square Belt	1 ea. green, blue, white		F
Ring Belt	1 ea. green, white, rust	13 bone rings of 1⅛" diam 6 of ⅝" diam	F
Green Belt	1	buckle	G
Red/white Belt	1 ea. color	4 shank buttons ¾" diam	G
Braided Belt	1 ea. red, white, blue	2 metal rings 2½" diam	F
Blue Shoulder Tote	7		G
Drawstring Pouch	2 white, 1 pink, 1 green		F
Hot Pink Bag	6		H
Zipped Argyle Bag	7 black, 1 ea. red, yellow, white	12" zipper	F

(18 sc). **Rnd 3:** * 1 sc in each of next sc, 2 sc in next sc; rep from * around (24 sc). **RND 4:** * 2 sc in each of next 3 sc, 2 sc in next sc; rep from * around (30 sc). **Rnd 5:** * 1 sc in each of next 4 sc, 2 sc in next sc; rep from * around (36 sc). **Rnd 6:** * 1 sc in each of next 5 sc, 2 sc in next sc; rep from * around (42 sc). Continue to inc 6 sts in every rnd, having 1 st more between incs each time, until a total of 12 rnds and 78 sc. Join with sl st to first sc of last rnd. **Rnd 13:** Thru *back* loops only, work 1 sc in each sc, inc 2 sts in rnd. Join. **Rnd 14:** Ch 3, 1 dc in each of next 2 sc, sk 2 sc, * in next sc work (2 dc, ch 2, 2 dc) group (gr), sk 3 ch, 1 dc in each of next 3 sc, sk 2 ch; rep from * to last 3 sts, gr in next sc, sk last 2 sc, join with sl st to top of ch-3. **Rnd 15:** Ch 3, 1 dc in each of next 2 dc, gr in ch-2 sp of next gr, * 1 dc in each of next 3 dc, gr in ch-2 sp of next gr; rep from * around. Join. Rep Rnd 15 until total of 6 pat rnds. **BRIM (worked entirely in sc):** 1 sc in each dc and in each ch around. Join, ch 1. **Rnd 2:** Inc 1 sc in every 9th sc (90 sc). **Rnd 3:** Inc 1 sc in every 5th sc (108 sc). **Rnd 4:** Inc 1 sc in every 9th sc (120 sc). **Rnd 5:** 1 sc in each sc. **Rnd 6:** Inc in every 12th sc (130 sc). **Rnd 7:** 1 sc in each sc. **Rnd 8:** Inc in every 26th sc (135 sc). **Rnd 9:** 1 sc in each sc. Join with sl st and fasten off. **CORD:** Cut 4 strands 3½ yards in length. Make twisted cord and weave thru first row of brim. (See Index.)

PILL-BOX

GAUGE: 4 sc = 1 inch, 4 rnds = 1 inch

CROWN: Work same as white hat, ending with Rnd 12 and 78 sc. Join with sl st to first sc of rnd. **Rnd 13:** Ch 1 and thru *back* loops only, work 1 sc in each sc around. Join with sl st to first sc. **Rnd 14:** Ch 1 and thru *both* loops, work 1 sc in each sc around. Join with sl st to first sc. Rep last 2 rnds 8 times more. Work 3 rnds sc, join and fasten off.

TO FRINGE: When you worked the rnds thru the back loops, a definite line of single strand sts was formed. These are the sts to be fringed. When fringing, hold center of crown toward you and fold along line. Wrap yarn around a 2-inch cardboard and cut at one end, forming 4-inch strands. Fold 1 strand in half, insert hook under st, draw fold thru, draw cut ends thru fold and tighten knot under fringe.

TWEED CLOCHE

GAUGE: 3 dc = 1 inch, 5 rnds = 3 inches

Hat is worked with double yarn in dc, always working in back loop of sts. With 1 strand each A and B chain 4. Join with a sl st to form a ring. **Rnd 1:** Ch 2 (counts as 1 dc) work 7 dc in ring. 8 dc. Mark end of each rnd. **Rnd 2:** 2 dc in each dc. 16 dc. **Rnd 3:** * Dc in 1 dc, 2 in next dc; rep from * around. 24 dc. **Rnd 4:** * Dc in each of next 2 dc, 2 dc in next dc; rep from * around. 32 dc. Continue to inc 8 sts every rnd, having 1 st more between incs each rnd until there are 56 dc in rnd. Join with a sl st to first dc of last rnd. Cut B strand. Join a 2nd strand A. **Rnd 8:** Ch 3 (counts as 1 dc), dc in each of next 12 dc, 2 dc in next dc, * dc in each of next 13 dc, 2 dc in next dc; rep from * around. 4 incs. **Rnd 9:** Inc 4 sts evenly spaced. Join as before. Cut 1 strand A. Join 1 strand B. With A and B, inc 4 sts in each of next 2 rnds. With A and B, work 72 dc. Join. Cut B. Join 1 strand A. **Rnd 13:** Ch 3, dc in next st, 2 dc in next st, * dc in each of next 2 sts, 2 dc in next st; rep from * around. 100 dc. **Rnd 14:** Inc 4 sts evenly around. **Rnd 15:** Work 104 dc. Join, fasten off. Weave in ends and block.

HAT

GAUGE: 4 sc = 1 inch, 4 rnds = 1 inch

CROWN: With G hook, chain 4. Join with sl st to form a ring. Work 6 sc in ring. Mark beg of rnds, do not join at end of rnds. **Rnd 1:** Work 2 sc in each sc (12 sc). **Rnd 2:** * 1 sc in next sc, 2 sc in next sc; rep from * around

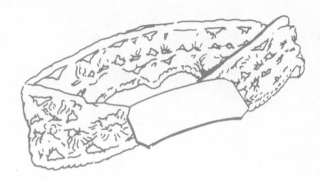

BELT

SIZE: Finished width 3 inches. Lengthwise stripe at center is worked first, then shells are worked around.

GAUGE: 4 groups (grs) = 3 inches in length

Chain 6 (narrow end). **Row 1:** In 6th ch from hook work (1 dc, ch 2, 1 dc). Ch 5, turn. **Row 2:** Under ch-2 work (1 dc, ch 2, 1 dc) gr. Ch 5, turn. Rep Row 2 to desired length. The total number of groups must be a multiple of 4 plus 3. Do not turn. **Rnd 1:** * In next ch-5 lp work (4 dc, ch 1, 4 dc) shell; rep from *, ending with shell in last ch-5 lp on side, work a gr in gr to the left, 4 dc under first ch-5 on other side, shell in each ch-5 lp, ending 4 dc in last lp. Ch 1, turn. **Rnd 2:** 1 sc in first dc, * ch 5, 1 sc in sp at center of next shell; rep from *, ending 1 sc in sp of last shell, ch 5, sk 7 dc, 1 sc in each of next 2 dc, 1 sc in ch-2 sp, 1 sc in each of next 5 dc, 1 sc in shell, ch 5 and work to correspond to other side, ending 1 sc in center of last shell, 1 sc in each of next 5 dc, 1 sc in next sp. Join with sl st to first sc. Ch 1, turn. **Rnd 3:** 1 sc in each sc and in each ch around. Join and fasten off. Weave in ends and block. Fasten with buckle, or as desired.

HAT

GAUGE: F hook, single strand—4 sts, 5 rows = 1 inch
G hook, double strand—3 sts, 4 rows = 1 inch

With F hook and single strand, beg at center crown, chain 4. Join with sl st to form a ring. **Rnd 1:** 7 sc in ring. Mark to indicate end of all rnds and do not join. **Rnd 2:** 2 sc in each st. **Rnd 3:** * Sc in next st, 2 sc in next st; rep from * around (7 incs in rnd). Inc 7 sts in each rnd (do not inc directly over previous incs) until 5½ inches in diameter. Work 2 rnds even. **Next Rnd:** Inc 7 sts, evenly spaced. Work even until 5½ inches from center. Sl st in next st.

BRIM—Rnd 1: Working thru *front* lps only, 1 sc in each st. Join 2nd strand and work with 2 strands and G hook. **Rnds 2 and 3:** Work sc thru *both* lps. **Rnd 4:** Inc 14 sts around, evenly spaced. **Rnd 5:** Sc in each st. Place a marker after last st to indicate center back. **First Short Row:** Work around to within 4 inches of center back, sl st in next st, turn. **2nd Short Row:** Sk sl st, work sl st thru *back* lp only of next 5 sts, sc thru both lps to within 4 inches of center back, sl st in next st, turn. **Rnd 6:** Sk the sl st, work sl st thru *back* lp only of next 5 sts, sc thru both lps to sl sts of previous row, working over the sl sts work sc in next 5 sts of sc row below, sc to end. Do not turn. **Rnd 7:** Sc to sl sts of previous rnd, working over the sl sts, work sc in next 5 sts of sc row below, sc to end. **Rnd 8:** Inc 1 st in each st around. **Next Row:** Sc to within 3 inches of center back, sl st in next st, turn. **Next Row:** Sk the sl st, work sl st thru *back* lp only of next 5 sts, sc thru both lps to within 3 inches of center back, sl st in next st, turn. **Rnd 9:** Rep Rnd 3. **Rnd 10:** Sc to sl sts of previous row, work over sl sts as before, inc 1 st in every 5th st to within 3 inches of center back, sc to end. **Rnds 11 and 12:** Sc in each st around. Sl st in next st and fasten off. Weave in ends.

FINISHING: Block brim lightly.

TRIM: With G hook and single strand CC, chain 4. **Row 1:** In 4th ch from hook work (yo, draw up lp, yo and thru 2 lps) 4 times, yo and thru 5 lps. Ch 4, do not turn. Rep Row 1 to desired length, join ends and fasten off. Tack in place around hat as desired.

BELT

GAUGE: Width = 1¼ inch

Chain 4. Join with sl st to form a ring. **Row 1:** Ch 3, 3 dc in ring, ch 2, 4 dc in ring. Ch 3, turn. **Row 2:** 3 dc under ch-2, ch 2, 3 dc under same ch-2, 1 dc in top of turning ch. Ch 3, turn, Rep Row 2 for pat and work to desired length. Fasten off. Sew buckle at one end, bringing tongue thru belt and tacking end on wrong side. Block lightly.

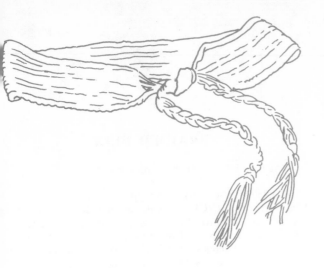

in same sp (corner), ch 1: * 3 dc in next sp, ch 1, 3 dc in same sp (corner), ch 1; rep from * twice, join with a sl st to top of ch-2. Fasten off. **Rnd 3:** Join C in ch-1 sp of any corner, 2 sc in same sp, * sc in each dc and ch-1 sp to next corner, 3 sc in corner sp; rep from * ending sc in same sp as joining. Join to first sc. **Rnd 4:** Ch 1, 2 sc in same st, sc in each sc, 3 sc in each corner sc, ending sc in same st with 2 sc. Join, fasten off. Make number of motifs for length desired.

FINISHING: Taking up back loop only of sc, overcast motifs tog. Fasten with hooks and eyes or as desired.

STRIPED BELT

GAUGE: 4 sc = 1 inch, 5 rows = 1 inch

Every row is worked from the same side in the following color sequence: Red, Blue, Green, Blue, Red, Green, Blue, Green; rep first 5 colors. Make a sl knot 20 inches from end of Red, insert hook and make a chain of desired length (allowing for belt to tie at front) and cut yarn 20 inches from hook, drawing cut end thru lp. **Row 1:** Make a sl knot 20 inches from end of same color, insert hook in loop and in first ch of original ch, draw yarn thru, yo and thru 2 lps, 1 sc in next and in each ch to end. Cut yarn and fasten off as before. **Row 2:** Make knot as before in next color, insert hook in lp and thru *back* lp of first sc of last row, draw yarn thru, yo and thru 2 lps, 1 sc thru *back* lp of next and each sc to end. Cut and fasten off as before. Rep Row 2, following color sequence and ending with Red. Cut and fasten off. **Last Row:** Make sl knot in Red, *turn work,* join as before in *front* loop of *last sc* of *last row,* 1 sc thru *front* lp of next and each sc to end. Cut and fasten off as before. **Braided Tie:** Divide strands at one end into 3 groups of 5 strands and braid, beg braid about 1 inch from end of belt and ending about 4 inches from cut ends. Tie knot to hold and trim ends evenly. Make other braid the same. Block.

BELT

SIZE: Length without ties 24(27–29) inches.

GAUGE: 4 dc = 1 inch

Chain 147(156–165) to measure approx 34(37–39) inches. **Foundation Row:** 1 dc in 4th ch from hook and in each to end, ch 42 for other tie; 1 dc in 4th ch from hook and in each ch. Join with sl st to next foundation ch. Do not turn. **Row 1:** Ch 3, 1 dc in each of next 5 foundation chs, * ch 3, sk 3 chs, 1 dc in each of next 6 chs; rep from * until there are 12(13–14) 6-dc grs. Turn. **Row 2:** Ch 4 (count as first tr), leaving the last lp of each tr on hook, work 1 tr in each of next 2 dc, yo and thru 3 lps (3-tr cluster), ch 5, 3-tr cluster over next 3 dc, * ch 5, 1 sc under ch-3, (ch 5, 3-tr cluster over next 3 dc) twice; rep from *, ending with 3-tr cluster over last 2 dc and in top of turning ch. Ch 1, turn. **Row 3:** Sl st in top of cluster, sl st in first lp; Ch 3, in same lp work 11 dc, * ch 3, sk next 2 lps, 12 dc in next lp; rep from * to end. Join and fasten off. Weave in ends and block.

GRANNY SQUARE

GAUGE: Each Motif = 2½ inches square

MOTIFS: With A ch 3. Join with a sl st to form a ring. **Rnd 1:** Ch 2 (counts as 1 dc), 2 dc in ring, ch 1 (3 dc in ring, ch 1) 3 times. Join with a sl st to top of ch-2. Fasten off. **Rnd 2:** Join B in any ch-1 sp, ch 2, 2 dc, ch 1, 3 dc

RING BELT

Large Rings—Make 4 Rust, 3 Green, 6 White as follows: **Rnd 1:** Work 28 sc tightly over ring, join with a sl st to first sc. **Rnd 2:** Ch 3, turn. Sk first sc, dc in next 27 sc, join with a sl st to top of ch 3, fasten off. Sew in ends. **Small rings**—2 each color: **Rnd 1:** Work 18 sc tightly over ring, join with a sl st to first sc. Fasten off. Sew in ends.

CORDS: Cut 3 strands of each color, 3½ yards long. Knot strands tog 9 inches from one end. Holding the 3 strands of each color tog, braid to within 9 inches of opposite ends and knot.

FINISHING: Using W, overcast rings tog across 6 sts, catching back lps only, in following color sequence; R, (W, G, W, R) 3 times.

TO LACE: Fold cord having one end slightly longer than other. Insert tied ends from wrong side thru end ring, leaving a 2″ loop extending from under ring, and sew securely. Weave cord over 2 rings, then under 2 rings ending with cord extending over outer edge of last ring. Smooth cord and adjust so belt is flat, then tack cord securely at end of belt. Trim cut ends so that all strands of one color are even, but colors are of slightly different length. Join to 3 sc of ring of matching color and weave in ends. Tack cord in place on wrong side where rings meet. Tie by pulling one end of cord thru loop.

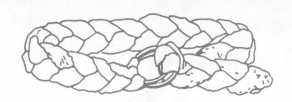

BRAIDED BELT

GAUGE: 5 dc = 1 inch, 2 rows = 1 inch

BELT: With A, work 5 sc tightly over both rings held tog, turn. **Row 1:** Ch 3 (counts as first dc), sk first sc, dc in next 4 sc, turn. **Row 2:** Ch 3, dc in next 3 dc, dc in top of turning ch. Rep Row 2 to 6 inches more than desired finished length. Beg each of other 2 colors over rings in same way, work to same length.

FINISHING: Braid the 3 strips loosely, taking care to keep strips flat. At end, tack strips tog to form a point. Weave in ends and block.

CORDED BELT

With 3 strands yarn held tog, work a chain of desired length. Work a sl st loosely in 2nd ch from hook and each ch to end. Fasten off. **Tassels (Make 2):** Wrap yarn around a 5-inch cardboard 10 times. Cut yarn at 1 end. Fold 8 strands in half, tying tog at top with other 2 strands. Wrap another strand several times tightly around folded strands ½ inch below fold, tie ends of the wrapped strand and draw to middle of tassel. Fasten a tassel to each end of belt.

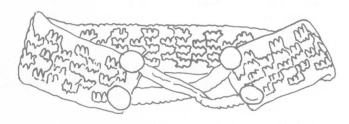

CHECKED BELT

GAUGE: 5 dc = 1 inch, Width = 2¼ inches

With R make a chain approx 4 inches less than desired length that is a multiple of 6 plus 4. **Row 1:** Dc in 3rd ch from hook, dc in next ch (working off last 2 lps with B), * 1 dc in each of next 3 ch (working off last 2 lps of last dc with A), 1 dc in each of next 3 ch (working off last 2 lps of last dc with B); rep from * to end. Ch 2, turn. **Row 2 (always change colors as in Row 1):** 1 dc in each of next 2 dc, * 1 A dc in each of next 3 dc, 1 B dc in each of next 3 dc; rep from * to end, ending with last B dc in top of turning ch. Work 3 more rows as Row 2, alternating colors. Ch 1, do not turn. **Edge:** 10 sc along narrow end, 3 sc in corner, sc in each st along edge, 3 sc in corner, 10 sc along narrow end, 3 sc in corner, sc in each st along edge. Join with sl st to first sc and fasten off.

FINISHING: Weave in ends. Block lightly. Sew button at each corner.

CLOSING BANDS (Make 2): Ch 24, 1 sc in 7th ch from hook and in each ch to end. Ch 6 and work 18 sc along other side of ch. Join and fasten off. Block. Close belt by buttoning bands to cross (top button on one end to lower button on opposite end). Tack bands on wrong side where they cross.

DRAW STRING POUCH

SIZE: Approx 10 x 12 inches

GAUGE: 2 pats (2 shells and 2 sc) = 3 inches,
7 rnds = 3 inches

Color Sequence by Rounds: * 3 B, 3 A, 3 C, 4 A. With B, chain 84 to measure approx 21 inches. Join with a sl st to form a ring, taking care not to twist chain. **Rnd 1:** Ch 3 (counts as 1 dc), 4 dc in same place with joining, sk 2 ch, sc in next ch, sk 2 ch, * 5 dc in next ch (shell), sk 2 ch, sc in next ch, sk 2 ch; rep from * around. Join with a sl st to top of ch-3, sl st in each of next 2 dc. **Rnd 2:** Ch 1, sc in same st with last sl st, shell in next sc, * sc in center dc of next shell; shell in next sc; rep from * around. Join with a sl st to first sc. Draw next color thru loop on hook. Cut other color. **Rnd 3:** Ch 3, 4 dc in same st with joining, sc in center dc of next shell, * shell in next sc, sc in center dc of next shell; rep from * around. Join, sl st in each of next 2 dc. Work as in rnds 2 and 3 in color sequence until there are 23 rnds from beg, ending with 1 rnd A. Join. **Beading Rnd:** Ch 3, dc in same place with joining, * sk 2 dc, shell in next dc, sk 2 dc, sc in next dc; rep from * around. Join, draw B thru lp. Work 2 more rnds, fasten off. **Draw Strings (make 2):** With A, chain 28 inches. Work sl st in 2nd and each ch to end, fasten off. Fold with 7 shells front and back. Overcast foundation chain tog for lower edge. Beg at side weave drawstring over and under 3 dc of beading row. Weave other drawstring from opposite side over and under same dc. **Trim:** Join B at 1 end of drawstring, ch 3, work 4 dc in same place, ch 3, turn. Work sc in first dc, (ch 3, sc in next dc) 4 times. Fasten off. Trim other 3 drawstring ends in same way.

BAG

SIZE: Approx 13 x 15 inches without fringe

GAUGE: 7 sc = 2 inches, 9 sc rnds = 2 inches

Beg at top of bag, chain 90 to measure 26 inches. Join with a sl st to first ch to form a ring. **Foundation Rnd:** Ch 1, work sc in same ch with joining and in each ch around. Join with a sl st to first sc. **Rnd 1:** Ch 3; in same sc with joining, work sc, ch 2, dc; sk 2 sc; * in next sc,

work dc, sc, ch 2, dc, (shell); sk 2 sc; rep from * around, join with a sl st to top of ch-3, 30 shells. **Rnd 2:** Ch 3, in sp between last shell and first shell of Rnd 1, work sc, ch 2 and dc; * shell in sp between next 2 shells; rep from * around, join with sl st to top of ch-3. **Rnd 3:** Ch 1; draw up a ½-inch lp in sp between last shell and first shell of Rnd 2, yo and thru 2 lps, (long sc—lsc); ch 3, * work lsc in next sp between shells, ch 3; rep from * around, join with a sl st to top of first lsc. **Rnd 4:** Ch 1, sc in first lsc, 2 sc in ch-3 sp, * sc in next lsc, 2 sc in next ch-3 sp; rep from * around, join. 90 sc. **Rnds 5 thru 10:** Ch 1, sc in each sc, join with a sl st at end of each rnd. Rep from Rnd 1 four times. Fasten off.

FINISHING: Fold and overcast at lower edge. Join yarn at side of lower edge. **Row 1:** Work shell pat across lower edge, skipping 2 sts between shells, ch 1, turn. **Row 2:** Sc in each st. Fasten off.

FRINGE: Wind yarn around a 6-inch cardboard. Cut yarn at 1 end. Fold 12 strands in half, insert hook in sp between first 2 shells on lower edge, draw fold thru, draw ends thru fold, pull to tighten knot. Knot fringe in sps between shells and in ch-2 sp of first and last shells. **Drawstring:** With 4 strands yarn, work 2 chains of about 40 inches each, or desired length. Beg at a side edge, weave 1 chain thru first rnd of lsc, weave or sew ends tog; beg at opposite side, weave other chain thru same rnd and join ends as before.

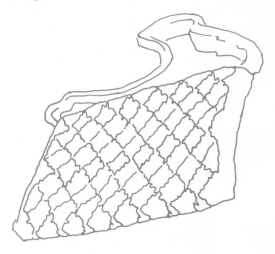

ZIPPED ARGYLE BAG

GAUGE: 9 dc = 2 inches, 8 rows = 3 inches

Note: Carry color not in use loosely across back of work. When changing colors, draw next color to be used thru last 2 lps of last dc.

FRONT AND BASE: With B, chain 58 to measure 13½ inches. **Foundation Row (wrong side):** Dc in 3rd ch from hook (the 2 skipped ch counts as 1 dc), dc in each ch to end, turn. 57 dc. **Row 1:** Ch 2, draw R thru lp on hook, dc in each of next 7 dc, working off last 2 lps of last dc with B, (dc in next dc, working off last 2 lps with R; dc in each of next 7 dc, working off last 2 lps with B) 6 times, dc in top of turning ch with B. Turn. **Row 2:** Ch 3, 1 dc in next dc, working off last 2 lps with R, * dc in each of next 5 dc, working off last 2 lps with B; dc in each of next 3 dc, working off last 2 lps with R; rep from * ending with B and dc in last dc, dc in top of turning ch, turn. **Row 3:** Ch 2, dc in each of next 2 dc working off last 2 lps with R; * dc in each of next 3 dc working off last 2 lps with B; dc in each of next 5 dc working off last 2 lps with R; rep from * ending with 3 B sts. Beg with Row 4 on chart and work until 40 rows are complete. Last row will be a repeat of Chart Row 8. **BACK:** With B only, continue working dc in each dc for 35 rows. Fasten off.

GUSSETS AND SHOULDER STRAP: With B, Ch 11 to measure 2½ inches. Dc in 3rd ch from hook and in each ch to end. 9 dc. Turn. Row 2: Ch 2, dc in each of next 7 dc, dc in top of turning ch. Rep Row 2 to approx 60 inches from beg. Fasten off.

FINISHING: Pin each end of strip along the last 5 pat rows (the base) of bag; pin edges of strip to front and back of bag forming gussets. Shoulder strap remains free. With B from right side, work sc on all pinned edges, working thru double thickness. Insert a 2-inch wide piece of belting or heavy cardboard in base of bag, line if desired. Sew in zipper to close.

SHOULDER TOTE

SIZE: Approx 12 x 14 inches
GAUGE: 4 sts = 1 inch, 6 rows = 1 inch

FRONT: Chain 48 to measure approx 12 inches. **Foundation Row:** 1 sc in 2nd ch from hook and in each ch to end. Ch 1, turn. **Row 1:** Sc in first and in each sc. Ch 1, turn. **Row 2:** Sc in each of first 3 sc, * 1 dc *around* next sc 2 rows below (post dc), sk next sc (behind post dc), 1 sc in each of next 3 sc; rep from * to end. Ch 1, turn. **Rows 3, 5 and 7:** Sc in first and in each st to end. Ch 1, turn. **Row 4:** Sc in each of first 4 sc, * dc *around* post dc below, sk next sc, sc in each of next 3 sc; rep from *, ending sk next sc, sc in each of last 2 sc. Ch 1, turn. **Row 6:** Sc in first sc, dc *around* post of next sc 2 rows below, * sk next sc, sc in each of next 3 sc, dc around post dc below; rep from *, ending sk 1 sc, sc in last sc. Ch 1, turn. **Row 8:** Sc in each of first 2 sc, * dc around post dc below, sk next sc, sc in each of next 3 sc; rep from *, ending sk 1 sc, sc in each of last 4 sc. Ch 1, turn. Rep from Row 1 for pat and work until a total of 77 rows, ending with a post dc row. Ch 1, do not turn. Work in sc along side, spacing sts to keep edge flat, 3 sc in lower corner, sc in each ch along lower edge, 3 sc in corner, sc along other side, being sure to have the same number of sts as on first side, 3 sc in corner, sc in each sc across top, ending with 3 sc in corner. Join with sl st to first sc, fasten off.

BACK: Work same as front for a total of 103 rows, working sc around all 4 sides as on front.

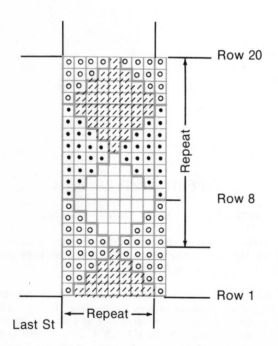

Row 20

Repeat

Row 8

Row 1

← Repeat →

Last St

☒ RED   ☐ WHITE   ☺ YELLOW   ◉ BLACK

STRAP: Leaving about 6 inches (for sewing), chain 108, to measure approx 27 inches. Work sc in 2nd ch from hook and in each ch to end. Ch 1, turn. Sc in first sc and in each sc. Fasten off, leaving a 6 inch end.

FINISHING: Pin front to back, right sides out and lower edges together. Join yarn at top corner of front and work with front toward you. Insert hook under single inner strand of first st on front and under single inner strand of matching st on back, draw yarn thru, ch 1, * insert hook thru next sts in same manner, draw yarn thru, yo and thru 2 loops (sc); rep from * around entire bag. Fasten off at opposite corner of front. Sew ends of strap securely at each side, across top of seam sts.

PILLOWS

Pillows are continually in fashion for home decor. Those that follow are either crocheted or knitted or done in needlepoint. The designs may be worked in or embroidered. There is also a variety of choices as to size and shape and style as well as the method of making.

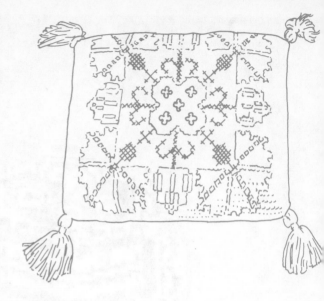

EMBROIDERED PILLOW

SIZE: 16" x 16".

MATERIALS: Spinnerin Deluxe Knitting Worsted or Germantown Deluxe or Marvel Twist (4-oz. skeins) 4 MC and 1 each A, B and C. Foam rubber pillow 16" x 16", about 3" deep at center, edges beveled.

EQUIPMENT: Afghan Hook Size J or size to give gauge.

GAUGE: 7 sts = 2 inches, 5 rows = 2 inches.

Pillow top and bottom are worked in afghan st; design is worked in cross-stitch when pieces are complete. See pages 207 and 208 for method.

PILLOW COVER (Make 2 pieces): With 2 strand MC, chain 58 to measure 16½ inches. Work afghan st for 43 rows. Bind off. Block to 17 inches square.

EMBROIDERY: Following Chart, work cross st, beg first row on first row of afghan st and completing the 22 charted rows. Then turn Chart upside down and, omitting Row 22, work to Row 1.

TASSELS (Make 4): Lay 2 eight-inch strands MC at top of a 5-inch cardboard and wrap MC 25 times around cardboard. Tie strands at top tightly around wrapped yarn, slip from cardboard and cut yarn at point opposite tie. Wind a strand MC around tassel 1 inch from top and knot, draw ends into center of tassel.

FINISHING: With wrong sides of pillow cover tog, overcast 3 edges, insert pillow, sew 4th edge.

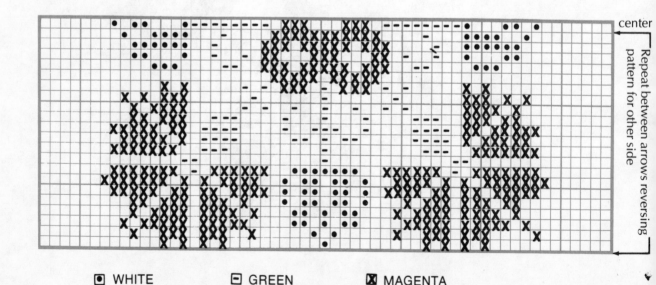

center

Repeat between arrows reversing pattern for other side

⊡ WHITE   ⊟ GREEN   ⊠ MAGENTA

226

If design is to be embroidered in duplicate st, K 33rd row and mark for first chart row of embroidery. Continue St St for 78 rows more. Bind off.

EMBROIDERY: Following Chart, work duplicate st (See illustration page 228) beg on 37th st of marked row.

TAPESTRY PILLOW COVER

SIZE: 16″ x 16″.

MATERIALS: Spinnerin Deluxe Knitting Worsted or Germantown Deluxe or Marvel Twist (4-oz. skeins) 1 each MC and CC and small amounts of 2 shades of green and 2 shades of rose in Tapestry Yarn or Wintuk (2-oz. skeins) 2 each MC and CC and small amounts of 2 shades of green and 2 shades of rose in Tapestry Yarn. 16″ zipper.

EQUIPMENT: Knitting Needles No. 8 or size to give gauge. Crochet Hook Size F.

GAUGE: Stockinette Stitch: 9 sts = 2 inches, 6 rows = 1 inch. Pattern Stitch: 9 sts = 2 inches, 15 rows = 2 inches.

NOTE: Top of pillow is worked in Stockinette Stitch (K 1 row, P 1 row). Floral design can be knit in (using a separate bobbin of each color), or can be embroidered in duplicate stitch after pillow top is completed. The same Chart is used for either method. Back of pillow is worked in pattern stitch. Both front and back are shown, in different color combinations.

PILLOW TOP: With MC, cast on 80 sts. Work in St St (K 1 row, P 1 row) for 32 rows. **With Design Worked In—Next row—**Chart Row 1: Picking up color to be used under color previously used and twisting yarns to prevent holes in work, K 36 MC, 1 dark green, 6 MC, 1 dark green, 36 MC. Continue to follow Chart for 47 rows more. With MC, work 32 rows. Bind off.

PILLOW BACK: With MC, cast on 81 sts. P 1 row. When working pat given, carry color not in use loosely across back of work. **Row 1 (right side):** With CC, K 1,* yarn at *back* sl 1 as to P, K 1; rep from * to end. **Row 2:** With CC, P 1,* with yarn at *back* sl next 3 sts as to P, bring yarn to *front,* P 1; rep from * to end. **Row 3:** With MC, K 1,* P 1; K 1; rep from * to end. **Row 4:** With MC, P 1,* K 1, P 1; rep from * to end. **Row 5:** With CC, K 1,* yarn at *back* sl 1, insert right needle upward under CC loop of Row 2 and in next st on left needle, K this st, drawing needle under loop, sl 1, K 1; rep from * to end. **Row 6:** With CC and yarn at back when slipping sts, sl 2 *, P 1, sl 3; rep from *, ending last rep sl 2. **Row 7:** Rep Row 3. **Row 8:** Rep Row 4. Twist colors to form CC loop on right side. **Row 9:** With CC, * insert needle under loop and K next st as before, yarn at *back* sl 1, K 1, sl 1; rep from *, ending insert needle under last loop and next st, K as before. **Row 10:** Rep Row 2. Rep Rows 3 thru 10 sixteen times more, then rep Rows 3 thru 9 once. **Next row:** Rep Row 2, slipping sts with yarn at *front.* Rep Row 3 once. Bind off as to P.

FINISHING: Block pieces to 18 inches square. Join top and back. Holding right sides tog and beg at lower right corner of top, join MC and work sc with MC thru double thickness of 3 edges, working 80 sc on each edge and 3 sc on each corner. Work 80 sc on 4th edge of top (single thickness) and 80 sc on 4th edge of back (also single thickness). On top 4th edge (to cover zipper), work 3 rows of 1 sc in each sc with ch 1, turn, at end of first 2 rows; fasten off at end of 3rd. Sew in zipper. Tack ends of cover over ends of zipper tape.

Fringe: Wrap MC around a 5-inch cardboard. Cut yarn at 1 end. Fold 2 strands in half, insert crochet hook from back of pillow in center sc at corner, draw fold thru, draw ends thru fold and tighten knot. Knot fringe in every 2nd sc around. Knot CC fringe in same way at each side of corner and in each skipped sc around. With adjoining 2 strands of same color form double knot fringe. (See illustration).

DUPLICATE STITCH

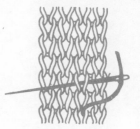

⊙ HUNTER

△ LIME

◎ RUST

⊟ CORAL

▲ PEACH

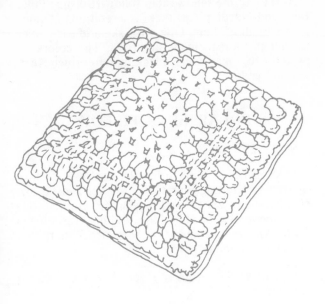

in corner work 2 hdc, ch 2, 2 hdc, (ch 1, 2 hdc in next sp) 4 times; rep from * twice, ch 1, work corner as before, ch 1, 2 hdc in next sp, ch 1, 1 hdc in last sp, join. 48 hdc. **Rnd 7:** Ch 3, work hdc pat around. 56 hdc. **Rnd 8:** Ch 2 instead of 3, then rep Rnd 7. 62 hdc. Draw A thru loop. Cut C. **Rnd 9:** Ch 2, then work popcorn rnd. 36 popcorns. Draw D thru loop. Cut A. **Rnd 10:** Ch 2, work hdc pat around. 80 hdc. Draw E thru loop. Cut D. **Rnd 11:** Rep Rnd 10. 88 hdc. Draw D thru loop. Cut E. **Rnd 12:** Ch 1, sc in each hdc and ch around, join with sl st to first sc. Fasten off.

FINISHING: Steam the 2 pieces lightly on wrong sides. With wrong sides tog and using D, overcast each pair of 3 edges tog, taking up back loop of each st. Insert pillow. Overcast 4th edges same as others.

FIVE-COLOR PILLOW

SIZE: 12″ x 12″.

MATERIALS: Spinnerin Homespun (4-oz. skeins) 1 skein each A, B, C, D and E. 12″ x 12″ foam rubber pillow, beveled edge.

EQUIPMENT: Crochet Hook Size K or size to give gauge.

GAUGE: 2 hdc and ch 1 = 1 inch, 2 rnds = 1 inch.

COVER (Make 2 pieces alike): With A, ch 4. Join with a sl st to form a ring for center. **Rnd 1:** * (Yo hook, insert hook in ring and draw up loop) 3 times, yo and thru 7 loops on hook, (popcorn), ch 2; rep from * 3 times, join with a sl st to top of first popcorn. Draw B thru loop on hook. Cut A. **Rnd 2:** With B, ch 2 (which counts as 1 hdc, Ch-1), (in next sp between 2 popcorns, work 2 hdc, ch 2, 2 hdc, ch 1) 3 times; in next sp, work 2 hdc, ch 2, 1 hdc; join with a sl st to first B ch, 4 corners. **Rnd 3:** Ch 2, 1 hdc in first ch-1 sp, (ch 1; in corner ch-2 sp, work 2 hdc, ch 2, 2 hdc; ch 1, 2 hdc in next ch-1 sp) 3 times, ch 1; in next ch-2 corner sp, work 2 hdc, ch 2, 2 hdc; ch 1; join with a sl st to top of ch-2. **Rnd 4:** Ch 3, 2 hdc in first sp, * ch 1; in corner sp, work 2 hdc, ch 2, 2 hdc; (ch 1, 2 hdc in next sp) twice; rep from * twice, ch 1, work in corner sp as before, ch 1, 1 hdc in next sp, join to 2nd ch of ch-3. 32 hdc. Draw A thru loop. Cut B. **Rnd 5:** Ch 2, popcorn in first sp, ch 1, popcorn in next sp,* ch 1; in corner sp, popcorn, ch 2, popcorn; (ch 1, popcorn in next sp) 3 times; rep from * twice, ch 1, work corner as before, ch 1, popcorn in next sp, ch 1, sl st in first A ch. Draw C thru loop. Cut A. **Rnd 6:** Ch 2, (2 hdc in next sp, ch 1) twice, * ch 1,

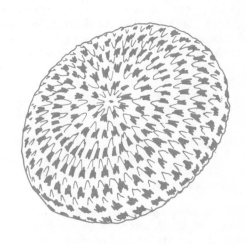

ROUND PILLOW

SIZE: 16″ in diameter; 3″ in depth.

MATERIALS: Spinnerin Deluxe Knitting Worsted or Germantown Deluxe or Marvel Twist (4-oz. skeins) 1 skein each A, B, C and D. Round Foam rubber pillow 16″ in diameter, 3″ in depth.

EQUIPMENT: Crochet Hook Size H or size to give gauge.

GAUGE: 2 dc and ch 2 = 1 inch, 7 rnds = 3 inches.

Work only 1 rnd of each color, A, B, C, D in rotation, cutting yarn at end of each rnd. **To Change Color and Join:** Insert hook in top of the ch-2 at beg of rnd, draw new color thru both the ch and the loop on hook (a sl st). Tighten and ch 2. Cut color just used, leaving an end long enough to weave in later. **THE CH2 AT BEG OF EACH RND IS NEVER COUNTED AS A DC.**

PILLOW COVER (Make 2 pieces): With A, ch 6, join with a sl st to first ch to form a ring for center. **Rnd 1:** With A, ch 2, work 10 dc in ring. Change color and join as above. **Rnd 2:** Dc in first dc, ch 2,* dc in next dc, ch 2; rep from * around. 10 dc. **Rnd 3:** Drawing loop up to ¾ inch, work 2 dc in first dc of Rnd 1 (2 dc group gr), ch 2, * 2 dc gr in next dc of Rnd 1, ch 2; rep from * around. 10 grs. **Rnd 4:** Work 2 dc, ch 2 in each dc of Rnd 2. **Rnd 5:** Work 2 dc gr between the dc's of first gr of Rnd 3, ch 3, * 2 dc between dc's of next gr, ch 3; rep from * around. **Rnd 6:** Work 3 dc between the dc's of first gr of Rnd 4 (3 dc gr), ch 3; * 3 dc gr between dc's of next gr of Rnd 4, ch 3; rep from * around. **Rnd 7:** Work same as Rnd 6, working between dc's of grs of Rnd 5. **Rnd 8:** Work 2 dc gr in first dc of Rnd 6, ch 2, sk next dc, 2 dc gr in next dc, ch 2, * 2 dc gr in first dc of next 3 dc gr, ch 2, 2 dc gr in 3rd dc of same group, ch 2; rep from * around. **Rnd 9:** Work 2 dc gr in first ch-3 loop of Rnd 7, ch 2, 2 dc gr in center of next gr of Rnd 7, ch 2, * 2 dc gr in next ch-3 loop, ch 2, 2 dc gr in center of next gr, ch 2; rep from * around. **Rnd 10:** Working into Rnd 8, work 3 dc grs with ch 2 between grs as in Rnd 6. **Rnd 11:** Working into Rnd 9, work same as Rnd 5. **Rnd 12:** Working into Rnd 10, work same as Rnd 8. **Rnd 13:** Work 2 dc gr in each ch-3 loop of Rnd 11. **Rnd 14:** Work 2 dc gr between dc's of first gr 2 rnds below, ch 2, * 2 dc gr between dc's of next gr, ch 2; rep from * around. Rep last rnd 5 times. **Rnds 20 thru 24:** Work as for Rnd 5. **Rnd 25:** With A, * sc in each of 2 dc of Rnd 24, 2 dc gr between dc's of next gr of Rnd 23; rep from * around. Join; fasten off.

FINISHING: Steam pieces lightly on wrong sides. With wrong sides tog, overcast edges (taking up both loops of each st) for half of circle, insert pillow, complete sewing.

NOTE: In the pillows that follow (Bolster, Polar Bear and Needlepoint) there is a repitition of some colors in all of them. One 4-oz. skein of each color is enough yarn to make all styles. The colors repeated are aqua, white, black, green, brown, rust, red and yellow.

POLAR BEAR PILLOW

SIZE: 29″ x 29″.

MATERIALS: Spinnerin Germantown Deluxe or Deluxe Knitting Worsted or Marvel Twist (4-oz. skeins) aqua, white, black, green, brown, rust. See note above. 30″ of 60″-wide white fake fur, muslin for backing crochet insertion, shredded foam rubber or desired stuffing.

EQUIPMENT: Afghan Hook Size I or size to give gauge.

GAUGE: 4 sts = 1 inch, 3 rows = 1 inch.
Insertion is worked in basic afghan stitch, following chart. See pages 207 and 208 for directions on working afghan stitch and changing colors.

TO BIND OFF: Slip st across row as follows — * Draw loop thru bar and thru loop on hook; rep from * across. Break yarn and draw thru last loop.

TO COUNT ROWS: Count only vertical bars. Each bar represents one complete row.

INSERTION: With A, chain 65 to measure 16 inches. Work afghan st, following Chart for colors, reading first row from right to left to center, then complete row by reading from left to right. Complete the 49 rows of Chart. Bind off. Weave in all ends. Block.

FINISHING: See diagrams 1 and 2. Mark exact center of fur fabric. Mark exact size of crochet insertion (centered) upon fur fabric, then mark edges ½ inch inside first markings (*toward center*) for seam allowances and cut on these lines. Clip into corners to first outline. Cut muslin larger than crochet insertion and lay under cut out space. Turn edges of fur fabric at first outline and sew to muslin. Sew insertion in place with blind stitch. With right sides tog, fold fur fabric so that selvages plus seam allowances meet at center back. Leaving center back open, seam other edges of pillow cover. Turn right side out, fill with desired pillow stuffing, sew back seam.

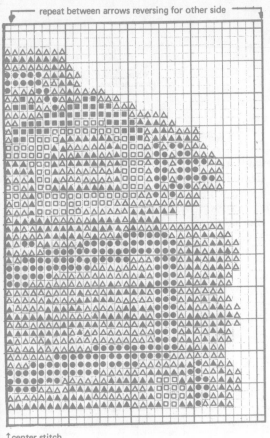

□ = Green
▲ = Black
△ = White
● = Red
■ = Brown

↑center stitch

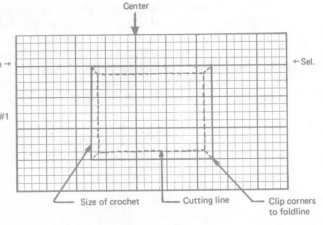

Center

age →

←Sel.

#1

— Size of crochet   — Cutting line   — Clip corners
                                        to foldline

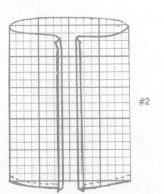

#2

BOLSTER

SIZE: Length: 36″, diameter: 8″.

MATERIALS: Deluxe Knitting Worsted or Germantown Deluxe or Marvel Twist (4-oz. skeins) 3 Maroon (MC). Additional colors (see note above): aqua, white. 2 buttons, 1½″ diameter. Bolster form 36″ long, 8″ diameter.

EQUIPMENT: Knitting Needles No. 7 or size to give gauge.

GAUGE: 5 sts = 1 inch, 6 rows = 1 inch.

231

■ = Blue
□ = White
Background is MC

NOTE: Chart is given for working designs. Use a separate ball or large bobbin of A or W for each motif. MC is carried across back of work. When changing colors, pick up color to be used under color previously used, twisting yarns to prevent holes. Take care to maintain gauge when carrying colors across back of work.

COVER: With MC, cast on 175 sts. P 1 row. Working St St (K 1 row, P 1 row), follow Chart, repeating the 18 charted rows 8 times, then repeating first 15 rows once more. P 1 row. Bind off. Sew in ends.

SIDE PIECES (Make 2): With MC, cast on 132 sts. P 1 row. **First dec row:** K 11, sl 1 as to P, K 1, psso,* K 1, K 2 tog, K 16, sl 1, K 1, psso; rep from * 4 times, K 1, K 2 tog, K 11. 12 decs. P 1 row. K1 row. P 1 row. **2nd dec row:** K 10, sl 1, K 1, psso, * K 1, K 2 tog, K 14, sl 1, K 1, psso; rep from * 4 times, K 1, K 2 tog, K 10. Continue in this way, dec 12 sts every 4th row, having 1 st less before first and after last dec and 2 sts less between other decs until there are 60 sts in last dec row. P 1 row. Break yarn, leaving an 8-inch end. Thread end into tapestry needle, draw thru sts on knitting needle, pull tog tightly and fasten. Weave ends of rows tog, forming circular piece.

FINISHING: Steam cover and weave seam. Draw cover over bolster form and pin ends to ends of form. Pin end pieces to edges of cover and sew neatly in place.

Button Covers (Make 2): With MC, cast on 12. Work St St for 1½ inches. Bind off. Place button in center of piece. Draw edges of piece tog at back of button. Sew a button to center of each side piece.

FOR WORKING NEEDLEPOINT PILLOWS

HALF CROSS STITCH MUST BE USED, by either Method A or Method B as shown. Cut length of yarn to measure, approximately 48 inches and use double.

Method A: Starting at upper left hand corner, draw needle and yarn through at 1, down at 2 and out at 3, down at 4 and out at 5. Continue in this manner across row, always starting each row at left hand side. Do not turn piece upside down and work back. Weave ends under preceding rows when starting and finishing a strand of yarn.

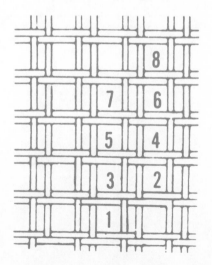

Method B: Starting at lower right hand corner, draw needle and yarn through at 1, down at 2 and out at 3, down at 4 and out at 5. Continue in this manner up row, always starting each row at lower right hand corner. Do not turn piece upside down and work back. Weave ends under preceding rows when starting and finishing a strand of yarn.

232

LARGE NEEDLEPOINT PILLOW

SIZE: Needlepoint 13″ x 13″.

MATERIALS: 14″ x 14″ canvas, 7 meshes to 1 inch. Finished pillow. Spinnerin Germantown Deluxe or Deluxe Knitting Worsted or Marvel Twist (4-oz. skeins) aqua, white, black, brown. See note page 230.

EQUIPMENT: Tapestry needle.
This pillow is made by working only the needlepoint, following the chart. The piece is then added to any type of pillow, as shown or as desired.

FINISHING: Dampen wrong side thoroughly. Stretch piece diagonally to straighten. Lay on a flat surface and tack down so that worked section measures 13 x 13 inches. Allow to dry. Clip corners of canvas to with ½-inch of needlepoint design. Turn unworked edges to wrong side and blind stitch in place on pillow.

□ = White
▲ = Aqua
● = Black
○ = Brown

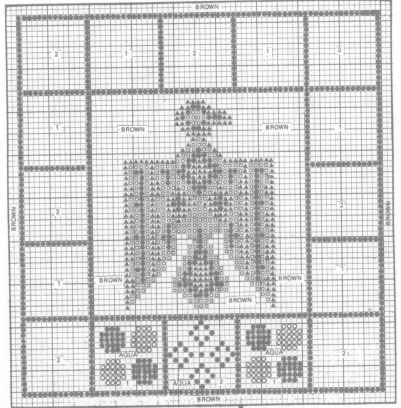

Repeat these instructions
alternately around all sides

233

SMALL NEEDLEPOINT PILLOW

SIZE: 12″ x 12″.

MATERIALS: 14″ x 14″ canvas, 7 meshes to 1 inch. 14″ square of desired fabric for back. Pillow form 12″ x 12″ x 3″. Spinnerin Germantown Deluxe or Deluxe Knitting Worsted or Marvel Twist (4-oz skeins) aqua, white, black, green, red, yellow. (See note page 230).

EQUIPMENT: Tapestry needle.

Following Chart, work needlepoint design on canvas.

FINISHING: Dampen wrong side thoroughly. Stretch piece diagonally to straighten. Lay on a flat surface and tack down so that worked section measures 12 x 12 inches. Allow to dry. Clip corners of canvas to with ½-inch of needlepoint design. Turn unworked edges to wrong side. Fold edges of fabric to wrong side to match size of needlepoint. With right sides together, overcast canvas and fabric along 3 sides. Turn right side out. Insert pillow form and blind stitch open sides together.

TASSELS (Make 3): Lay an 8-inch strand of a color at top of an 8-inch cardboard. Wrap same color 20 times around cardboard. Tie strand at top tightly around wrapped yarn. Cut yarn at other end. Wind a strand of same color around tassel 1 inch from top, knot and draw ends into center of tassel. Use colors and join to pillow as shown.

Across lower edge work from A to B, repeat from A to C. Along side edge work from B to D, repeat from B to E.

- ▨ RUST
- ⊡ BLACK
- ⊙ RED
- ▲ GREEN
- △ YELLOW
- ✕ WHITE
- ☐ AQUA

A   C   B

BASHFUL BOA

MATERIALS: 6 skeins Spinnerin Homespun (4-oz. skeins).

EQUIPMENT: Crochet Hook No. K, or size to give gauge.

GAUGE: 4 sts. = 3 inches.

Chain 75 loosely to measure approx. 1½ yards. In 6th chain from hook, work 12 tr (pulling loops to 1 inch); work 3 hdc in next and each chain to within 14 chains from end; work 3 sc in each of next 4 chains; work 2 sc in each of next 4 chains; work 1 sc in each of next 4 chains; sl st in each of last 2 chains. Fasten off and weave in end.

POMPON: Use remaining yarn and wrap over a 3-inch diameter pompom maker or 2 cardboard circles. Form head by tying pompom to first and last of the 12 dc's.

EYELASHES: Cut 8 slits in each piece of felt to within ⅛ inch of end, spread and glue to head as shown.

EYES: Glue paillette over eyelashes, then glue 2nd paillette, overlapping the first, then glue eye in place.

TONGUE: From CC, cut off two 2 inch pieces. Divide remainder into 3 equal lengths. Braid and tie each end securely with short pieces. Glue or sew in place as shown.

SIMPLE SIMON HATS
WITH
SLINKY SCARVES

MATERIALS	FOR HATS	FOR SCARVES
Spinnerin Marvel Twist or Germantown DeLuxe (4-oz. skeins)	1	2
OR Frostlon Petite (1-oz. balls)	4	6
NEEDLES:	No. 35	No. 17

GENERAL INSTRUCTIONS: Both hats are worked with 4 strands of yarn. Where necessary, divide the yarn being used into 4 separate balls before starting. Both scarves are worked with 2 strands of yarn, working from 2 skeins.

GOLD SEED STITCH SET
PATTERN STITCH:

Row 1: * K 1, P 1, rep from *, ending K 1. Rep Row 1 for pattern.

HAT

GAUGE: 3 sts = 2 inches
5 rows = 2 inches

With 4 strands of yarn, cast on 31 sts. Work 18 rows in pat. Cut yarn, leaving a long end. Draw end of yarn thru sts, pull tightly and fasten securely. Weave seam. Use remaining yarn to make one large pompon and sew to top of hat. Blocking not necessary.

SCARF

GAUGE: 2 sts = 1 inch
3 rows = 1 inch

With 2 strands of yarn, cast on 7 sts., Work 1 row, increasing to 21 sts by (K 1, P 1, K 1) in each st. Work pat for 216 rows. K 3 tog across row. Cut yarn, leaving an end. Draw yarn thru sts, pull tightly and fasten securely. Use remaining yarn for 2 large pompons and sew to ends as shown. Block to desired length.

RED POPCORN SET
PATTERN STITCH:

Row 1 (right side): Purl.
Row 2: * In next st (K 1, P 1, K 1), P 3 tog, rep from *.
Row 3: Purl.
Row 4: * P 3 tog, in next st (K 1, P 1, K 1), rep from *, Rep these 4 rows for pattern.

HAT

GAUGE: 6 sts = 7 inches
1 row = 1 inch

With 4 strands of yarn, cast on 32 sts. Work 18 rows in pat. Cut yarn, leaving a long end. Draw end of yarn thru sts, pull tightly and fasten securely. Weave seam. With 2 strands of yarn, make a 7 inch chain and fasten off. Draw chain thru top of hat and sew in place, having one end slightly longer than the other. Use remaining yarn for 2 pompons and sew to ends of chain. Blocking not necessary.

SCARF

GAUGE: 5 sts = 4 inches
3 rows = 2 inches

With 2 strands of yarn, cast on 20 sts. K 2 rows. **Keeping 2 sts at each side in garter st** (K every row) and center 16 sts in pat, work 172 rows (86 popcorn rows). P next 2 rows, then bind off as to P. With remaining yarn, make 8 pompons and sew 4 to each end as shown. Block to desired length.

NEEDLEPOINT BELT

SIZE: Width of belt, 1½″; buckle, 2⅜″ x 4⅜″.

MATERIALS: ¼ yard double mesh needlepoint canvas, 10 meshes to 1″; approx. 6 skeins tapestry yarn; tafetta for lining; 2″ x 4″ rectangle of heavy cardboard for buckle back; skirt-type hook and eye closure.

EQUIPMENT: Tapestry needle, fabric glue.

PREPARING CANVAS: To conserve canvas and thereby save money, the canvas is cut in two pieces and joined in the making. Cut canvas to measurement to insure having the amount required for the buckle. Cut 2 strips of canvas 3″ wide and 2″ longer than half the waist measurement. Cut a rectangle 4⅜″ x 6⅜″.

NEEDLEPOINT: Use checkerboard shadow stitch on page 93. For belt work boxes of 9 diagonal stitches; for buckle work boxes of 5 diagonal stitches. Start needlepoint at short end of long strip, allowing 1″ for hem on end and ¾″ top and bottom for turning. Work in rows of 3 checkerboard boxes until 1″ from end of long strip. Overlap second strip and work 1 row of boxes through 2 thicknesses of canvas. Cut away excess canvas and continue belt until desired length for waist. For buckle, work 8 smaller boxes to a row, centering buckle on canvas to allow for hem all around.

FINISHING: Block pieces. Turn under all excess canvas, mitering corners, pin and steam on wrong side. Allow to dry thoroughly. Glue all hems in place with fabric glue following manufacturer's directions. Cut pieces of tafetta (allowing for hems) for belt and buckle backing. Turn under and press hems. Insert cardboard backing under hem of buckle lining and glue lining securely to back of canvas; glue belt lining in place. Center finished buckle over one end of belt and sew in place through lining. Sew skirt hook on back of other end of buckle and hook eye on front of belt.

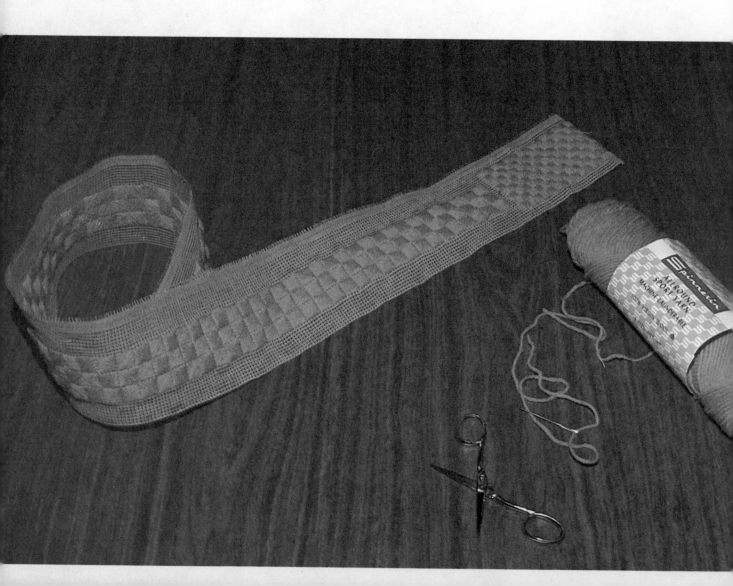

BAG BUDDIES

MATERIALS: Spinnerin Wintuk Featherton (2-oz.)

For Boy: 1 skein each MC, A and B.
2 small buttons.

For Girl: 1 skein each MC, A, B and C, few yards D.

For Frog: 2 skeins MC, 1 skein each A and B.

For Mouse: 1 skein each MC, A and B.

For All Styles: 2 button eyes.

EQUIPMENT: Size H crochet Hook or size to give gauge.

GAUGE: 7 sc = 2 inches, 7 rows = 2 inches.

NOTE: All pieces are worked with double yarn.

BOY

BODY and HEAD: With MC ch 4. Join with a sl st to form a ring. Ch 1. **Rnd 1:** Work 6 sc in ring. Mark end of rnds. **Rnd 2:** 2 sc in each sc. 12 sc. **Rnd 3:** * Sc in next sc, 2 sc in next sc; rep from * around. 18 sc. Continue to inc 6 sts each rnd, having 1 st more before inc each rnd, 3 times more. 36 sc. **Rnd 7:** * Sc in each of next 3 sc, 2 sc in next sc; rep from * around. 9 incs. 45 sc. **Rnd 8:** * Sc in each of next 4 sc, 2 sc in next sc; rep from * around. 54 sc. Join with sl st to first sc. **Rnd 9:** Thru back loop only, work 1 sc in each sc. **Rnds 10 thru 21:** Thru both loops, work sc in each sc. Join with a sl st, draw A thru loop on hook, break MC. With A work 13 rnds. Join with a sl st, fasten off. With B make a sl st knot in yarn. Holding yarn at inside of bag, insert hook from outside between 2 sc of last MC row and draw loop of sl st thru to outside, work sl st over each sc of this row. Fasten off.

HAT: With B, work same as body until 7 rnds are completed and 45 sts in rnd. **Rnd 8:** * Sc in each of next 8 sts, 2 sc in next st; rep from * around. 50 sc. **Rnd 9:** Thru back loop work sc in each sc. **Rnds 10 thru 14:** Thru both loops work sc in each sc. **Rnd 15:** Sc in each of next 9 sc, 2 sc in next sc. 55 sc. **Rnds 16 thru 19:** Sc in each sc. Ch 1, turn. **Visor:** Thru back loop only, sc in each of next 20 sc. Ch 1, turn. Work 3 rows of 1 sc in each sc. Ch 1, turn. **Last Rnd:** 2 sc in first sc, sc in each of 7 sc, 2 sc in each of next 4 sc, sc in each of next 7 sc, 2 sc on side edge, sc in each sc around lower edge, 2 sc on side edge of visor, sc in first sc of rnd. Join.

NOSE: With A ch 5. **Row 1:** Sc in 2nd ch from hook and each ch to end. 4 sc. Ch 1, turn. Work 7 rows of 1 sc in each sc. Ch 1, turn at end of each row. Work 1 row sc around all edges. Fold lengthwise. Thru double thickness, join by working sc in each st and on 1 side, leaving other side open. Stuff with cotton. Overcast open edges tog, leave end for sewing.

MOUTH: With MC chain 14. Fasten off, leaving an end for sewing.

HANDS (Make 2): With A work same as nose, working 10 rows instead of 7 rows sc.

FEET (Make 2): With B work same as hands. Sew buttons on body as shown to mark center front, on 4th and 8th rnds below A.

ARMS: Wrap double strand MC around an 8-inch cardboard 12 times. Cut at 1 end (24 strands). **Arms:** On 2nd row below A, mark 8th st at each side of button. Insert hook under marked st and draw cut ends of 8 strands thru st; (draw ends of 8 more strands thru next st toward back) twice. Pull all 48 cut ends to same length. Using 16 strands for each section, braid lightly for 4 inches. Wrap a piece of yarn tightly at end of braid to hold. Trim extra length about 1/2 inch from tie. Insert braid into hand and over cast open edges of hand tog catching braid. Rep for other arm.

LEGS: Wrap double strand MC around a 10-inch cardboard 15 times. Cut at 1 end forming 20-inch strands. Mark diameter of lower circle of bag. Using 10 strands draw thru 2nd, 4th and 6th row to right and left of center (as arms). Braid 5½ inches. Finish and insert in feet same as hands.

CORD (Make 2): With B, beg 3 inches from end of yarn make a chain 24 inches long. Fasten off. Cut yarn leaving 3-inch ends.

To Attach Cords to Bag and Hat: On last rnd of bag, mark each side. Draw end of a cord from wrong to right side at marker. Draw 2nd cord thru 1 st to left of first cord. Draw ends thru other side in same way. Knot ends at each side tog. Draw loop of both cords thru center top of hat, then tie knot 3 inches from top of cords.

FINISHING: Mark center front of head at 6th rnd from top. With eyes touching at markers, sew between 6th and 7th rnds. Center nose at eyes and sew in place 1 row below eyes. Sew mouth as shown.

GIRL

HEAD: With MC ch 4, and work 6 rnds as for Boy. 36 sc. **Rnd 7:** Sc in each of 2 sts, 2 sc in next st (sc in each of 5 sts, 2 sc in next st) 5 times, sc in each of 3 sts. 42 sc. **Rnd 8:** (Sc in each of 6 sts, 2 sc in next st) 6 times. 48 sc. **Rnd 9:** (Sc in each of 15 sts, 2 sc in next st) 3 times. 51 sc. **Rnd 10:** Thru *back* loop, work sc in each sc. Thru *both* loops work 15 sc rnds. Join, fasten off.

SKIRT: With right side facing, (open edge toward you), join A in front (single loop) of first st of 8th rnd. **Rnd 1:** Sc in front loop of each st. 51 sc. **Rnd 2:** (Sc in each of 2 sts, 2 sc in next st) 17 times. 68 sc. Work 2 rnds even. **Rnd 5:** (Sc in each of 7 sts, 2 sc in next st) 8 times, sc in each st to end. 76 sc. Work 3 rnds even. Join with a sl st

to first sc. **Last Rnd:** * Ch 3, sk 1 sc, sl st in next sc; rep from * around. Fasten off.

HAT: With C, ch 4. Join with a sl st to form a ring.
Rnd 1: Work 8 sc in ring.
Rnd 2: 2 sc in each st. 16 sc.
Rnd 3: (Sc in next st, 2 sc in next st) 8 times. 24 sc.
Rnd 4: (Sc in each of next 2 sc, 2 sc in next st) 8 times. 32 sc.
Rnd 5: Sc in next sc, 2 sc in next sc, (sc in each of next 3 sts, 2 sc in next sc) 7 times, sc in each of next 2 sc. 40 sc.
Rnd 6: (Sc in each of 7 sc, 2 sc in next sc) 5 times. 45 sc.
Rnd 7: Sc in each of next 4 sc, 2 sc in next sc, (sc in each of next 8 sc, 2 sc in next sc) 4 times, sc in each of next 4 sc. Join with a sl st to first sc. 50 sc.
Rnd 8: Thru *back* loop work sc in each sc. Thru *both* loops work 5 sc rnds. Join with a sl st. Fasten off.

HAIR: Wrap double strand C 18 times around an 8-inch cardboard. Cut at 1 end forming 16-inch strands. Mark a st at each side of hat. (See arms for boy for detailed instructions). Draw 6 strands thru marked st and 6 strands each thru st to right and st to left of first st. Braid to within 2 inches of end. Tie double strand several times tightly around all strands and trim ends. Place and braid hair at other side in same way.

LEGS: Wrap double strand C 15 times around a 10-inch cardboard. Cut at 1 end forming 20-inch strands. Attach same as for boy. Braid, leaving 2 inches for foot. Tie a short strand several times around end of braid and tie tightly. Trim ends.

NOSE: With MC ch 2, work 4 sc in 2nd ch from hook. **Next Rnd:** 2 sc in each sc. 8 sc. Work 2 rnds of 1 sc in each sc. Join with a sl st. Fasten off, leaving an end for sewing. Stuff with cotton. With tapestry needle, sew opening. Leave end.

FINISHING: Mark center front of head at 6th rnd from top, with eyes touching at marker, sew between 6th and 7th rnds. With yarn attached to nose, sew 2 rnds below, centered between eyes. With tapestry needle and D work long sts for mouth over 3 sts 2 rows below nose.

Cheeks—(Make 2): With D ch 3. Join with a sl st to form a ring. **Rnd 1:** Work 6 sc in ring. **Rnd 2:** Work 2 sc in each sc. Join with a sl st. Fasten off. Sew at sides as shown.

CORDS: Same as for Boy.

OWL

BODY (make 2 pieces): With MC, chain 21 to measure 6 inches. **Row 1:** Sc in 2nd ch from hook and each ch to end. Ch 1, turn. 20 sc. **Row 2:** Sc in each sc. Ch 1, turn. Rep Row 2 until there are 18 rows from beg. Ch 1, turn. **Next Row:** Draw up a loop in each of first 2 sts, yo and thru 3 loops on hook (a dec), sc in each sc to last 2 sc, dec. Ch 1, turn. Rep last row twice. 14 sc. Ch 1, do *not* turn. Work 1 sc in end of each row on side to foundation ch, 2 sc in first ch, sc in each ch to last ch, 2 sc in last ch, sc in each row on other side. Fasten off.

HEAD CIRCLES: With MC, ch 2. **Rnd 1:** Work 6 sc in 2nd ch from hook. Mark end of rnds. **Rnd 2:** 2 sc in each sc. 12 sc. **Rnd 3:** (Sc in one st, 2 sc in next st) 6 times. 18 sc. **Rnd 4:** Sc in one st, 2 sc in next st, (sc in each of 2 sts, 2 sc in next st) 5 times, sc in last st. 24 sc. **Rnd 5:** (Sc in each of 3 sts, 2 sc in next st) 6 times. 30 sc. **Rnd 6:** Sc in each of 2 sts, 2 sc in next st, (sc in each of 4 sts, 2 sc in next st) 5 times, sc in each of 2 sts. 36 sc. Join with a sl st to first sc. Cut yarn. Draw A thru loop on hook. **Rnd 7:** (Sc in each of 8 sts, 2 sc in next st) 4 times. 40 sc. Join with a sl st to first sc. Fasten off. Make another piece in same way. Do *not* fasten off. **To Join Circles:** Holding wrong sides of circles tog, thru double thickness, work sl st in each of 6 sts. Fasten off. Make and join 2 more circles in same way.

EYES (Make 2): With A work first 3 rnds same as for head. Join with a sl st to first sc. Fasten off leaving an end for sewing.

FEET (make 2): With A, ch 6. **Rnd 1:** Sc in 2nd ch from hook and each ch to end. Ch 1, turn. Work 11 more sc rows, ch 1, turn at end of every row. Fold piece in half. Join all sides by working thru double thickness. Join with a sl st, fasten off, leaving 12-inch end.

NOSE: With B, ch 11. **Rnd 1:** Sc in 2nd ch from hook and each ch to end. Work 9 more sc rows. Ch 1, turn at end of each row. Fasten off, leaving an end for sewing. Fold with opposite points tog (to form triangle) and overcast thru double thickness along one side, turn so seam is

at center. Fold top corner down to seam and tack in place.

FINISHING—Front: Sew button eye to center of crochet eye. Sew crochet eyes over center of 2 head circles. Mark off 2 center st of front body piece.

To Join Front Head and Body: With wrong side of head circles to side of body, join A to first sc at top of body, insert hook in same sc of body and in 9th st from joining of head circles. Thru double thickness, join 5 more sts; sc in each of 2 center sc of body; sk 3 sc from joining of other circle and join 6 sc as before. With wrong sides of back and front tog, work sc thru double thickness of sides and bottom, working 2 sc in lower corners, join, fasten off. Join head circles to back and finish as front. With front facing, holding wrong side of front and back tog, join A to first free sc at right edge of joining of head and body. Thru double thickness with sc, join 11 sts of front and back of head. Join with a sl st. Fasten off. Join at other side to correspond.

To Join Feet: With back facing, sk 2 sts on lower edge of body, with yarn attached to foot, sl st foot to body. Join other foot in same way.

To Join Nose: Sew straight edge below eyes as shown.

HANDLE: Wrap double yarn 18 times around an 11-inch cardboard and cut at one end. (36 22-inch strands). Tie a strand of yarn tightly 1-inch above cut ends at one end. Divide in 3 equal sections and braid to within 1-inch of other end. Tie tightly as before. Tack one end securely in place at center top of head, letting ends of fringe form bangs on right side. Tack other end in same manner at center top of back. Trim ends.

MOUSE

BODY (Make 2 pieces): With MC, chain 4. Join with sl st to form ring. **Rnd 1:** Work 5 sc in ring. Mark end of rnds. **Rnd 2:** Work 2 sc in each sc. 10 sc. **Rnd 3:** (Sc in one sc, 2 sc in next sc) 5 times. 15 sc. **Rnd 4:** (Sc in each of 2 sc, 2 sc in next sc) 5 times. 20 sc. Continue to inc 5 sts *every* rnd twice more, having one st more between incs every rnd. 30 sc. **Rnd 7:** (Sc in each of 4 sc, 2 sc in next sc) 6 times. 36 sc. **Rnd 8:** (Sc in each of 5 sc, 2 sc in next sc) 6 times. 42 sc. **Rnd 9:** Sc in each of 3 sc, (sc in each of 6 sc, 2 sc in next sc) 5 times, sc in each of last 3 sc. 48 sc. **Rnd 10:** (Sc in each of 5 sc, 2 sc in next sc) 8 times. 56 sc. **Rnd 11:** Sc in each of 3 sc, 2 sc in next sc, (sc in each of 6 sc, 2 sc in next sc) 7 times, sc in each of last 3 sc. 64 sc. **Rnd 12:** (Sc in each of 7 sc, 2 sc in next sc) 8 times. 72 sc. **Rnd 13:** (Sc in each of 7 sc, 2 sc in next sc) 9 times. 81 sc. **Rnd 14:** Sc in each of 4 sc, 2 sc in next sc, (sc in each of 8 sc, 2 sc in next sc) 8 times, sc in each of last 4 sc. 90 sc. **Rnd 15:** (Sc in each of 8 sc, 2 sc in next sc) 10 times. 100 sc. Join with sl st to next sc and fasten off.

EARS: With MC, work 2 circles same as circles for head of Owl (40 sc on last rnd). Do not fasten off at end of 2nd circle. **To Join:** Holding wrong sides tog. thru double thickness, sl st in each of 26 sc and fasten off, leaving about a 14-inch end. Work same for other ear.

Join to Body: Insert one body circle into open section of ear and sew one free edge of ear to body. Join other ear, leaving 7 sc between ears. Sew other edge of ears to other body circle to correspond.

NOSE: With A, ch 3. Join with sl st to form ring. **Rnd 1:** Work 5 sc in ring. **Rnd 2:** 2 sc in each sc. **Rnd 3:** (Sc in next sc, 2 sc in next sc) 5 times. 15 sc. Work 2 rnds of 1 sc in each sc. Join with sl st and fasten off, leaving a long end for sewing. Stuff with cotton, draw tog tightly and sew at center front of body.

EYES (Make 2): With A, ch 2. Work 6 sc in 2nd ch from hook. Work 2 sc in each sc. 12 sc. Join and fasten off, leaving end for sewing. Sew a button eye to center of each circle. Sew in place on front, above nose as shown.

MOUTH: With B, make a ch 4-inches long. Sew on as shown.

WHISKERS: Cut 8 strands of A, 5-inches long. Fold 4 strands in half. Insert hook under a st on right side of body to right of nose, draw fold thru, draw cut ends thru fold and tighten knot. Fasten other 4 strands to left of nose in same way. Trim ends.

TAIL (not shown): Wrap double strand A around a 7-inch cardboard 6 times and cut at one end. On back, insert hook on right side under center st at lower edge, 2 rnds above edge, and pull cut ends thru. Pull ends at each side to be even, divide in 3 sections and braid to within 2 inches of ends. Wrap strand of yarn tightly at end of braid and tie. Trim ends.

FEET (Make 2): With A, ch 8. **Row 1:** Work sc in 2nd ch from hook and in each ch to end. Ch 1, turn. Work 11 rows of 1 sc in each sc. Ch 1, turn at end of every row. Fold piece in half and join sides by working sl st thru double thickness, 7 sts across top and lower edge, 6 sts at each side. Fasten off, leaving long end.

FINISHING: With MC, from right side and working thru double thickness, join front and back body with sl st, beg at one ear and ending at the other. Leave top open. Mark 4 center sts at lower edge and sl st feet to body.

HANDLES: Work and join to body same as for Owl.

FROG

BODY (Make 2 pieces): With MC, work same as Mouse for 14 rnds (90 sc). Join and fasten off.

EYES (Back): Make 2 circles with MC, following instructions for head circles of Owl and ending with Rnd 6 and 36 sc. Join and fasten off. **Eye (Front):** With A, work 3 rnds as for back, working off last sc with MC. Drop A. Work Rnds 4 thru 6, join with sl st and draw A thru loop. Fasten off MC. **To Join Eyes:** With wrong side of a back and front eye tog, thru double thickness work sc in each of 24 sts. Join and fasten off. Make other front eye and join to back in same way. Sew button eye to each front eye. Mark center 6 sts on last rnd of body for top. Sew eyes to front and back as for Mouse, with the 6 center sts between eyes.

MOUTH: With MC, ch 2 and work 6 rnds as for back eye (36 sts). **Rnd 7:** (Sc in each of 7 sc, 2 sc in next sc) 4 times (40 sc). **Rnd 8:** (Sc in each of 3 sc, 2 sc in next sc) 10 times. Join with sl st, draw A thru loop, fasten off MC. **Rnd 9:** (Sc in each of 9 sc, 2 sc in next sc) 5 times. 55 sc. Join and fasten off.

INNER MOUTH: With B, ch 18 to measure 5 inches. **Row 1:** Sc in 2nd ch from hook and in each ch to end. Ch 1, turn. **Row 2:** Draw up a loop in each of next 2 sc, yo and thru 3 loops (a dec), sc in each sc to last 2 sc, dec. 15 sc. Ch 1, turn. Continue as in Row 2, dec 1 st each side every row 5 times more. Ch 1, turn. Work 1 sc in each of 5 sc. Fasten off. With right side of mouth facing, sew foundation ch of inner section in place across diameter of MC circle. With A, work 1 rnd sc around mouth, working thru double thickness to join inner section to MC circle. Join with sl st and fasten off. With right side of mouth facing, fold MC top of mouth over inner mouth and sew to body along fold 6 rows below top edge of body, centered below eyes.

FINISHING: Join A at inner top joining of eye. From right side, thru double thickness of front and back, work sc in each sc around eye, around body and around other eye, ending at inner eye; work 6 sc across center top of front, then of back. Join and fasten off.

LEGS: Wrap double strand of A 15 times around a 7-inch cardboard and cut at one end. (30 strands of 14-inches). Mark center st at lower edge of body. Divide strands in 3 groups of 10. Draw a group thru each of the 3 sts to left of marked st. Pull ends (all cut ends—a total of 60) to even length and braid (there will be 20 strands in each of 3 sections) to within 2 inches of ends. Tie a strand of yarn tightly around end of braid. Trim ends. Make other leg the same, drawing strands thru the 3 sts to right of center.

HANDLE: Same as for Owl.

Finishing Touches

Finishing Touches

Needleworkers are almost always blessed with generous spirits. They want to share their ideas, patterns, experiences and pleasures with you. There is space here for only a few suggestions that we hope will be helpful.

HEMMING

On household linens you probably trued up the fabric and basted a hem before doing the needlework. If not, baste in a hem of the desired width, mitering corners as described in the directions immediately following. Thread a sewing needle with sewing thread of a color to match your fabric. Place work wrong side up with hem edge toward you. Work from right to left. Fasten thread in fold of hem. Take a tiny stitch (1 or 2 threads of fabric) in the piece itself, then slide needle along $1/8''$ to $1/4''$ inside the fold of the hem. Repeat, keeping stitches even. Secure the last stitch by making several stitches one on top of the other; run thread through hem and clip off.

Some experts prefer a more pronounced hem. On coarse linens or cottons they work a stitch in every thread of their background fabric. This emphasizes the line where the hem is stitched.

MITERING HEMS

For neat corners on napkins, tablecloths and such items miter the hems as follows:

1. Crease along inside and outside hem lines (A and B in Diagram 1).
2. Unfold hem and clip off corner diagonally (dotted line, Diagram 1).
3. Turn down corner (Diagram 2).

4. Now refold hem along lines A, then lines B. Pin, baste and sew hem, slip-stitching along miter at each corner (Diagram 3).

Helpful Hint: Never use permanent knots at the ends of threads in any form of needlework. To start a new thread leave a 2″ end, hold it out of the way on *top* of work until your first few stitches have been made. Later draw end to back of work, insert it in a needle and slip it under a few stitches. Also draw final ends of thread through a few stitches on the back of work and clip off.

WASHING EMBROIDERY

If your needlework has become soiled during the making and it is made of washable and color-fast fabric and threads, it can be hand laundered successfully. Just gently swish the piece through warm water and mild soap suds. Do not squeeze or twist. Rinse thoroughly in clear water. Do not wring out. Roll up loosely in a clean towel. When piece is ready, press or block.

Note: If piece cannot be washed, remove spots and freshen it up with cleaning fluid or take it to a fine dry cleaner.

PRESSING EMBROIDERY

Use a well-padded ironing board and a steam iron or a regular iron and a press cloth. Place embroidery face down and steam press lightly, being careful not to allow the weight of the iron to flatten embroidery. Press the rest of your piece—hems, etc.—as you would any linen or cotton item.

BLOCKING EMBROIDERY

If your needlework has been made in a frame, has been kept clean and does not require hemming or other finishing, it will probably need only blocking to prepare it for framing or the like. Leave it in the embroidery frame (or large hoop), lay a clean wet

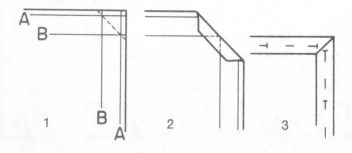

cloth on the right side of the piece and allow it to remain until dry.

If you have had to wash your embroidery, mark out the exact size of the piece on heavy paper mounted on a large board. While piece is still wet, but not dripping, line up with your marked area. Fasten with rust-proof push pins or thumb tacks at each corner, then in the center of each of the 4 sides. Keep adding pins halfway between those just added, alternating sides, until they are no more than ½" apart. Allow to dry thoroughly.

Just a Suggestion: If you are left-handed, you may need to adapt a stitch or technique to your own way of doing things. If a stitch diagram is difficult to adapt, try holding a little mirror along the side of the diagram and at a right angle to the page. The mirror image may be easier for you to follow.

FRAMING NEEDLEWORK

We'll assume that you made your embroidery to fit a given frame or that you have found a frame of the proper size and proportions to fit your needlework. Remember that a frame should be large enough to allow a certain amount of plain fabric to extend beyond the embroidered area. This fabric border is usually the same width on top and sides, just a little wider at the bottom. On modern pictures the fabric border may be even all around or omitted entirely.

Remove all little wire nails, hooks and picture wire at back of frame. Refinish frame if necessary.

Cut a piece of firm cardboard to fit into the rabbet which holds the picture at the back of the frame but make it just a hair's breadth narrower all around. Place cardboard in desired position on back of embroidery; draw excess fabric over it. Insert a few straight pins into each edge of cardboard to anchor fabric. If the extra fabric is more than 1½" to 2" wide, trim evenly. Make sure that the threads of the background fabric line up squarely on the front of the picture, then fasten down the extra fabric at the top and bottom of the back with masking tape. Repeat at each side of picture.

In some cases if the double folds of fabric at the corners are too bulky, cut away the under layer. This is necessary with certain heavy or stiff fabrics like needlepoint canvas.

Insert the cleaned and polished glass in the frame, then place the picture face down in the frame. Fasten picture in place by carefully hammering a fine wire nail into the center of each side of the rabbet. Larger frames require 2 or 3 nails per side. If a dust cover is desired, run a line of glue around the back of the frame and lay a sheet of brown paper over the entire back. Trim paper close to frame. Replace hooks or picture wire.

A Good Idea: If it is difficult to find suitable background fabric for embroidery, take a look at artists' canvas available by the yard in art supply stores. It is often 54" wide, comes in both cotton and linen and has a good texture.

MAKING WALL HANGINGS

The easiest way to make a wall hanging is as follows: True up the edges of your needlework piece. Machine stitch or sew by hand narrow hems on the sides, then on the lower edge of your piece. Finally turn down a hem 1" (or more) wide at the top of the hanging; stitch across, leaving ends of hem open. Width of turndown depends on thickness of dowel or metal rod that you are using. Insert dowel or rod in top hem. If desired, dressmaker's weights can be sewed to the back of the hanging spaced evenly along the lower edge. Another way to keep the bottom of the wall hanging from buckling is to make the lower hem like the top hem to accommodate a matching dowel or rod. The ends of the dowels can be whittled down to fit into large wooden beads if a decorative trim is desired.

A slightly more complicated way of making a wall hanging is described in the directions for the Butterfly Wall Hanging in the Pretend Appliqué section. The more professional results are well worth the little extra effort. Adapt the directions to any size wall hanging by using the appropriate number of hanging tabs of a size suitable for the piece.

MAKING A TWISTED CORD

There are two popular methods for making a twisted cord, one of which requires two people, so choose whichever you prefer.

Regardless of method, determine the number of strands necessary for the required thickness of the finished cord and cut strands three times the desired length of the finished cord.

This method requires two people. Tie knots in the ends of the strands forming loops through which to slide two pencils. The two people face each other and keeping the yarn taut, twist the pencils in opposite directions. (1) When the yarn is taut and begins to kink, catch center of the cord over a door knob or let one person hold the center of the yarn. Bring the pencils together allowing yarn to twist. (2) If necessary run your hand down the twisting cord to keep it smooth. Cut the center loop and tie the ends. Trim ends.

If there is no one to hold the other pencil and you are on your own, try this method. Cut strands as above, place one looped end over a door knob and a pencil in the other end. Holding the pencil in your hand, keeping the yarn taut, rotate the pencil until yarn has twisted taut and starts to kink. Slide the larger finger grip of your sewing shears over the pencil to the center of twisted cord. Bring the pencil close to the door knob and allow the scissors to rotate freely and twist the cord. Cut both ends, tie and trim.

MAKING A TASSEL

Cut a piece of cardboard the length desired for tassel and 3 or 4 inches wide. Lay a 12-inch strand of yarn along top of cardboard. Wind yarn over cardboard and strand at top as many times as necessary for desired thickness. Tie the strands tightly together at top and cut through loops at bottom of cardboard. Wind a strand of yarn several times tightly around strands ½ to 1 inch below the knot and fasten securely. Trim ends.

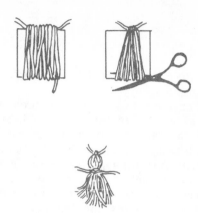

MAKING A POMPOM

Cut two cardboard circles the size desired for the pompom; cut a ¼ or ½-inch hole in the center of each. Thread a needle with two long strands of yarn. Place the circles together and wind the yarn thickly over the circles, working through the center hole. When circle is covered, slide a scissors between the circles and cut all strands along outside edge. Draw a strand of yarn between the cardboard circles and wind tightly several times around the center of the pompom. Tie a secure knot and leave ends for attaching pompom. Slide cardboard circles off, fluff pompom and trim ends.

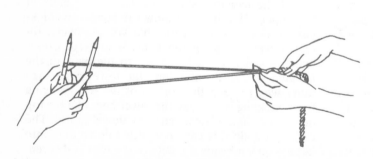

"KNITTING IN" BUTTONHOLES

Buttonholes may be very easily knitted right into a garment. First, knit the side of the garment on which the buttons are to be placed. When finished, choose the button and mark for button-hole placement. The button must be chosen before making the buttonholes so that there are no problems in finding a button to fit the buttonhole. While knitting the other side match the two pieces carefully and work buttonholes opposite the markings in this manner. On the right side row, bind off as many stitches as necessary for button to pass through. On wrong side row, cast on the same number of stitches as bound off on previous row. After knitting has been completed, buttonholes must be finished with a buttonhole stitch (see page 25) in matching yarn to avoid stretching. If garment is faced with ribbon or lined, slash the fabric behind buttonholes and work buttonhole stitch catching in the edge of fabric.

WEAVING A SEAM

Vertical seams in knitted garments can be woven together invisibly. This method is far superior to the outdated whipping of the knots on wrong side. Weaving is done on the right side of a garment with matching yarn and a tapestry or blunt needle. Examine the edge of the knitted piece and you will notice that every other row ends in a knot; weaving is done under these knots. Place the two edges together and bring needle up through first stitch on left edge. Insert needle down through center of first stitch on right edge, pass it under the knot and bring out through next stitch. Insert needle down in corresponding row of left side, pass under the knot and bring out through next stitch to right side. Work back and forth from side to side, always inserting needle down in last stitch worked and under next knot.

FACING A CARDIGAN WITH RIBBON

Grosgrain ribbon provides the best body for facing front edges of cardigan, however it must be washed before attaching to allow for shrinkage. Use matching ribbon slightly narrower than front band. Turn sweater inside out and lay flat on a table. Turn under ½-inch of ribbon at neck edge and pin in place, one stitch in from front edge and below neck edge. Taking care not to stretch front edge place pins horizontally down length of ribbon turning ½-inch under at lower edge. Measure carefully and be certain that the pieces of ribbon for each side are the same length. Blind stitch ribbon along each edge top and bottom. If buttonholes were knitted in, slash the ribbon and work buttonhole stitch catching in the ribbon.

CROCHETING BUTTONS

Covered Button Form. Use the top half of a "cover your own" button form or an old button about ⅛-inch smaller than desired finished button. Since the crochet must be very tight, use the smallest hook possible to catch the yarn. If the yarn is heavyweight, carefully separate strands of sufficient length to cover button and use these finer strands of yarn.

Ch 2, work 6 sc into 1st ch, join with sl st and mark for beginning of rnd. Ch 2, work 2 sc into ea st of previous rnd, join with sl st. (12 sts) Rnd 3: ch 1, * work 2 sc into next st, 1 sc into next st; rep from * to end of rnd. (18 sts) If circle must be larger than this to cover the face of the button, continue to crochet additional rnds increasing 6 sts evenly spaced on each rnd. When circle is sufficient size, work 1 rnd even. Dec. rnd: * sc in 1st st, skip next st *. Rep this dec rnd until back of form is covered; fasten off leaving a 12-inch end for sewing.

Covered Plastic Ring. A plastic of bone curtain ring may be used for a very attractive, easy to make button. Work 1 row sc tightly over the ring and join with a sl st. Ch 1, work a sc tightly into ea st; fasten off leaving a 12-inch end for weaving. Thread the end into a blunt needle and work a running st through the top loops of crochet stitches. Pull the thread, drawing the stitches tightly together. As you pull the work will turn and fill the inside of the ring. Fasten. If desired, a small button may be sewn in the center of ring for a more decorative effect.

Crocheted Ball Button. Rnd 1: Ch 2, work 6 sc tightly into first ch. (Do not join.) Rnd. 2: Work 2 sc into ea st of previous rnd. Work 2 more rnds even. If you are using a bead to stuff button, check to see if cup is deep enough; if not, continue to sc even rnds until proper depth. Dec rnd: * skip 1 sc, sc in next st; rep from * until closed. If you are not using a bead to stuff button, after working the 2 rnds even, fill cup firmly with yarn, then beg to dec.

Crocheted Ball Button

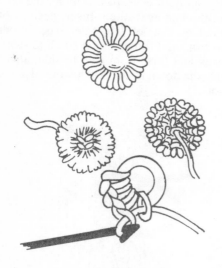

Covered Plastic Ring

Covered Button Form

STANDARD BODY MEASUREMENTS

Infants and Toddlers

Size	6 mos.	1	2
Breast	19	20	21
Waist	19	19½	20
Hip	20	21	22
Height*	22	25	29

Boys

Size	3	4	6	8	10	12	14	16
Chest	22	23	24	26	28	30	32	34
Waist	20½	21	22	23	24	25½	27	29
Neck			11	11½	12	12½	13½	14
Hip	22	23	25	27	29	31	33	35½
Height*	31	33	37	41	45	49	53	55

Girls

Size	3	4	6	8	10	12	14
Breast	22	23	24	27	28½	30	32
Waist	20½	21	22	23½	24½	25½	26½
Hip	23	24	26	28	30	32	34
Height*	31	33	37	41	45	49	53

Young Juniors/Teens

Size	7/8	9/10	11/12	13/14
Bust	29	30½	32	33½
Waist	23	24	25	26
Hip	32	33½	35	36½

Juniors

Size	7	9	11	13	15
Bust	31	32	33½	35	37
Waist	22½	23½	24½	26	28
Hip	33	34	35½	37	39

Misses

Size	8	10	12	14	16	18
Bust	31½	32½	34	36	38	40
Waist	23	24	25½	27	29	31
Hip	33½	34½	36	38	40	42

Women

Size	38	40	42	44	46	48
Bust	42	44	46	48	50	52
Waist	34	36	38	40½	43	45½
Hip	44	46	48	50	52	54

Men

Size	34	36	38	40	42	44
Chest	34	36	38	40	42	44
Waist	30	32	34	36	38	40

* From nape of neck to floor while wearing shoes.

Index